CONFLICT
and
COOPERATION
in the
GLOBAL COMMONS

CONFLICT
and
COOPERATION
in the
GLOBAL COMMONS

A Comprehensive Approach

for International Security

SCOTT JASPER, EDITOR

Georgetown University Press/Washington, DC

Library of Congress Cataloging-in-Publication Data

Conflict and cooperation in the global commons : a comprehensive approach for international security / Scott Jasper, editor.
   p. cm.
Includes bibliographical references and index.
ISBN 978-1-58901-922-5 (pbk. : alk. paper)
1. Security, International.   2. Global commons.   3. International cooperation.   4. National security—United States.   I. Jasper, Scott.
JZ6005.C66 2012
355'.0335—dc23

                                                          2011051795

∞ This book is printed on acid-free paper meeting the requirements of the American National Standard for Permanence in Paper for Printed Library Materials.

15 14 13 12   9 8 7 6 5 4 3 2   First printing

Contents

Illustrations

Foreword

Contested Superiority
in the Commons

The United States has a long-standing interest in protecting access to the global commons. Since the founding of the Republic, the US military has safeguarded American lives and trade abroad. Military power not only has provided security and prosperity for the nation, it also has protected international airspace and the high seas to guarantee the free flow of ideas, commerce, and travel around the world. The global community must have unimpeded access to space and cyberspace together with the air and maritime domains. The ability to protect the commons is paramount to the progress, well-being, and stability of the entire international community.

Today the United States and its allies and partners face the most complex and challenging security environment in recent memory. First, an international coalition is engaged in the fight against violent extremist organizations such as al-Qaeda and its affiliates: a protracted conflict with irregular adversaries using unconventional means and hybrid tactics that spans the globe. Quite apart from the war in Afghanistan, this conflict will generate significant demands for forces for the foreseeable future.

Second, it is clearly necessary to deal with regional antagonists such as North Korea and Iran, two nations that threaten US allies and friends as well as stability of key regions of the world. North Korea possesses nuclear weapons and a missile arsenal that are being leveraged to sustain an oppressive regime with open scorn for international law. For its part, Iran has sought nuclear weapons and intercontinental ballistic missile capability and employed terrorist groups such as Hezbollah and its own clandestine services as instruments of foreign policy.[1]

Third and potentially most significant is the rise of China. The modernization of the People's Liberation Army affects the balance of power in ways that threaten the United States and its allies in the Pacific. Beijing is acquiring weapons tailored to weaken the capabilities of US forces. Not only do these advanced systems challenge free access to areas of vital strategic importance, they may undermine the alliances that have served effectively as the foundation of stability across the Asia-Pacific region for over half a century.[2]

Each of these situations represents a threat to international order and poses barriers to free access to the global commons. Al-Qaeda and its associates offer nothing short of a brutal attack on the international system. They do not recognize national sovereignty or respect international boundaries. Rather, they exploit these norms for their own purposes. Indeed, extremists use the instruments of globalization that they claim to despise—the unfettered flow of information and ideas in open societies, goods and services, capital, people, and technology—to further their goals. Similarly, rogue states such as North Korea and Iran have demonstrated their deep contempt for international norms. Pyongyang has been implicated in drug smuggling and counterfeiting, whereas Tehran has supported terrorists. And for its part, China is pursuing a mercantilist policy and has promulgated a novel interpretation of the law of the sea to support its territorial designs.

Dealing with these challenges will require versatile military forces that will continue to play an important role in the struggle to defeat violent extremist organizations such as al-Qaeda. The projection of military power can disrupt the capability of terrorist groups to strike globally, bolstering the ability of local regimes to deal with insurgents in their own territory. To achieve success, the US military and its allies and partners must develop and sustain their proficiency in irregular warfare as they retain an ability to engage in high-end conventional conflicts.

Military power will also play a crucial role in dealing with regional rogues, particularly those who either possess or seek nuclear weapons. The threat of military force plays a central role in deterring these nations and their surrogates from aggression. However, thinking about deterrence went out of fashion with the demise of the Soviet Union and only recently has begun to stage a comeback. A revival is needed in both understanding deterrence and developing new approaches to compete with North Korea and Iran in the long term. Both US and allied military forces must improve their ability to defend against missile attacks that rogue states may launch as well as counter the threats posed by international terrorism and conventional warfare. The decision by the North Atlantic Alliance at the Lisbon Summit to "develop a missile defence capability to protect all NATO European populations, territory and forces" is a welcome start.[3]

Finally, military forces will play important roles in dealing with China. In particular, the United States must maintain the preponderance of power in the Pacific to reassure allies and partners and ensure continuing access to the global commons. US and allied forces also must develop asymmetric responses to Chinese military capabilities that put them at risk.

In addition to these broad challenges, the operational environment is likely to change in the coming years. Specifically, the spread of precision-strike capabilities and cyber warfare will give states and nonstate actors greater leverage in contesting access to the global commons. For example, some US bases in the Western Pacific already come within the range of Chinese precision-guided ballistic and land-attack cruise missiles, whereas others will become vulnerable when the Chinese field longer-range weapons. Eventually, the ability of US forces in the region to deter aggression as well as reassure US allies and partners will diminish.

This threat to bases in the Pacific calls into question the model that the United States has used to project power in recent decades. Without access to ports and airfields in Saudi Arabia and across that region, for example, it would have been harder for a US-led coalition to eject Iraqi forces from Kuwait in 1991. Any future operations conducted against adversaries armed with precision-guided weapons may resemble the invasion of Normandy and Iwo Jima during World War II more than the relatively unopposed incursions into Afghanistan and Iraq.

Although it is axiomatic that national strategies must be formulated and implemented with constrained resources, it appears inevitable that fiscal constraints will threaten to limit the power projection capabilities of the United States in the coming years. For reasons of domestic politics as well as economics, it is likely that the priority and allocation of resources for national security will gradually decline. Such constraints make it increasingly clear that the United States cannot counter threats by throwing money at them. In other words, the nation cannot simply afford to do more of the same instead of developing a comprehensive strategy for the long term.

Policymakers should consider innovative ways to close the gap between ends and means. The United States should develop networks of intelligence, surveillance, and reconnaissance in the Western Pacific through coalitions and collective responses to crises and acts of aggression. Linking airborne sensors would build a common picture of the region. Such an approach could represent a significant deterrent to hostile action. It would be difficult for an adversary to strike any network with impunity because it would represent an attack on the entire coalition.

In addition, the United States should help bolster the submarine forces of its allies as well as seek to link them together. Undersea warfare provides a comparative advantage to both US and allied forces, and one that will be increasingly relevant in the future. For example, a recent initiative by the Canberra-based Kokoda Foundation urged the Royal Australian Navy to either buy or lease *Virginia*-class nuclear-powered attack submarines from the United States.[4] Those boats would provide the speed and endurance needed to protect the maritime domain.

The contributors to this volume investigate each domain in the global commons. Equally important, their analyses present insights on the fact that military primacy is being increasingly contested in the commons. Each chapter points to the need for comprehensive approaches that emphasize the importance of leveraging all the instruments of national power including use of force. The range of political, diplomatic, and economic tools is brought to bear in dealing with security challenges in each domain. In sum, US allies and partners will play critical roles in ensuring access to the global commons and protecting freedom of action within their domains. This volume will fuel a timely debate on the challenges facing the United States and its allies and partners in international airspace, the high seas, outer space, and cyberspace.

THOMAS G. MAHNKEN
Jerome Levy Chair of Economic
Geography and National Security at the
Naval War College and Visiting
Scholar at Philip Merrill Center for
Strategic Studies at Paul H. Nitze
School of Advanced International
Studies, Johns Hopkins University

NOTES

1. National Air and Space Intelligence Center, *Ballistic and Cruise Missile Threat* (Dayton, OH: National Air and Space Intelligence Center, April 2009), 19.
2. See US Department of Defense, *Military and Security Developments Involving the People's Republic of China, Annual Report to Congress* (Washington, DC: Office of the Secretary of Defense, 2011).
3. North Atlantic Treaty Organization, "Lisbon Summit Declaration," November 20, 2010, www.nato.int/cps/en/natolive/official_texts_68828.htm.
4. Kokoda Foundation, *Australia's Strategic Edge in 2030* (Canberra: Kokoda Foundation, 2011).

Acknowledgments

This volume was inspired by the escalating impact of widespread threats to the global commons. In exchanges with US and international students at the Naval Postgraduate School, I have come to realize that they and their compatriots will be committed in harm's way at some point in the defense of our access to the commons. I trust the ideas in this book will lead to collective solutions to the threats our nations will confront in protecting the global commons.

I want to thank Vice Admiral Daniel T. Oliver, USN (Ret.), president of the Naval Postgraduate School, for his direct involvement during the initial stages of this project. Thanks also are due to Richard Hoffman, director of the Center for Civil-Military Relations, who provided encouragement throughout the development and completion of the book.

Each of the contributors to this volume deserves special recognition for sharing expertise and insights on unique issues related to the global commons. Together they represent both the United States and allied nations as well as both the public and private sectors engaged in challenges in the maritime, air, space, and cyberspace domains.

In addition, I want to acknowledge the assistance of Robert A. Silano, who edited the manuscript prior to publication. Moreover, the efforts of both Ian M. Cool, who created the maps, and William A. Rawley, illustrator, enliven the text. Also, I would like to recognize Scott Moreland for his extensive and diligent literature search. My sincere appreciation goes to Don Jacobs and the staff at Georgetown University Press for facilitating the review and publication of this volume.

Finally, I want to acknowledge Annie, my dear wife and best friend, and Christopher, Kevin, and Brian, our wonderful boys, for their enduring support.

Abbreviations

AA/AD	anti-access/area denial
ABC	American Broadcasting Company
ABM	antiballistic missile
AIS	Automatic Identification System
APT	advanced persistent threat
ASAT	antisatellite (weaponry)
ASBM	antiship ballistic missile
BIOS	basic input-output system
BMD	ballistic missile defense
C4ISR	command, control, communications, computers, intelligence, surveillance, and reconnaissance
CCU	Cyber Consequences Unit
CERT	Cyber Emergency Response Team
CD	Conference on Disarmament
CEP	circular error probability
CFO	chief financial officer
CHOC	Charleston Harbor Operations Center
COPUOS	Committee on the Peaceful Uses of Outer Space
CPU	central processing unit
DNA	deoxyribonucleic acid
DOD	Department of Defense
EEZ	exclusive economic zone
EU	European Union

FDA	Food and Drug Administration
G-7	Group of Seven
G-20	Group of Twenty
GLCM	ground-launched cruise missile
GPS	global positioning system
ICAO	International Civil Aviation Organization
ICC	Interorganizational Collaborative Capacity
ICS	industrial control system
ISC	Information Sharing Centre
INF	Intermediate-Range Nuclear Forces
IP	Internet protocol
ISP	Internet service provider
IT	information technology
JHOC	Joint Harbor Operations Center
LACM	land-attack cruise missile
MRBM	medium-range ballistic missile
MSSIS	Maritime Safety and Security Information System
MSP	Malacca Strait Patrols
MUC	Maritime Unified Command
NATO	North Atlantic Treaty Organization
OST	Outer Space Treaty
PLA	People's Liberation Army
PLAAF	People's Liberation Army Air Force
PLAN	People's Liberation Army Navy
PRC	People's Republic of China
R&D	research and development
ReCAAP	Regional Cooperation Agreement on Combating Piracy and Armed Robbery against Ships in Asia
SCADA	supervisory control and data acquisition
SRBM	short-range ballistic missile
S&T	science and technology
START	Strategic Arms Reduction Treaty
TCBM	transparency and confidence-building measure
UAV	unmanned aerial vehicle
UC	unified communications

Abbreviations

UK	United Kingdom
UN	United Nations
UNCLOS	UN Convention on the Law of the Sea
URL	uniform resource locator
USNS	United States Naval Ship
VHF	very high frequency
WMD	weapons of mass destruction

Introduction

A Comprehensive Approach

❖

SCOTT JASPER and SCOTT MORELAND

America, working in conjunction with allies and partners around the world, will seek to protect freedom of access throughout the global commons—those areas beyond national jurisdiction that constitute the vital connective tissue of the international system.

—*Sustaining US Global Leadership: Priorities for 21st Century Defense*

National security and economic prosperity depend on safeguarding the global commons, which are the "domains or areas that no one state controls but on which all rely."[1] The *global commons* comprise four domains: maritime, air, space, and cyber.[2] The maritime and air domains are international oceans and skies that are not under the sovereign control of any individual nation. Outer space begins at that point above the earth where objects can remain in orbit, whereas cyberspace is a digital world generated through computer networks. Although cyberspace relies on the infrastructures of individual nations, it is globally connected and requires cooperation to secure like other domains. These shared spaces provide conduits through which an international system of commerce, communication, and governance prospers. Recent disruptions in transit and access points have revealed the risks associated with globalization. The commons have become an arena for conflict through intrusion, exploitation, and attacks by myriad competitors that threaten nefarious actions and violent trends on a daily basis.

A PRESSING IMPERATIVE

The promotion of democracy, open markets, and social progress are some of the benefits of the global system. Yet international order, on which that system thrives, is susceptible to profound and unsettling changes in the global distribution of power.[3] Rising nations and nonstate actors have extended their influence and reach dramatically.[4] Such emerging centers of influence may offer alternative, cynical, even alarming worldviews, manifest in actions to exploit the freedom of the commons. Recent disruptions in the commons reflect some ominous new trends, ranging from the proliferation of weapons of mass destruction and transnational terrorism to economic and political instability and worldwide competition for increasingly scarce resources.

The stability of the international order and economy depends on reliable and unhindered access to the global commons. The maritime domain serves as the conduit for more than 90 percent of global trade, valued at some $14 trillion in 2008.[5] Essential space services such as communications networks, satellite imagery, and global positioning netted the US aerospace sector an estimated $214 billion in 2009.[6] Moreover, e-commerce amounted to more than $3.3 trillion in 2009 via cyber networks that rely on private sector security.[7] With regard to international security, the United States and allied nations use many of the same cyber networks and space systems to enable movement of forces and operations in the air and maritime domains.

Although armed force can serve as the primary instrument for projecting national power, the responsibility to prevent, deter, and resolve conflicts in the commons does not fall entirely to the military. The protection of vulnerable but indispensable systems in the commons requires cooperation by private, governmental, and international partners to identify problems and find solutions. Only through a comprehensive approach that totally aligns the parties based on shared interests, complementary opportunities, and mutual procedures will continued access to the global commons be assured.

CHALLENGES IN THE COMMONS

It is ironic that some beneficiaries of the global system have become its most problematic users. As one senior Pentagon official noted: "We are entering a new period of sustained competition and potential conflict in domains that previously have been the purview of very few states, and virtually no non-state actors."[8] For instance, newly developed antisatellite systems threaten not only the military but also commercial services and scientific research in space.[9] Cyber intrusions by state-sponsored and criminal hackers that compromise economic data and transactions demonstrate the growing confluence of illegal interference, traditional espionage, and the militarization of cyberspace.[10] Advanced air defense systems threaten the ability of US and allied forces to set conditions for success in other domains.[11] Likewise, a startling range of maritime security threats from shore-based antiship ballistic missiles to acts of piracy on the high seas hamper unfettered access to international trade and energy resources.[12]

Awareness of attacks and responses to them can be problematic. It took months before Google, Intel, Adobe, and Yahoo realized that malware attacks thought to come from China had stolen data.[13] The Stuxnet worm began infecting nuclear power plant systems, primarily inside Iran, more than eighteen months before public exposure by an obscure Belarusian security company.[14] In the more obvious denial-of-service attacks that targeted websites in the United States and South Korea, suspicion of North Korean complicity proved to be dubious once the attacks were traced to sixteen nations, including the United States and South Korea, although not North Korea.[15] These events raise issues over whether such attacks constitute acts of war and whether governmental responses might be appropriate, particularly military. Thus far the private sector has dealt with these threats, but when will they become national security issues?

The global community depends on space for communications networks, navigational and timing data, weather forecasting, and commercial remote sensing in addition to financial, travel, and other services.[16] Attacks in space disrupt those activities and can spoil the less-than-pristine environment of space. For instance, the Chinese test of an antisatellite weapon in January 2007 against the Fengyun-1C satellite generated 2,691 bits of debris, many of which remains in low-Earth orbit as hazards to satellite constellations such as Iridium, Orbcomm, and Globalstar.[17] Identifying the source of attacks and deterring them are just as difficult in space as in cyberspace. Although direct-ascent weapons like the Chinese antisatellite system are exceptions, the origin of transitory harassing interference from ground-based sources may become harder to detect.

Despite the complexity of security issues, the global order cannot and should not become the prey of rogue actors and criminals. Governments and other sectors must cooperate to prevent, deter, and resolve conflicts. A coordinated approach to safeguarding the commons must account for the nature and impact of conflict and cooperation dynamics to protect the commons.

HYBRID THREATS

Conflict in the global commons is symptomatic of a security environment that is more troubled now than in the past. Moreover, as one defense analyst pointed out: "Future contingencies will more likely present unique combinational or hybrid threats that are specifically designed to target US vulnerabilities."[18] Attacks launched in or through the commons may produce strategic, political, and operational effects on US, allied, and other international parties. A range of state and nonstate actors with competing interests of their own, which may include transnational syndicates operating from ungoverned sanctuaries or cyber factions attempting to exfiltrate technical data, are conspiring to undermine Western norms and disrupt the fragile global order.

The audacity of those spoilers who flout asymmetric challenges to international security reflects a global perception of declining Western superiority.[19] Iran has demonstrated resolve in aggressively controlling the Strait of Hormuz through the use of small-boat swarming tactics and indigenously produced surface-to-surface missiles designed to saturate and destroy warships as part of an explicit strategy of area denial.[20] Highly capable combat elements of the Iranian hornet's nest include Bavar-2 sea-skimming amphibian seaplanes, Zulfikar fast patrol boats armed with the Nasr-1 medium-range antiship missiles, and the hard-to-detect Ghadir minisubmarines.[21] As Rear Admiral Farhad Amiri, the head of research and self sufficiency for the Iranian Navy, has claimed, "When this submarine submerges, it can easily target and hit an aircraft carrier passing nearby."[22] In disputed waters off the Korean Peninsula in 2010 the South Korean corvette *Cheonan* was sunk without warning by a North Korean minisubmarine in a power mismatch that demonstrated the viability of this threat of asymmetric warfare.[23]

Prospective competitors recognize that the United States and its allies want to maintain their conventional military primacy. In response those competitors employ a combination of traditional means, irregular warfare, terrorism, and criminal activities—aided by cyber attack and malevolent information campaigns—to circumvent or negate conventional defenses. This amalgam of capabilities not only targets opposing militaries but also threatens the political, economic, and social order of nations. Recent offensive actions by Hezbollah illustrate this rising hybrid threat. In thirty-four days of conflict with Israel in 2006, this militant group fielded disciplined units equipped with antitank guided missiles against armored forces while launching thousands of rockets to terrorize Israeli citizens.[24] Hezbollah also utilized the Internet as well as sympathetic cable networks to publicize its military successes.[25]

Hezbollah also introduced a maritime dimension by attacking the Israeli corvette *Hanit* with two radar-guided C-802 Silkworm antiship missiles, although it was not the first instance in which a hybrid threat fired shore-based missiles. Iranian Silkworm missiles hit the American-owned Liberian-flagged tanker *Sungari* and the Kuwaiti tanker *Sea Isle City* in 1987. Over the course of Operation Earnest Will, the US naval convoy effort that escorted tankers during the Iran–Iraq conflict, the major concern of the task force commander was unconventional threats: swarms of small boats armed with rockets, grenade launchers, and machine guns supported by frigates, fighter bombers, mining operations, and cruise or surface-to-air missiles.[26]

Emerging hybrid threats signal that the age of uncontested projection of US and allied seapower and airpower supported by space-based assets and cyber networks is waning. Specifically, several nations are seeking to increase the costs of leveraging power in areas of vital interest.[27] They are likely to employ anti-access capabilities in the future, which will be enhanced by high-tech antisatellite weapons and cyber warfare. This trend is evident in the Chinese development of air superiority fighters (Su-27s and J10s), two-stage, solid-fueled, medium-range ballistic missiles (DF-21Cs), long-range land-attack cruise missiles (DH-10s), and antiship ballistic missiles (DF-21Ds) in addition to antiship cruise missiles (SS-N-22 Sunburns and SS-N-27 Sizzlers) and underwater combat systems (Song SS, Kilo SS, and Shang SSN).[28] As newer systems like the J-20 prototype fifth-generation combat aircraft or the blue-water aircraft carrier *Shi Lang* and carrier-capable J-15 aircraft are developed and fielded, high-end capabilities will more openly threaten forward bases and operational sanctuaries that support the projection of conventional allied forces.[29]

The force modernization of competitors increases the chance of their militaries gaining diplomatic advantage, and it will eventually increase their leverage in disputes. Nevertheless, military-to-military exchanges may reduce mistrust, enhance mutual understanding, and broaden cooperation. Interaction can encourage constructive participation in missions that address mutual security concerns such as peacekeeping, humanitarian assistance, and countering piracy. However, the United States and its allies have a responsibility to monitor force modernization and deter conflict. Maintaining both peace and stability may be enhanced by building alliances and partnerships and capability development.[30]

One promising development at the joint level is the agreement by the US Navy and US Air Force to collaborate on an air-sea battle concept.[31] The concept will address naval and air capabilities that may be integrated to defeat anti-access systems and guide the advent of power-projection capabilities. Such initiatives might include land- and seabased kinetic and nonkinetic air and missile defenses; long-range strike capabilities for unmanned combat air systems and stealthy intelligence, surveillance, and reconnaissance; both offensive and defensive cyber assets; space hedge (rapid-launch and micro satellites) and control, undersea, and air refueling capabilities; and base hardening, rapid base repair, and regeneration.[32] None of these many systems can be developed in isolation but rather must be pursued within the context of a cooperative strategy that fully engages government agencies, the commercial sector, and international partners.

COLLECTIVE STRATEGIES

The modes of conflict employed by Hezbollah demonstrate that security competitors embrace strategies that integrate every source of influence at their disposal including military, political, diplomatic, societal, and informational resources. Hezbollah is more than a military force, which is a lesson that developed nations must fully appreciate to effectively mitigate similar crises.[33] Threats to security require coordination of the instruments of national power. As Secretary of State Hillary Clinton explained: "We are shifting from mostly direct exercise and application of power to a more sophisticated and difficult mix of indirect power and influence."[34]

A comprehensive approach to US national security must integrate all the capabilities of allies and coalition partners, international and nongovernmental organizations (NGOs), and the private sector.[35] At the Bucharest Summit in 2008 the North Atlantic Treaty Organization (NATO) endorsed an action plan to develop and implement contributions of a comprehensive approach.[36] Afghanistan and the Balkans have demonstrated the importance of including relevant actors in the planning and conduct of operations, especially those with skills in areas such as institution building, development, and governance. That approach is relevant not only in stabilization and reconstruction but also more broadly in addressing other security challenges of the twenty-first century such as protecting against cyber attacks and countering the threat of piracy.[37]

Although military action remains the established means of applying hard power in the commons, civilian agencies and commercial stakeholders also can play a role in containing or resolving conflicts. Using deterrent and cooperation incentives, a comprehensive approach may harmonize the objectives of various partners to ensure the well-being of their constituencies. Such an approach is centered on the shared "principles and collaborative processes that enhance the likelihood of favorable and enduring outcomes within a particular situation."[38]

The initial step in implementing a comprehensive approach for the global commons is establishing policies, mechanisms, and incentives for cooperation. For example, those states with unclear intentions should be encouraged to participate in multilateral operations in the maritime domain where their interests align, such as the proliferation of weapons of mass destruction or broader maritime security.[39] In the space domain there are potent incentives to cooperate in mutually beneficial activities including research, operations, and exploration.[40] In cyber defense of critical infrastructure and key resources, public and private sector partnerships could create or enhance shared situational awareness of network vulnerabilities, threats, and events.[41]

FLEXIBLE DETERRENCE

Deterrence remains a critical element of a comprehensive approach to the commons. Efforts by competitors to gain asymmetric military advantages reveal that attempts to deter them have not produced optimal results. Strategies that threaten military action are not always effective. The motivations of potential enemies can be hard to fathom much less counter, although established dependencies provide them with vulnerable targets. This is especially true of cyberspace and outer space as defenses and countermeasures attempt to keep pace with networked command, communication, surveillance, and engagement systems. The escalating effects of retaliatory strikes in cyberspace and outer space have given rise to "a new form of mutually assured destruction—or at least mutually assured disruption."[42] Moreover, in view of recent events, Beijing "clearly sees Internet and mobile innovation as a major driver of its global economic competitiveness."[43]

Deterrence mechanisms of retaliation and denial become even more problematic in the commons due to factors such as attribution, proportionality, and escalation. For those nations aspiring to collaborate in the global order, the focus of deterrence in the commons must shift toward incentivizing compliance with international norms and behaviors while maintaining the will to promote the ideals of liberal democracy.[44] Would-be powers must recognize that their self-interests dictate the formation of an international regime to protect the interests of all parties in ensuring responsible, sustainable, and cooperative use of shared domains.

Economic entanglement is one potentially effective deterrent incentive. Nations become entangled in the global system through economic and by extension political relationships that create dependencies that provide a disincentive for conflict.[45] Entanglement is based on the notion that economics is the major driver of conflict and generally overrides political, ideological, and cultural factors and that global players will tend to act out of self-interest.[46] This approach has been augmented in recent years by an additional means of comprehensive entanglement in the form of information access. The free flow of information has proven to be a compelling way to persuade autocratic or isolated governments to balance control over their citizens against the accessibility of sufficient global information to maintain the health of their economy.

Strategic alignment is the endeavor to identify mutual interests and work cooperatively toward beneficial outcomes. Militaries can support this alignment by planning and training for cooperative security in spaces and transit points strategically important to the international community. Threats to economic prosperity are powerful incentives for cooperation with forces from rising centers of influence. The concerted international response to piracy off the coast of Somalia is one encouraging example of the willingness of the international community to act in concert to protect and secure the global commons out of shared economic interests.[47]

Ultimately, an effective comprehensive approach to security in the commons will rely on national governments, global industries, and international agencies working together in a unified and coherent fashion to combine traditional disincentives with the more effective application of incentives such as international norms, economic entanglement, and strategic alignment.

MITIGATION INCENTIVES

Operating within the commons imposes new and unfamiliar risks.[48] As one defense expert has observed: "The prevalence of complex contingencies and the military's heavy involvement in them call for a new approach to judging risk and ultimately a new grand bargain to align our capabilities and requirements."[49] Threats range from competitors engaging in hybrid modes of warfare to adept criminals exploiting vulnerabilities. In all cases, however, conflicts are characterized by a high degree of uncertainty, transnational influences, and adaptive strategies that respond to shifts in economic, cultural, and geopolitical conditions. To achieve success in this environment it is critical to understand current global activities, identify changes, and anticipate and prepare for likely futures.[50] Although each shared space in the commons implies unique challenges and levels of integration, cooperation remains critical to developing strategies to mitigate risk when confronted by hostile threats.

Cyberspace Risk

The chief of naval operations stated that much of what we rely on "to operate and conduct business and even to socialize today, lives in the cyber domain without adequate defense."[51] Cyberspace is defined as an "interdependent network of information technology infrastructures, including the Internet, telecommunications networks, computer systems, and embedded processors and controllers."[52] US Cyber Command conducts activities to direct the operations and defense of specified Department of Defense information networks whereas the US Department of Homeland Security protects federal civilian department and agency networks.[53] Although both departments share information with the private sector, which owns roughly 85 percent of cyber infrastructure, industry protects itself.[54] The unsettling reality is that the military remains highly dependent on the private sector to provide connectivity and information.[55]

Cyber commerce relies on public confidence in cyber security. For that reason economic incentives that compel the business community to assure cyber security have reversed traditional relationships whereby the public sector depends on the private sector for research, expertise, and tools to guarantee cyber security. Moreover, business firms that depend on consumer confidence in the cyber marketplace are reluctant to trust government in countering cyber threats because of fears over intrusive oversight or perceptions that public bodies lack competence and jurisdiction to secure the cyber domain, which is not contained within sovereign boundaries.[56]

Such unusual security relationships create some significant impediments for public and private sector cooperation. Aside from the inherent difficulty of attributing cyber attacks, other considerations like market impacts, customer confidence, legal concerns, proprietary data, and inadequate law enforcement negatively impact on information sharing and cooperation between the public and private sectors. In fact, the US Government Accountability Office acknowledges that before companies decide to report cyber incidents they must "weigh the cost and impact of the incident with the time and effort needed to support an investigation and prosecution."[57]

The international community recognizes that the best weapon against online criminals, spies, and terrorists who threaten national security and global trade is the international private-public coordination of cyberspace. First, a unified effort must expose anonymous players who threaten cyberspace. Because the Internet is an integral part of the political, social, and economic landscape, there are no incentives for providing sanctuary to cyber rogues.[58] Although the private sector may assist in threat attribution, the public sector must pursue cyber criminals. The cyber domain is unlike other domains in that its physical infrastructure of computers, manufacturers, and personnel is situated in sovereign national territory and owned by someone. In contrast, it is like other domains in that it transcends national jurisdictions and requires an international legal regime to enforce penalties for serious violations.[59] Second, governments must develop financial incentives to encourage the private sector to improve security that include tax breaks, limitations on liability, and standard certifications. One journalist who reports on the field commented that "attacks are relatively easy and cheap, and the gains from them can be enormous. On the other hand, defense can be costly and the perimeter to defend is virtually infinite."[60]

Outer Space Risk

Aerodynamic lift yields to centrifugal force sixty-two miles above sea level at the Von Karman line, which defines the edge of outer space. Both military and commercial orbital systems have become critical to the economic, scientific, and defense communities. Space systems provide communications, navigation, and digital information and entertainment for millions of people. As one senior allied officer described this trend: "History shows that humans have fought for dominance over every medium which contributes to commerce. Space may well prove to be no different."[61] Institutions engaged in space research offer the best understanding of Earth and its environment as well as the outer limits of space. The military depends on satellites to locate enemies, target weapons, detect missiles, and secure global command and control.[62]

Critical space assets are extremely vulnerable to accidental and hostile actions. There are estimated to be more than 22,000 man-made objects in space ranging from satellites, research systems, and commercial assets to space junk, which hurtle at thousands of miles an hour on an unsynchronized orbital speedway. Spacefaring nations such as the United States and China have demonstrated the ability to precisely target and destroy systems in orbit. Militaries around the globe, both friendly and hostile, are constantly studying the US military operations supported by space assets in order to gain insights on vulnerabilities and strengths.[63]

Dependence on the space domain assumes the protection of access to space systems. One way of mitigating unnecessary risk is through space situational awareness that identifies the location, status, and purpose of space assets. This awareness can enable spaceflight safety and avoid orbital collisions. It also can determine when an incident in space is hostile, unintentional, or simply a malfunction.[64] Space situational awareness provides a means of implementing and monitoring compliance with international treaties, agreements, and standards.[65]

Norms can regulate appropriate behavior for nations that deploy, utilize, and influence space-based assets. The *National Space Policy* published in 2010 made a commitment to an arms control policy that is "equitable, effectively verifiable, and enhances the national security of the United States and its allies."[66] For instance, the national development of offensive space capabilities should be considered within the broader context of compliance to a legitimate code of conduct that discourages first-strike targeting of vital and vulnerable space assets.[67]

An effective way to mitigate risk in space calls for augmenting and reconstituting space capabilities. The operational responsive space concept presents a three-tiered solution including rapid deployment of on-call ready-to-field assets in days or weeks.[68] This concept has potential to enhance the synergistic application of instruments of power by reducing barriers to the space sector. Coalitions might deploy a constellation of small, special-mission satellites through shared investments for mutual benefit.[69] Moreover, commercial entities may contribute in various ways to assure spacepower, like the Commercially Hosted Infrared Payload program that has taken advantage of excess payload capacity to attach responsive military sensor packages.[70]

Maritime Domain Risk

International waters comprise the oceans beyond the twelve-mile limit measured in accordance with the UN Convention on the Law of the Sea.[71] These waters pose challenges for the international community as terrorists and other criminals leverage this unregulated domain to mask and facilitate their illicit activities. Identifying and tracking such threats are critical to ensuring security and economic prosperity.[72] According to one commentator, "The sea is the lifeblood of our global economy and it is appropriate [that] the Coalition, NATO and other international partners work together to address this problem [of piracy]."[73]

Maritime security partnerships that incorporate governmental and commercial entities in consortiums for mutual security can greatly enhance global awareness.[74] For example, selected commercial partners may act as sensor enhancements to existing information-sharing networks. The top three firms operate about three times as many vessels as the 1,200 bottoms found in all the navies of the world and have large economic interests in enhanced maritime awareness.[75] If commercial ships were connected to the naval and security networks that are regionally controlled, they could vastly improve network visibility and coverage.

The power of naval-commercial cooperation is evident in the pirate-infested waters of the Gulf of Aden. Vessels voluntarily share their movements with the United Kingdom Maritime Transportation Office in Dubai, United Arab Emirates, or the European Union Maritime Security Centre–Horn of Africa, and in return, they get updates on pirate activity and shipping lane security.[76] As the benefit of maritime information sharing becomes more evident, commercial vessels could be more fully integrated into sensor networks and form a regional maritime security consortium. This concept may be implemented by providing commercial partners with both interoperable tracking and standardized incident reporting systems to establish something akin to a maritime neighborhood watch.[77]

Airspace Risk

Air superiority enables precision-strike forces to be deployed from forward positions and engage targets anywhere in the world.[78] In the case of Asia-Pacific security the senior US commander in the region warns that "China continues to develop weapons systems, technologies and concepts of operation that support anti-access and area denial strategies in the Western Pacific by holding air and maritime forces at risk at extended distances."[79] The United States and its allies must be capable of striking from beyond the anti-access zone to ensure theater security and to deter nonstate actors that might assume they can threaten vital national interests with impunity.[80]

One concern is that relatively short-range F-35 Joint Strike Fighters, which are touted as a game changer because of stealth, supersonic, and sensor capabilities, will be deployed from forward bases at sea or on land but rendered untenably vulnerable.[81] For example, the combat radius of the F-35C carrier variant is 640 miles or inside the 900-mile-plus threat envelope of Chinese DF-21D anti-ship ballistic missiles that feature maneuverable high-speed (Mach 10–12) reentry vehicles.[82] The current status of this anti-access missile is determined to have achieved the initial operational capability of a comparable, existing US weapons system.[83]

Enhanced long-range strike options including both penetrating platforms and standoff weapons systems are essential capabilities for a concerted response to unstable threats, such as failing or aggressive nuclear powers, and to anti-access threats in the commons. Unmanned air systems such as the Predator, Reaper, and Global Hawk can address to some extent the anti-access threat through their persistent surveillance and strike ability.[84] Next-generation unmanned aircraft including the X-47B Naval Unmanned Combat Air System, which has a combat radius of 1,500 miles, promises revolutionary advances in long-range surveillance and strike ability through the development of stealth technologies and carrier-based launch.[85] The X-47B demonstration program has successfully completed first test flights for two prototype aircraft, exhibiting the viability of a tailless, fighter-sized aircraft and the navigation system that allows it to fly without a pilot on board.[86] These emerging systems have potential to counter threats and reduce risk of pilot casualties. In order to achieve success in contested airspace, these systems must be hardened against GPS-denial and communication or data link-out situations as well as partially hardened against both land-based and aerial threats.[87]

VOLUME INTENT

The global commons are congested, contested, and competitive. The four domains are distinct yet have many similarities and are closely interwoven. It is insufficient to conceptualize or deal with them independently; differentiate among civil, commercial, and military spheres; or segregate military roles. In the face of persistent or unfamiliar threats and their consequences, the global commons can serve as an organizing principle or construct for developing strategy, policy, and capabilities. Toward those ends this volume provides a forum for the contributors to describe the nature and impact of conflict and cooperation dynamics within and among the four domains.

The work is organized to identify and explore in order and depth the trends, contexts, and implications of persistent conflict and opportunistic cooperation. The authors provide considerations that can enhance, influence, and align commercial industry, civil agency, and military department perspectives and actions in a comprehensive approach for the commons. The chapters describe emerging developments and methods in conflict and, in response, suggest novel policies, mechanisms, incentives, and norms for cooperation. The aim of the volume is to embrace security precedents and best practices in order to recommend strategies and partnerships for responsible and sustainable use of the commons.

Part I, Security Dynamics, frames the competing interests and motivations that threaten security and prosperity in the global commons. In the first chapter Sandra Leavitt considers the uses and misuses of the commons as sources of global public goods, examines impediments to forming collective action groups for the security of the commons, and proposes three strategies to resolve these problems. Ian Adam then rehearses the causes and character of conflict in the commons to include the range of threats, vulnerabilities, and features. To conclude, Schuyler Foerster focuses on concepts of deterrence for actors inclined to wage conflict in and on the commons that serve as strategic environments for securing shared interests.

Part II, Conflict Methods, posits that because the oceans and airspace above them formed the first internationally recognized global commons, they can serve as the models for addressing the emerging space and cyberspace domains. To lay the groundwork, Sam Tangredi outlines the legal, diplomatic, and economic contexts of the maritime commons in peace and war that guide naval presence and power in the face of two major maritime disputes. Then Mark Stokes and Ian Easton portray how the integrated application of asymmetric air and space capabilities in coercive campaigns threatens regional stability and why accession to standing treaties might help resolve tensions. Following their analysis, Kevin Coleman details the cyber attack process with associated weaponry characteristics and modes drawn from actual incidents and discusses the value yet difficulties of cyber arms control.

Part III, Cooperative Opportunities, shapes thinking on how government, commercial, and military stakeholders can collaborate in defense of the commons. First, Susan Hocevar applies a conceptual model framework to examine structures and methods of cooperation among multiple nations and agencies with shared interests and complementary capabilities. Then, in a look at joint operational access, Paul Giarra explores the way that concepts and doctrine codify defense planning and military operations for countering competitor strategies designed to undermine traditional advantages and preferred means. To conclude this section, Marc Berkowitz examines domain interdependency in terms of the necessary measures and constructs for a comprehensive, whole-of-nations approach to protect and execute operations in space and cyberspace.

Part IV, Interface Mechanisms, provides insights on the various types of forums, practices, and incentives used in implementing a comprehensive approach. Gordan Van Hook begins by reflecting on the necessity for public-private efforts because of threats on the high seas to the global economic system and offers sample initiatives and activities to achieve maritime domain awareness. Next, Larry Clinton rounds out the section with an explanation of how business economics influences decisions in the private sector related to cyber security and thus why a market incentive system that embraces best practices is necessary to stimulate investment.

Part V, Behavioral Norms, focuses on those rules that advance peace and stability in the international environment by delineating how actors should work together to meet obligations. Michael Krepon makes the case for a code of conduct that establishes standards, expectations, and responsible behavior necessary for space. That discussion is complemented by Eneken Tikk, who describes the concept of rules for responsible state and stakeholder behavior for cyber security derived from existing legal frameworks, in the final chapter of the book.

The commons are probed, penetrated, and threatened daily through nefarious actions and disturbing developments. Military departments, civilian agencies, and commercial stakeholders all play roles in preventing, containing, or resolving conflicts. This volume is intended to provide the perspectives and methods for them to cooperate in a comprehensive approach for security.

NOTES

The epigraph appeared in new strategic guidance issued by the Secretary of Defense titled *Sustaining US Global Leadership: Priorities for 21st Century Defense* (Washington, DC: Office of the Secretary of Defense, January 5, 2012), 3.

1. United States Department of Defense, *Quadrennial Defense Review Report* (Washington, DC: Office of the Secretary of Defense, February 1, 2010), 8.
2. Mark A. Barrett, Dick Bedford, Elizabeth Skinner, and Eva Vergles, "Assured Access to the Global Commons" (Norfolk, VA: Supreme Allied Command Transformation, April 3, 2011), 5.
3. [Stewart M. Patrick], "International Institutions and Global Governance Program: World Order in the 21st Century" (Washington, DC: Council on Foreign Relations, May 1, 2008), 6.
4. C. Raja Mohan, "Rising India: Partner in Shaping the Global Commons?" *Washington Quarterly* 33 (July 2010): 133–38.
5. Abraham M. Denmark and James C. Mulvenon, "Contested Commons: The Future of American Power in a Multipolar World" (Washington, DC: Center for a New American Security, January 2010), 5.
6. Aerospace Industries Association, *2009 Year-End Review and 2010 Forecast* (Arlington, VA: AIA Research Center, December 15, 2010), www.aia-aerospace.org/assets/year -end-09_Review_and_Analysis.pdf.
7. US Census Bureau, Economics and Statistics Administration, "E-Stats" (Washington, DC, May 26, 2011), www.census.gov/econ/estats.
8. Kathleen Hicks, remarks presented at a conference on the "2010 Cooperation and Conflict in the Global Commons," sponsored by the Naval Postgraduate School, National Defense University, US Joint Forces Command, and Allied Command Transformation, Virginia Beach, Virginia, June 29, 2010.
9. Ian Easton, "The Great Game in Space: China's Evolving ASAT Weapons Program and Their Implications for Future US Strategy" (Washington, DC: Project 2049 Institute, June 20, 2009), 2–7.
10. Ron Deibert and Rafal Rohozinski, "Shadows in the Cloud: Investigating Cyber Espionage 2.0" (Toronto: Information Warfare Monitor, Munk School of Global Affairs, University of Toronto, April 6, 2010), 4–6, http://shadows-in-the-cloud.net.
11. See, for example, Inigo Guevara, "Venezuela Eyes Russian S-300 System Banned from Iran," *Jane's Defence Weekly*, October 27, 2010, 5. See also Sebastien Falletti, Duncan

Lennox, and Ted Parsons, "Pyongyang Shows Off Hardware and New Heir," *Jane's Defence Weekly*, October 26, 2010, 4–7.

12. Eric Talmadge, "Chinese Missile Could Shift Pacific Power Balance: US Naval Planners Are Scrambling to Deal with Carrier-Killing Weapon," Associated Press, August 5, 2010, www.msnbc.msn.com/id/38580745/ns/world_news-asiapacific/.

13. William Matthews, "Cyber Chief: US Needs 'Situational Awareness' of Computer Attacks," *Defense News*, June 7, 2010, 27.

14. Kim Zetter, "Clues Suggest Stuxnet Virus Was Built for Subtle Nuclear Sabotage," *Wired*, November 15, 2010, www.wired.com/threatlevel/2010/11/stuxnet-clues/#.

15. William Matthews, "US Security Experts Differ on Impact of Cyberattacks," *Defense News*, July 13, 2009, 14.

16. Edward M. Morris, "A Day without Space: Economic and National Security Ramifications," remarks presented at the George Marshall Institute and Space Enterprise Council, Washington, DC, October 16, 2008, 2–8, www.marshall.org/article.php?id=695.

17. TS [Thomas Sean] Kelso, "How International Collaboration Is Improving Space Situational Awareness," *High Frontier* 6 (February 2010): 23.

18. Frank G. Hoffman, "Conflict in the 21st Century: Rise of the Hybrid Wars" (Arlington, VA: Potomac Institute for Policy Studies, December 2007), 7.

19. Tim Lister, "Analysis: Saber-rattling in Strait of Hormuz," *CNN.com*, December 28, 2011, http://articles.cnn.com/2011-12-28/middleeast/world_meast_iran-hormuz_1 _strait-iranian-warship-iranian-oil-platforms?_s=PM:MIDDLEEAST.

20. Scott Peterson, "Iran War Games Begin with New 'Ultra Fast' Speed Boat," *Christian Science Monitor*, April 22, 2010, http://defensetech.org/2010/04/26/hybrid-war-at-sea -irans-great-prophet-5-exercises/. See Jeremy Binnie, "Iran Flexes Sea Denial Muscles," *Jane's Defence Weekly*, January 11, 2012, 16.

21. Tamir Eshel, "Updated: Iran's Hornets Nest at Bandar Abbas," Defense Update, September 30, 2010, http://defense-update.com/wp/20100930_irans-hornets-nest-at-bandar -abbas.html.

22. Jeremy Binnie, "Iranian Sub Fleet Continues to Expand," *Jane's Defence Weekly*, February 22, 2012, 16.

23. Pauline Jeliner, "Ship Sinking Was Near US, Korean Exercises," *Monterey County Herald*, June 6, 2010.

24. Frank G. Hoffman, "Hybrid Warfare and Challenges," *Joint Force Quarterly* 54 (2009): 34–39.

25. Stephen D. Biddle and Jeffrey A. Friedman, "The 2006 Lebanon Campaign and the Future of Warfare: Implications for Army and Defense Policy" (Carlisle Barracks, PA: US Army War College, Strategic Studies Institute, September 2008), 4.

26. Frank G. Hoffman, "Hybrid Threats: Neither Omnipotent nor Unbeatable," *Orbis* 54 (Summer 2010): 446–52.

27. Andrew F. Krepinevich, "Why AirSea Battle?" (Washington, DC: Center for Strategic and Budgetary Assessments, 2010), 7–11.

28. Mark A. Stokes and Ian Easton, "Evolving Aerospace Trends in the Asia-Pacific Region" (Washington, DC: Project 2049 Institute, May 27, 2010), 12–18; Ronald O'Rourke, "China Naval Modernization: Implications for US Navy Capabilities: Background and Issues for Congress" (Washington, DC: Congressional Research Service, February 8, 2012), 7–15.

29. On the former, see Reuben F. Johnson, "China's J-20 Clocks Up 18-Minute Maiden Flight," *Jane's Defence Weekly*, January 19, 2011, 4; on the latter, see Wendell Mimmick, "China's Navy Set to Launch First Carrier This Year: Paper," *Defense News*, March 19,

2012, 22, and Reuben F. Johnson, "Images Suggest Shenyang Making Progress on Carrier-Capable J-15," *Jane's Navy International*, March 2012, 11; Ben Iannotta, "Red Scare? Navy Intel Director Outlines Threats from China's New, High-Tech Weapons," *Navy Times*, January 17, 2011, 6.

30. United States Department of Defense, *Military and Security Developments Involving the People's Republic of China* (Washington, DC: Office of the Secretary of Defense, 2010), 1, 56.

31. Dave Majumdar, "U.S. AirSea Battle Takes Shape amid Debate," *Defense News*, October 10, 2011, 70.

32. Jan Van Tol, Mark Gunzinger, Andrew F. Krepinevich, and Jim Thomas, "AirSea Battle: A Point-of-Departure Operational Concept" (Washington, DC: Center for Strategic and Budgetary Assessments, May 18, 2010), 36.

33. Russell W. Glenn, "Thoughts on 'Hybrid' Conflict," *Small Wars Journal* (February 24, 2009): 3–4, http://smallwarsjournal.com/blog/journal/docs-temp/188-glenn.pdf.

34. Hillary R. Clinton, "Previewing the Obama Administration's National Security Strategy: A Conversation with Secretary of State Hillary Clinton," remarks presented at the Brookings Institution, Washington, DC, May 27, 2010, www.brookings.edu/~/media/Files/events/2010/0527_secretary_clinton/20100527_national_security_strategy.pdf.

35. Stephan J. Hadley and William J. Perry, "The QDR in Perspective: Meeting America's National Security Needs in the 21st Century" (Washington, DC: US Institute of Peace, July 29, 2010), 31–32.

36. North Atlantic Treaty Organization, "Bucharest Summit Declaration," April 3, 2010, www.nato.int/cps/en/natolive/official_texts_8443.htm.

37. Ibid., "A Comprehensive Approach," August 10, 2010, www.nato.int/cps/en/natolive/topics_51633.htm.

38. United Kingdom, Ministry of Defence, "The Comprehensive Approach," joint discussion note 4/05 (Shrivenham: Joint Doctrine and Concepts Centre, 2006), 1–4 to 1–5, www.mod.uk/NR/rdonlyres/25A7F4A2-31C2-49D8-A857-4D31750CBD6F/0/20071218_jdn4_05_U_DCDCIMAPPS.pdf.

39. Gidget Fuentes, "Keeping the Pacific Peaceful: From N. Korean Threat to Chinese Growth, US Regional Commander Outlines Challenges," *Defense News*, July 19, 2010, 38.

40. Michael F. O'Brien, "NASA, Exploring the Boundaries of International Cooperation," *High Frontier* 6 (February 2010): 26–29.

41. United States, Executive Office of the President, *The Comprehensive National Cybersecurity Initiative* (Washington, DC: The White House, March 5, 2010), 1–5.

42. Thomas M. Davis, "Schriever Wargame 2010: A Political Perspective," *High Frontier* 7 (November 2010): 3.

43. Rebecca MacKinnon, quoted in Melanie Lee and Jennifer Saba, "Google Gets Nod from China to Keep Search Page," Reuters Online (Shanghai/New York), July 9, 2010, www.reuters.com/article/idUSTRE6676L220100709.

44. Roger G. Harrison, Deron R. Jackson, and Collins G. Shackleford, "Space Deterrence: The Delicate Balance of Risk," *Space and Defense* 3 (Summer 2009): 8.

45. Chadwick I. Smith, "North Korea: The Case for Strategic Entanglement," *Orbis* 50 (Spring 2006): 352.

46. The notion of entanglement is used in game theory to predict cooperative and competitive behavior of well-informed rational actors based on economic self-interest. Access to information is fundamental for reliable outcomes. See John Von Neuman and Oskar Morgenstern, *Theory of Games and Economic Behavior* (Princeton, NJ: Princeton University Press, 1944).

47. Lauren Gelfand, "NATO Extends Piracy Mission off Somalia," *Jane's Defence Weekly*, March 17, 2010, 16.
48. James N. Miller, testimony before the House Committee on Armed Services, 111th Cong., 2nd Sess., March 16, 2010.
49. Thomas G. Mahnken, "A New Grand Bargain: Implementing the Comprehensive Approach in Defense Planning," *Joint Force Quarterly* 55 (2009): 13.
50. James N. Mattis, "The Joint Operating Environment" (Norfolk, VA: US Joint Forces Command, February 18, 2010), 4–5.
51. Gary Roughead, remarks presented at the commissioning of US Fleet Cyber Command and recommissioning of US Tenth Fleet, Fort George G. Meade, Maryland, January 29, 2010.
52. *DOD Dictionary of Military and Associated Terms*, Joint Publication 1-02, as amended (Washington, DC: Joint Chiefs of Staff, November 8, 2010), 49.
53. Keith B. Alexander, testimony before the Subcommittee on Emerging Threats and Capabilities, House Committee on Armed Services, 112th Cong., 1st Sess., March 16, 2011; Philip Rettinger, "Examining the Cyber Threat to Critical Infrastructure and the American Economy," testimony before the Subcommittee on Cybersecurity, Infrastructure Protection, and Security Technologies, House Committee on Homeland Security, 112th Cong., 1st Sess., March 16, 2011.
54. Janet Napolitano and Robert M. Gates, "Memorandum of Agreement between the Department of Homeland Security and the Department of Defense Regarding Cybersecurity," October 13, 2010, 1–5; William Matthews, "In Cyber War, Most of US Must Defend Itself," *Defense News*, June 7, 2010, 27.
55. Keith Rhodes, "Cybersecurity: Make It Work This Year," *Defense News*, June 11, 2010, 29.
56. John P. Mello Jr., "Cybercrime Costs US Economy at Least $117B Each Year," *TechNewsWorld, E-Commerce Times* News Network, July 14, 2010, www.ecommerce-times.com/story/58517.html?wlc=1279151574.
57. "Cybercrime: Public and Private Entities Face Challenges in Addressing Cyber Threats" (Washington, DC: US Government Accountability Office, June 2007), 37–38, www.gao.gov/new.items/d07705.pdf.
58. Varkan Sarkissian, "Interim Report from the First Worldwide Cybersecurity Summit" (Dallas, TX: EastWest Institute, May 28, 2010), www.ewi.info/interim-report-first-worldwide-cybersecurity-summit.
59. Eneken Tikk, Kadri Kaska, Kristel Rünnimeri, Mari Kert, Anna-Maria Talihärm, and Liis Vihul, "Cyber Attacks against Georgia: Legal Lessons Identified" (Tallinn: NATO Cooperative Cyber Defence Center of Excellence, 2008), 18–25.
60. William Matthews, "Cyber War's 'Front Lines' May Be in Private Hands: ISA," *Defense News*, December 7, 2009, 38.
61. Friedrich Wilhelm Ploeger, excerpt from "NATO Space Operations Assessment" (Kalkar: NATO Joint Air Power Competence Centre, January 30, 2009), ii.
62. Marion C. Blakey, testimony before the Subcommittee on Space and Aeronautics of the House Committee on Science and Technology, 111th Cong., 1st Sess., April 28, 2009.
63. Edward M. Morris, "The Importance of Space Commerce to National Power," *High Frontier* 3 (March 2007): 3–6.
64. Ploeger, "Operations Assessment," 33–34.
65. United States Department of Defense, *Space Operations*, Joint Publication 3-14 (Washington, DC: Joint Chiefs of Staff, January 6, 2009), II-7 to II-9.
66. United States, Executive Office of the President, *National Space Policy of the United States of America* (Washington, DC: The White House, June 28, 2010), 7.

67. Bruce W. MacDonald, testimony before the Subcommittee on Strategic Forces of the House Committee on Armed Services, 111th Cong., 1st Sess., March 18, 2009.

68. Peter M. Wegner, "Operationally Responsive Space: Not New, Just Bringing New Approaches to Space," *High Frontier* 6 (May 2010): 7. See Ben Iannotta, "Central Command's ORS-1 satellite goes fully operational," *C4ISR Journal* (March 2012): 12.

69. Joseph D. Rouge and John E. Puffenbarger, "Operationally Responsive Space: An Avenue to Evolving the Space Enterprise Architecture," *High Frontier* 6 (May 2010): 11–12.

70. See John T. Sheridan, "Operationally Responsive Space and the National Security Space Architecture," *High Frontier* 6 (May 2010): 3–4. See also Ben Iannotta, "Hosted Payload Launch Could Set Precedent," *C4ISR Journal* (October 2011): 12.

71. UN Convention on the Law of the Sea, updated July 21, 2010, part 2, 27–40, www.un .org/Depts/los/convention_agreements/convention_overview_convention.htm.

72. James T. Conway, Gary Roughhead, and Thad W. Allen, "Naval Operations Concept: Implementing the Maritime Strategy," remarks presented at the Navy League Sea-Air-Space Expo, National Harbor, Maryland, May 2, 2010.

73. Tim Lowe, quoted in "Two Million Somalis Survive on Food Aid Shipped Past Pirates," *Environmental News Service International Daily Newswire* (Rome), November 19, 2008, www.ens-newswire.com/ens/nov2008/2008-11-19-02.html.

74. Gordan E. Van Hook, "Maritime Security Consortiums," in *Cutting the Bow Wave, 2009–2010* (Norfolk, VA: Combined Joint Operations from the Sea Centre of Excellence, 2010), 22–24.

75. United States Department of Transportation, "Leading World Maritime Container Carriers by Fleet Size: September 2009" (Washington, DC: Research and Innovative Technology Administration, Bureau of Transportation Statistics, September 2009), www.bts.gov/publications/freight_transportation/html/table_13.html.

76. European Union, Naval Force Somalia, www.mschoa.org/links/pages/UKMTO .aspx.

77. Gordan E. Van Hook, "On the Horizon," *C4ISR Journal*, October 2010, 46–49.

78. United States Department of Defense, *Countering Air and Missile Threats*, Joint Publication 3-01 (Washington, DC: Joint Chiefs of Staff, March 23, 2012), I-2.

79. Robert F. Willard, testimony before the Senate Armed Services Committee, 111th Cong., 2nd Sess., March 23, 2010.

80. Abraham M. Denmark, "Managing the Global Commons," *Washington Quarterly* 33 (July 2010): 165–82, www.cnas.org/node/4695.

81. Caitlin Harrington, "F-35C Makes First Successful Flight-Test," *Jane's Defence Weekly*, June 16, 2010, 10; Karen Walker, "Beyond the Numbers, behind the Capabilities," *Armed Forces Journal* (July–August 2010): 14–18.

82. Lockheed Martin Corporation, "F-35 Lightning II, Capabilities, F-35C STOVL Variant," www.lockheedmartin.com/products/f35/f-35c-cv-variant.html; Andrew S. Erickson and David D. Yang, "Using the Land to Control the Sea?" *Naval War College Review* 62 (Autumn 2009): 53–79.

83. Andrew S. Erickson and Gabriel B. Collins, "China Deploys World's First Long-Range, Land-Based 'Carrier Killer,'" *China SignPost*, December 26, 2010, 1.

84. Robert F. Spaulding, "America's Two Air Forces," *Air and Space Power Journal* 23 (Summer 2009): 51–56.

85. Gidget Fuentes, "US Navy Carrier UAV Set to Fly in November," *Defense News*, July 20, 2009, 42; Thomas P. Erhard and Robert O. Work, "Range, Persistence, Stealth, and

Networking: The Case for a Carrier-Based Unmanned Combat Air System" (Washington, DC: Center for Strategic and Budgetary Assessments, 2008), 137–47.

86. Associated Press, "Unmanned Aircraft Passes Test Flight," *Monterey County Herald*, February 7, 2011. See also Marina Malenic, "USN Completes Second UCAS-D Test-Flight," *Jane's Defence Weekly*, December 7, 2011, 10.

87. Dave Majumdar, "Future UAVs Must Be Hardened: USAF Officers," *Defense News*, April 25, 2011, 22.

PART I

SECURITY DYNAMICS

CHAPTER 1

Problems in
Collective Action

❖

SANDRA R. LEAVITT

> Global public goods can only be attained if countries work
> together, and globalization has only increased this fundamental
> interdependence.
> —Kofi Annan, "Endorsements"

S oft and hard power are intrinsically tied to the measured use of global public
goods that exist in the global commons. Diplomatic power relies heavily on
unfettered access to airspace through which national interests are promoted by
governments, to oceans in which the balance of power is enforced in accordance
with the UN Convention on the Law of the Sea, and to both outer space and
cyberspace by which allies, partners, adversaries, and international organizations
communicate and inform the global public.[1] Ideological power encompasses for
many nations the ideals of democracy, free trade, universal human rights, and
advancement of scientific knowledge and is projected through the international
media and private citizens who travel and work abroad with relative ease. Today
economic and military power depend almost equally on unrestricted access to
and use of the resources within the air, maritime, space, and cyber domains. In
the final analysis national interests cannot be pursued or achieved without secure
access to the global commons.

Use of the commons must be maintained in concert with formal and informal
groups. Collaboration can provide efficient responses to threats, lower the cost of
unilateral action, and multiply influence and resources.[2] Some problems cannot
be resolved or goods supplied without the participation of large numbers of people
acting for the common good rather than simply out of self-interest. Such action

occurs when a member of a group "acts as a representative of the group and where the action is directed at improving the conditions of the group as a whole" and/or influencing others to adopt policies that favor the group's objectives.[3] This will not preclude acts of self-interest but it requires creating a shared identity, compromising in favor of the group, investing time and resources, and lessening the role of national sovereignty.

The fundamental difficulty of getting individuals and nations to create and nurture global public goods—like the global commons and the freedom, prosperity, and capabilities that they provide—is forging and maintaining collective action. Our understanding of this dynamic and how to overcome it has been the task of political and social scientists for several decades, both within their respective fields and through multidisciplinary research efforts. The conclusions of this academic collaboration indicate the importance of developing a practical, comprehensive approach to addressing the problems of generating collective action in the commons.

This chapter examines the security dynamics of forming collective action groups that are focused on securing the global commons. It elucidates the basic features of public goods that distinguish them from private goods and expounds on the global commons as sources of goods that are vital to international security. It also analyzes problems in collective action in terms of social mobilization, suboptimal collective nature of rational individual choices, free riders, and the tragedy of the commons. The tendency to overuse and misuse the commons is discussed in light of future conflicts and threats posed by negative externalities. Finally, three strategies are considered for resolving problems of collective action: capitalizing on the enabling dynamics of interpersonal relationships within groups, continuing to make investments in formal institutions that inculcate desired norms and values, and nurturing the development of informal transnational networks, which have proliferated as many nations become more interdependent on one another. Each speaks to shared benefits and individual incentives for collective action.

FEATURES OF PUBLIC GOODS

There are three features of public goods. The first is nonexcludability, which means that once supplied it is nearly impossible to deny the use of the goods to others.[4] The second feature is nonrivalry, or the dynamic that use of public goods by a person or nation typically does not detract from their use by others. And some scholars posit a third feature, namely, jointness of supply.[5] This suggests that public goods need voluntary cooperation to supply and maintain them because of the first two features or because "none could afford to supply them on their own."[6] These features can be contrasted with private goods, which are bought and sold

24

in a competitive market driven by the laws of supply and demand and furnished by exchanging labor for wages. Private goods primarily benefit those people who trade in them. By contrast, public goods assist more people who play no role in producing or maintaining them. Without market incentives to supply them, sovereign nations are called on to produce public goods with pooled taxes.

Global public goods share the core features of nonexcludability, nonrivalry, and jointness of supply to various degrees. According to one analysis, "public goods are considered global when they have universal benefits, covering multiple groups of countries and all populations."[7] Given the vast physical reach of global public goods, it is difficult to exclude those who do not contribute to their existence. It is more likely that self-interested individuals will overuse global public resources, which they perceive as infinite, or overconsume when they appear scarce. It is less likely that sovereign nations and private actors with diverse national self-interest will join together to supply them. In order for nations to act collectively they must agree on which global public goods must be provided, who will pay for their creation and maintenance, and who will enforce their contribution and sustainable use.

SOURCES OF PUBLIC GOODS

The global commons are best conceptualized as composed of physical or virtual domains that are not owned or controlled by a single nation or individual. They include international airspace, the high seas, outer space, and cyberspace. Over time, the global commons have become important to providing tangible and intangible global public goods that are vital to economic interests as well as national security. Tangible goods include food, clean air, ozone preservation, transportation routes, institutions like the United Nations, and sectors such as communications, biodiversity, medicine, and technology. Safe passage and unfettered access in the commons produce diverse and affordable goods to buy as well as markets to sell them. The nonproliferation of weapons of mass destruction and the protection of fissile material are additional tangible global public goods.

Intangible global public goods include concepts, norms, and values that make access to physical resources possible and add to human potentialities, among them peace and stability.[8] They have been provided largely by the projection of allied power, which generates favorable regional balances of power that contain adversaries without direct confrontation and promote democracy. Conflict prevention, another intangible public good, also has been created by the international norms of nonviolent conflict resolution, humanitarian aid, and universal human rights.[9] Security-related public goods are made possible by freedom of transit in the global commons. For example, airpower, enabled by the exploitation of outer space, has given the United States an "increasingly pronounced degree of freedom from attack and freedom to attack for all force elements," not only for its own national security but also to ensure peace and stability worldwide.[10]

Personal freedom represents another public good championed and protected by Western nations. As it has gained acceptance, many state and nonstate actors have come to respect this value, whether for utilitarian reasons or from personal conviction. Leaders in developing states may pay lip service to increasing personal freedoms for their fellow citizens in order to acquire access to higher levels of Western aid while at the same time placating their domestic constituencies, which have come to expect more personal freedoms. The spread of this value has also given the United States a multitude of nongovernmental organizations (NGOs) to consider as partners in furthering democratization and rule of law abroad. It can be argued that there are many others, who work collectively, that is, through private militia and authoritarian regimes, to limit others' personal freedoms; the values espoused by these groups, however, currently have limited legitimacy on the international stage.

The global commons provide freedom in various ways. The first is freedom to travel abroad to earn a living or education, experience foreign cultures, and conduct innovative research. The free-market economic system, which is highly reliant on the global commons, is in part based on notions of equal opportunity and competition. Democratic values, the rule of law, and universal human rights have spread widely, in part because of the influence of the transnational media and freedom of the press. Freedom from want and fear, as espoused by President Franklin D. Roosevelt, are intangible but critically important goals that have been internalized as key values that help people develop their own potential.[11] The adoption of these political ideals remains central to physical safety and economic prosperity as well as national security.

Finally, global public goods include the shared heritage of mankind. International organizations and NGOs work to preserve and make public uncommonly spoken languages, art, biodiversity, symbols and documents of major civilizations, and scientific knowledge. Although some artifacts find their way to the auction block and marketplace, many people respect them as belonging collectively to mankind. Mindful of this legacy the UN Educational, Scientific and Cultural Organization has designated more than 900 World Heritage Sites in some 151 nations since 1972.[12] Moreover, scientific and technological knowledge, which are key to addressing many global challenges, are themselves global public goods with security and economic ramifications.[13]

IMPEDIMENTS TO ACTION

The primary features of global public goods—nonexcludability, nonrivalry, and jointness of supply—often lead to problems of collective action that impede social mobilization. Nations and individuals operating in an anarchic international system, without legitimate regimes to firmly compel desired behavior, for the most part do not readily supply or protect goods that benefit noncontributors or curtail their own use of resources. As such, international cooperation is a form of organized volunteerism, even given the breadth and depth of international law that exists today.[14] The ability to opt out typically leads to an undersupply of global public goods as well as the depletion of resources in the global commons, even when nations and individuals realize that they would gain far more by working together.[15]

Social mobilization is the sustained organization of large, complex groups acting toward defined political goals involving society's power, resources, behavior, and participation.[16] Although social mobilization theory sought to understand when, why, and how people acted in rebellion against the state, its four analytical elements are applicable to mobilizing citizens to make extraordinary contributions as well as multilateral efforts to provide global public goods. These four elements are shared grievances, framing narratives, political opportunities, and resource mobilization.[17] The absence of any one can derail the best-intended collective efforts; on the other hand, their skilled application can motivate sacrifices on behalf of the group, sometimes entailing economic losses or even death.[18]

All collective actions start by recognizing shared grievances: the mutual understanding that a problem exists or is looming and that a change must take place in the public sphere to remedy harm, avoid future losses, or create something that is not being provided but is highly valued. Next, leaders must frame the problem by persuading others to join the cause, solidify the group, and make sacrifices that benefit them as well as noncontributors.[19] Ideology serves as a strong motivator for collective action when it is based on shared identity and action.

Political opportunities raise national and individual awareness and commitment levels.[20] These often involve catastrophic events, such as the terrorist attacks of September 11, 2001, global financial crises, and news about high-risk illicit activities, for instance, the A. Q. Khan nuclear-smuggling network. Finally, collective actions require considerable resources on a sustained basis. One of the most important is charismatic and competent leadership. Institutions and networks are needed to keep group members contributing, while masses of people are indirectly needed to supply sufficient resources. Other critical resources include allies, workers, intelligence, funding, communications, media access, meeting space, and transport.

When nations and individuals decide to act collectively they must make rational, strategic choices that weigh the costs and benefits of participation, uncertainties and risks involved, and discount rates, or how much they care about the future rather than the present. Their decisions "rest on their assessment of the probable actions of others . . . [whereas] personal outcomes depend on what others do."[21] Typically such choices are made with incomplete information. Given the human tendency to maximize their own immediate security, wealth, values, and influence, both nations and individuals often decide not to participate in collective action that will supply global public goods, thus resulting in nonrational aggregate behavior.[22]

Free Rider Dilemmas

Global public goods, including the global commons, are notionally available to everyone, which means that everyone has an incentive to benefit from them, whereas no one is incentivized equally to contribute to their creation, maintenance, and sustainability. As such they frequently can be undersupplied. The burdens of leadership and investments tend to be borne disproportionately. Both rich and poor nations benefit without investing proportionate shares in the risks or costs.[23] This phenomenon is called free riding. Aspiring nations watch others free ride and often have few incentives to join international efforts that supply and protect the global commons.

In one significant work on collective action, the author sought to explain "how a group of principals who are in an interdependent situation can organize and govern themselves to obtain continuing joint benefits when all face temptations to free ride."[24] This dynamic was certainly operative during the global economic crisis in 2007, which began in the United States and then spread globally. Initiatives by governments, the private sector, and the Group of Seven (G-7) were ineffective.[25] Subsequently, the Group of Twenty (G-20) discussed both individual and collective actions to respond to the worst such crisis since the Great Depression.

A complete collapse of the international banking system was a real possibility.[26] Even without that meltdown, losses were bringing down governments and spurring riots, communal violence, and mass protests in many nations and regions of the world. If this crisis were not comprehensively resolved, national security as well as economic prosperity would be threatened. Collective action was required to calm public fears, craft complementary policies, mitigate risks, and restore the global public good of a well-functioning banking system on which economic development and markets depend.

Finding a solution to the economic crisis was difficult. The costs of failure were high, considerable public resources were needed to keep the financial system afloat when even rich nations were facing staggering debts, and world leaders were focused on their own political survival, not the fate of international banks. Moreover, the burden of a solution rested with just twenty nations, which were unable to contribute proportionately. The world's other 172 nations and their populations would benefit without making any contributions, although there were no means of denying them use of the global public good that was a stable, well-functioning financial system. Hence, they, by definition, became free riders.

As a major seafaring nation, the United States pays disproportionately in providing naval forces to safeguard passage for fishing, cargo, cruise, research, and foreign naval ships. The forward deployment of the US Navy enables freedom of navigation as well as international peace and stability by balancing power in Asia and the Middle East. European and Asian nations have modernized their forces, largely to counter regional adversaries, although their investments represent only a comparatively small percentage of their gross domestic product.[27]

Some may argue that the private sector would do a better job of providing security than states with their cumbersome bureaucracies, politics, and militaries. Where the private sector provides its own security out of self-interest—such as in protecting merchant ships from pirates on the high seas by hiring private security forces and pooling private resources into insurance programs—the resultant safer passage for others might be considered nonexcludable and nonrival and thus a public good. However, unlike states, these private efforts are under no obligation to provide protection for state military vessels, private yachts, and non-consortium-paying merchant ships. Moreover, even if there are positive externalities to the public, these hired security services are private goods in that they are bought and sold in a competitive market. Indeed, the public role of governments remains crucial to these private efforts. States provide rule of law, infrastructure for prosecutions, and mechanisms for honoring and enforcing contracts between private entities. Governments have failed in many cases to act collectively in combating global problems such as trafficking in people, weapons, and drugs. Still, one could argue that the private sector has done even less in this regard; most of civil society lacks the resources to tackle such global problems, businesses often lack profit incentives to do so, and both lack the authority to arrest and stand up forces capable of taking on the heavily armed cartels that run smuggling networks.

The United States has led in the development and fielding of space capabilities alone or in partnership with selected allies and competitors. Efforts to track the position, condition, reentry, type, and origin of orbiting objects have been conducted by the US Space Surveillance Network. Since 1957 it has tracked more than 24,500 objects and shared the data with other nations as problems or potential problems arise. This has been true especially of a mission to "prevent a returning space object, which to radar looks like a missile, from triggering a false alarm."[28] The United States owns 441 of the 994 operational satellites in orbit around Earth that provide global connectivity and scientific data.[29] Although ten nations including India, Iran, and Israel are able to launch satellites, many other nations depend on these ten and a handful of private companies to launch their satellites into orbit, which are used for communications and global positioning, weather forecasting, monitoring illegal immigration and misuse of natural resources, and military command and control.[30] Certainly, not all states have the desire or geographic, economic, or technological requirements to become satellite-launching nations themselves. However, allowing them to utilize the scant number of launch systems that represent decades and billions in unshared investment costs provides the world with data on transnational problems and strengthens the capacities of key US allies and partners. Moreover, the number of free riders to satellite services may well be worth the investment made by space-faring nations in terms of controlling access to orbit, protecting assets, and opening up market opportunities internationally by critical linkages between outer space and cyberspace.

Tragedy of the Commons

Not all public goods in the commons are infinite. Although it may be physically impossible, cost prohibitive, or strategically ill-advised to deny the use of global public goods to the some 6.8 billion people in the world, the second principle of collective action, nonrivalry, is not that rigid. Intangible public goods of stability, peace, freedom, democracy, human rights, and sound financial policies are relatively safe from overuse, but not from undersupply or misuse. Tangible goods, however, risk depletion and overcrowding. Depletion most often threatens resources found in international waters, even though airspace, orbital space, and cyberspace appear threatened by overcrowding. As the wealth of nations increases and their yearnings for international prestige are realized, more nations of the world will tap into these vast but not unlimited global resources.

The commons have been termed "commonly owned and freely accessible resources that tend to become depleted or damaged if the population exploiting the resources is large enough."[31] Although everyone benefits from the global commons, they may pay none or only a fraction of the cost of husbanding them. If resources are perceived as infinite, few will be inclined to stop using them. And if resources are considered scarce, some may be tempted to grab their share before someone else does. Incomplete information both contributes to these misperceptions and is factored into the seemingly individual rational choices that lead to suboptimal, aggregated action of unsustainable practices.

As nations and individuals pursue their goals, they often put immediate gains before future losses. How much they discount the future depends on several factors.[32] First is the opportunity for rapid returns in other settings far from home. The second factor that severely discounts future gains is a personal or national level of economic security. Many cannot leave local safety nets or invest in another industry, and even the upwardly mobile middle classes are reluctant to risk their recently acquired wealth and status by practicing sustainable use of global public goods. Overuse of common resources will eventually force such individuals to adapt to new livelihoods, although they may hope that resources will be available through their lifetime and that of their children, who will be afforded opportunities for better educations in state-run schools.

Overfishing has become a global problem. From 1970 to 2000, the percent of overfished stocks climbed from approximately 15 to 25 percent.[33] Today this figure hovers around 66 percent.[34] Nearly one billion people rely on fish as a primary source of protein and almost an equal number are employed in fishing industries. These trends bode poorly for food security, environmental contagion, unemployment, and mass emigration. China has begun exploiting the waters off the coast of Africa, which eventually could threaten food supplies in that region. The efforts by international governmental organizations to address this problem have fallen short because resources and measures for collective action have been lacking.

CONFLICT IN THE COMMONS

The misuse or overuse of the commons has provoked conflict and insecurity among and within nations. The outcomes have been referred to as *public bads* if the intention was malicious or as *negative externalities* if they were unintentionally detrimental.[35] Such incidents are characterized by their impact on the global commons and potential for threatening the security of numerous communities around the world, most of whom play no role in their creation and spread.

Many transnational actors misuse the public goods of free access, safe passage, free trade, worldwide communication, and financial services. The abuses include smuggling drugs, people, and weapons; international terrorist organizations escaping capture, entering target nations, and obtaining and using weapons against noncombatants; and the proliferation of the knowledge, technologies, and materials to build and deliver weapons of mass destruction. Threats originate and operate mostly from within sovereign nations, preferably weak ones with modern infrastructure but little danger of interference. Yet these threats, which are designed to harm, often cross international waters or airspace through private or commercial transportation networks. Moreover, these illicit activities are facilitated by the use of cyberspace and outer space for coordinates for drop-offs, communication with loosely organized and scattered cells, wire transfers to fund activities, announcements via the media to claim responsibility for attacks, or Internet propaganda for recruitment and shaping of public opinion.[36]

Some transnational threats that utilize the global commons are not intended to cause harm but may be disruptive to the nations shielding them if they not are addressed by global collective action. For instance, 11.5 million economic refugees and asylum seekers in 2009 alone generated communal discord and heightened ethnic nationalism in host nations, a loss of international reputation for those who drove out the refugees, and heavy financial burdens for poorer nations.[37] Governments often are caught in a quandary: on one hand, they have a responsibility based on international law to accept and protect refugees if only temporarily, even though they are not responsible for the strife that led them to flee.[38] On the other hand, their first responsibility is the security and well-being of their citizens, which frequently conflicts with the plight of refugees. Moreover, accepting any and all refugees may encourage others to flee and overwhelm a nation's support capacity.

COOPERATION IN THE COMMONS

Despite the dynamics that often discourage cooperation, collective action in the global commons protects and provides global public goods. But why would nations and individuals choose to do so when global public goods have potential benefit to others who have not contributed and when making such an investment is often risky or costly? Research has shown that a number of factors can alter preferences and perceived risks to favor collaboration. Apart from further enclosing the commons and making them market driven, which would be cost prohibitive on the high seas and virtually impossible in cyberspace, problems in collective action could be overcome through the management of group relations and the creation of both formal, binding international institutions and informal, more flexible global networks. Once collective action groups are instituted—which is no small feat in itself—they can be influenced and shaped by norms, sanctions, and success.

Interpersonal Relations

Rewards bestowed through personal relationships within groups appear to play an important role in overcoming collective action problems. These include feelings of solidarity, trust, and respect, which are often built through frequent exchanges.[39] Forming a collective identity is especially important for developing and sustaining any social mobilization effort. The more features that people share, such as class or ideology, the easier it is to develop unity. The same could be said for their shared grievances and the interdependence of group members to carry out day-to-day operational functions to include achieving desired outcomes.[40] Interestingly, those leaders who disproportionately invest time and resources in group activities gain status in the eyes of group members, creating a feedback loop through which they subsequently are given a larger share of public goods by others and, in turn, furnish more to the group.[41] This dynamic speaks to the importance of being a lead player in the global commons as a means to secure access.

Smaller, more homogeneous groups have greater opportunities to interact with others and build trust through reciprocity and iterative exchanges as well as provide more transparency on who contributes to collective objectives.[42] It also has been argued that social mobilization costs for organizing large numbers of people are difficult to overcome and thus benefit small groups with fewer resources but more long-term commitment based on personal relations. In addition, smaller groups were more restrained in advocating personal interests over those of the group.[43]

International Organizations

A formal institution is defined as "the set of working rules that are used to determine who is eligible to make decisions in some arena, what actions are allowed or constrained, what aggregation rules will be used, what procedures must be followed, what information must or must not be provided, and what payoffs will be assigned to individuals dependent on their actions."[44] In short, formal institutions both constrain and shape group member behavior with organizational appropriateness often winning out over efficiency or outcome. They also offer benefits of predictability, acceptable methods of sanctioning members, and clearly articulated strategies and objectives.[45] Because their expectations are closely tied to positions, formal institutions can be maintained even at times of leadership change. Although their initial establishment can be costly, they incur lower transaction costs to maintain because of the standardization and shared burden of a greater number of members. Most institutions use combinations of established norms and formal measures to enforce rules and deter free riders.[46]

Today there are estimated to be one to three thousand formal international governmental organizations.[47] They have had some success in raising awareness of security concerns in the global commons, promoting universal human rights and liberal values, providing formal mechanisms for less powerful nations to participate in decision making, and contributing to global peace and security through deployment of peacekeeping forces. Research has revealed that "states experiencing negative externalities caused by other states' behaviors have incentives to devise international institutions to change those behaviors."[48] This tendency and increasing numbers of international governmental organizations suggest formal institutions with stiff sanctioning abilities may be effective at overcoming collective action problems. However, it also has been found that "escape clauses generate more durable and stable cooperative international regimes," indicating nations will seek collective objectives so long as they are in line with their self-interest.[49]

Informal Global Networks

Transnational government networks that directly bring together bureaucrats, security officials, and regulators in direct interaction have been on the rise since the end of the Cold War.[50] Today international relations are no longer the exclusive province of foreign ministries and diplomats, and often take place through disaggregated, nonhierarchical, and less structured forms of representation.[51]

Covering almost every aspect of governmental activity, they offer another method of collective action by which international concerns can be tackled including the global commons. Three initiatives launched in recent times have been carried out by informal transnational government networks including the Missile Technology Control Regime (1987), the Proliferation Security Initiative (2003), and the Global Nuclear Security Summit (2010).[52] In addition to world leaders and the members of NGOs, academe, think tanks, and nonstate actors have been invited frequently to work together on such initiatives through multinational coalitions.[53]

Transnational government networks cooperate through informal, nonbinding agreements, norms, and procedures.[54] They maintain a lower profile than formal state-to-state contact and their approach to issues is more flexible. These qualities are useful in dealing with the fast pace of change, expansion of data, information and knowledge, and rapid communication. Indeed, their relatively flat structures enable information and ideas to flow easily among local nodes based in multiple nations.[55] Their rise and staying power are believed to be driven by necessity. Today the interdependence found in meeting challenges by transnational government networks has been bred by globalization, including misuses and overuses of the commons, and by similarities in governmental organizational structures worldwide.[56]

Networks can overcome problems of collective action in several ways. First, networks are typically relatively small, which discourages free riding. Second, networks normally are focused narrowly, which makes consensus easier to achieve. Third, the informality, start-up costs, and maintenance of networks are relatively low, which encourages the participation of more actors. Finally, cooperation is based on trust fostered by reciprocity and the frequency of interaction. Although networks may seem ideally suited for the globalized world, they are complements of formal state-to-state relations and agreements rather than replacements for them. Their informal character makes defection easier, offers little by way of infrastructure and decision making, and provides few enforceable measures to sanction nonperformers or contributors.[57] Indeed, some nations would prefer that the Global Nuclear Security Summit results in a binding, verifiable fissile material cutoff treaty under which a few capable nations would bear a large share of the financial, technological, and organizational burdens to accomplish its goals.[58] As is always the case in collective action, especially on the global level, free riding remains a reality.

PROBLEMS in collective action that result in an undersupply or a misuse of global public goods create major challenges. The UN High-Level Panel on Threats, Challenges, and Change identified six global concerns: war between nations; violence within nations; nuclear, radiological, chemical, and biological weapons; terrorism; transnational organized crime; and poverty, infectious diseases, and environmental degradation.[59] All six use the global commons and misuse global public goods. Many of the same concerns were seconded by the International Task Force on Global Public Goods. Both organizations propose that the best way to overcome these abuses is through collective action that protects and promotes global public goods.

Generating unity of effort is often difficult but not impossible. Given public goods' core features of nonexcludability, nonrivalry, and jointness of supply, nations and individuals face sizeable obstacles in providing them on a global level and protecting the global commons on which they depend. Social mobilization remains challenging because of its complexity, the tendency of actors to ride free, and the inclination of some actors to overuse public goods, which creates a tragedy of the commons that belong to all of humanity. Although strong leadership, shared norms and values, formal institutions, and informal networks regularly mitigate such dynamics, it is difficult to bring these favorable conditions together.[60] Global leaders, for instance, can be weakened, distracted, and even eliminated by power struggles and crises within states. The world's sheer complexity and diversity of cultures, parochial concerns, and issue weariness often weaken commitments to universal norms as well as global objectives and efforts.[61] Overreliance on standardization through formal institutions often plays to the lowest common denominator while decreasing flexibility, initiative, and creativity. Informal networks may form to overcome some of these shortfalls, yet have less sanctioning ability and staying power.

A number of questions on collective action remain. First, how can the much-valued global public good of economic freedom be balanced against the misuse and overuse of the commons? Can new systems be designed to compel or entice free riders to contribute more equitably to the maintenance of the global commons and production of global public goods? Can the United States afford to lead and pay a disproportionately higher share of the costs and risks in protecting the commons and producing global public goods? Can it not afford to lead? What are the consequences of global powers not leading? The answers to these questions will influence the current international security environment as well as future generations who inhabit a world that is highly dependent on international systems and cooperation.

NOTES

The epigraph by Kofi Annan appeared in "Endorsements" (New York: United Nations Development Program, July 2002)[0].

1. Diana Owen, "Transnational Mass Media Organizations and Security," in *Grave New World: Security Challenges in the 21st Century*, Michael E. Brown, ed. (Washington, DC: Georgetown University Press, 2003), 240–41.

2. Christopher Hemmer and Peter J. Katzenstein, "Why Is There No NATO in Asia? Collective Identity, Regionalism and the Origins of Multilateralism," *International Organization* 56 (Summer 2002): 576.

3. Stephen C. Wright, "The Next Generation of Collective Action Research," *Journal of Social Issues* 65 (December 2009): 860, 870.

4. Inge Kaul, Isabelle Grunberg, and Marc A. Stern, "Defining Global Public Goods," in *Global Public Goods: International Cooperation in the 21st Century*, Inge Kaul, Isabelle Grunberg, and Marc A. Stern, eds. (New York: Oxford University Press, 1999), 3–4.

5. Russell Hardin, *Collective Action* (Baltimore, MD: Johns Hopkins University Press, 1982), 17.

6. International Task Force on Global Public Goods, *International Cooperation in the National Interest: Meeting Global Challenges* (Stockholm: International Task Force on Global Public Goods, 2006), 40.

7. Anders Hjorth Agerskov, "Global Public Goods and Development: A Guide for Policy Makers" (Kobe: World Bank Seminar Series, Global Development Challenges Facing Humanity, May 12, 2005), 2.

8. Ruben P. Mendez, "Peace as a Global Public Good," in *Global Public Goods: International Cooperation in the 21st Century*, Inge Kaul, Isabelle Grunberg, and Marc A. Stern, eds. (New York: Oxford University Press, 1999), 382–416.

9. David A. Hamburg and Jane E. Holl, "Preventing Deadly Conflict: From Global Housekeeping to Neighborhood Watch," in *Global Public Goods: International Cooperation in the 21st Century*, Inge Kaul, Isabelle Grunberg, and Marc A. Stern, eds. (New York: Oxford University Press, 1999), 366–81.

10. Benjamin S. Lambeth, "Airpower, Spacepower, and Cyberpower," *Joint Force Quarterly* 60 (2011): 47.

11. Franklin D. Roosevelt, "The Four Freedoms," annual address to Congress, January 6, 1941, http://docs.fdrlibrary.marist.edu/od4freed.html.

12. *Convention Concerning the Protection of World Cultural and Natural Heritage* (Paris: UN Educational, Scientific and Cultural Organization, November 16, 1972), http://whc.unesco.org/en/convention and http://whc.unesco.org/en/list.

13. Agerskov, "Global Public Goods," 5.

14. Christopher C. Joyner, ed., *The United Nations and International Law* (New York: Cambridge University Press and American Society of International Law, 1997).

15. Mancur Olson, *The Logic of Collective Action: Public Goods and the Theory of Groups* (Boston, MA: Harvard University Press, 1965).

16. Sidney G. Tarrow, *Power in Movement: Social Movements and Contentious Politics*, 2nd ed. (New York: Cambridge University Press, 1999).

17. See John D. McCarthy and Mayer N. Zald, "Resource Mobilization and Social Movements: A Partial Theory," *American Journal of Sociology* 82 (1977): 1212–41; Doug McAdam, *Political Process and the Development of Black Insurgency* (Chicago: University of Chicago Press, 1982).

18. Wright, "Next Generation," 867.

19. Examples of cultural ideas and symbols used by nonstate actors include self-determination, universal human rights, democracy, and religious freedom.

20. Russell Hardin, *Collective Action* (Baltimore, MD: Johns Hopkins University Press, 1982), 31.

21. Margaret Levi, "A Model, a Method, and a Map: Rational Choice in Comparative and Historical Analysis," in *Comparative Politics: Rationality, Culture and Structure*, Mark Irving Lichbach and Alan S. Zuckerman, eds. (New York: Cambridge University Press, 1997), 23.

22. Ibid., 22. See also Mancur Olson, *The Logic of Collective Action: Public Goods and the Theory of Groups* (Boston, MA: Harvard University Press, 1965).
23. Michael Mandelbaum, *The Case for Goliath: How America Acts as the World's Government in the Twenty-First Century* (New York: PublicAffairs, 2005).
24. Elinor Ostrom, *Governing the Commons: The Evolution of Institutions for Collective Action* (Cambridge: Cambridge University Press, 1990), 29.
25. Federal Reserve Bank of New York, "Timelines of Policy Responses to the Global Financial Crisis" (New York: Federal Reserve Bank, July 14, 2009), www.newyorkfed.org/research/global_economy/policyresponses.html.
26. Lee Hudson Teslik, "Timeline: Global Economy in Crisis" (New York: Council on Foreign Relations, 2009).
27. US Central Intelligence Agency, "Country Comparison: Military Expenditure," *CIA World Factbook Online Edition*, www.cia.gov/library/publications/the-world-factbook/rankorder/2034rank.html.
28. US Space Command, "Space Surveillance" (Colorado Springs, CO: Headquarters, US Space Command, n.d.), www.au.af.mil/au/awc/awcgate/usspc-fs/space.htm.
29. Union of Concerned Scientists, "UCS Satellite Database" (Cambridge, MA: Union of Concerned Scientists, 2011), www.ucsusa.org/nuclear_weapons_and_global_security/space_weapons/technical_issues/ucs-satellite-database.html.
30. Jorge Daniel Taillant and Romina Picolotti, "The Uses of Satellite Imagery: Linking Human Rights and Environment" (Washington, DC: Center for International Environmental Law and National Aeronautics and Space Administration, n.d.); Union of Concerned Scientists, "What Are Satellites Used For?" (Cambridge, MA: Union of Concerned Scientists, 2007), www.ucsusa.org/nuclear_weapons_and_global_security/space_weapons/technical_issues/what-are-satellites-used-for.html.
31. Garrett Hardin, "The Tragedy of the Commons," *Science* 162 (December 13, 1968): 1243–48.
32. Ostrom, *Governing the Commons*, 37.
33. On food scarcity and commodity markets, see Peter Timmer, "Food Security in Asia and the Changing Role of Rice" (San Francisco, CA: Asia Foundation, October 2010).
34. United Nations, "Fisheries at the Limit?" (Rome: Food and Agriculture Organization of the United Nations, 1995), www.fao.org.
35. Inge Kaul, Isabelle Grunberg, and Marc A. Stern, "Global Public Goods: Concepts, Policies and Strategies," in *Global Public Goods: International Cooperation in the 21st Century*, Inge Kaul, Isabelle Grunberg, and Marc A. Stern, eds. (New York: Oxford University Press, 1999), 456–57.
36. Diana Owen, "Transnational Mass Media Organizations and Security," in *Grave New World: Security Challenges in the 21st Century*, Michael E. Brown, ed. (Washington, DC: Georgetown University Press, 2003), 250.
37. United Nations, "2009 Global Trends Report: Refugees, Asylum-Seekers, Returnees, Internally Displaced, and Stateless Persons" (Geneva: UN High Commissioner for Refugees, June 15, 2010), www.unhcr.org/pages/49c3646c4d6.html.
38. David A. Martin, "Refugees and Migration," in *The United Nations and International Law*, Christopher C. Joyner, ed. (New York: Cambridge University Press and American Society of International Law, 1997), 162–63.
39. Mancur Olson, *The Rise and Decline of Nations* (New Haven, CT: Yale University Press, 1984), 23. Platforms such as Facebook can overcome the difficulty of bonding with people.
40. Jeff Goodwin and James M. Jasper, eds., *Rethinking Social Movements: Structure, Meaning and Emotion* (Lanham, MD: Rowman and Littlefield, 2004).

41. Robb Willer, "Groups Reward Individual Sacrifice: The Status Solution to the Collective Action Problem," *American Sociological Review* 74 (February 2009): 23–34.
42. Olson, *Rise and Decline of Nations*, 60.
43. Alexander Wendt, *Social Theory of International Politics* (New York: Cambridge University Press, 1999), 343.
44. Ostrom, *Governing the Commons*, 51.
45. James G. March and Johan P. Olsen, "The New Institutionalism: Organizational Factors in Political Life," *American Political Science Review* 78 (September 1984): 745.
46. Jonas Tallberg, "Paths to Compliance: Enforcement, Management and the European Union," *International Organization* 56 (Summer 2002): 643.
47. Harold K. Jacobson, William M. Reisinger, and Todd Mathers, "National Entanglements in International Governmental Organizations," *American Political Science Review* 80 (March 1986): 141.
48. Ronald B. Mitchell and Patricia M. Keilbach, "Situation Structure and Institutional Design: Reciprocity, Coercion and Exchange," *International Organization* 55 (Autumn 2001): 891.
49. Peter Rosendorff and Helen V. Milner, "The Optimal Design of International Trade Institutions: Uncertainty and Escape," *International Organization* 55 (Autumn 2001): 829; Kenneth Abbot and Duncan Snidal, "Hard and Soft Law in International Governance," *International Organization* 54 (Summer 2000): 421.
50. Anne-Marie Slaughter, "Disaggregated Sovereignty: Towards the Public Accountability of Global Government Networks," *Government and Opposition* 39 (2004): 159.
51. Mette Eilstrup-Sangiovanni, "Varieties of Cooperation: Government Networks in International Security," in *Networked Politics: Agency, Power, and Governance*, Miles Kahler, ed. (Ithaca, NY: Cornell University Press, 2009), 198–99.
52. The Missile Technology Control Regime was begun by the G-7 in 1987 to help combat the spread of weapons of mass destruction carrying missiles and technologies; the 2003 Proliferation Security Initiative seeks voluntary international collaboration in interdicting suspected carriers of weapons of mass destruction and their component materials in international waters; and the 2010 Global Nuclear Security Summit solicits support and designs programs to curtail illicit trade in nuclear materials and secure all fissile materials worldwide through international cooperation. Ibid., 218–22; United States Department of State, "Proliferation Security Initiative" (Washington, DC, 2011), www.state .gov/t/isn/c10390.htm; Andrew Riedy, "Fact Sheet: 2010 Global Nuclear Security Summit" (Washington, DC: Center for Arms Control and Non-Proliferation, December 9, 2009), http://armscontrolcenter.org/policy/nuclearweapons/articles/120909_global_nu clear_security_summit/.
53. Sidney Tarrow, *Power in Movement: Social Movements and Contentious Politics*, 2nd ed. (New York: Cambridge University Press, 1999), 176.
54. Robert O. Keohane and Joseph S. Nye, "Transgovernmental Relations and International Organizations," *World Politics* 27 (October 1974): 43.
55. Duncan J. Watts, *Six Degrees: The Science of a Connected Age* (New York: W. W. Norton, 2003), 280–81.
56. Kal Raustiala, "The Architecture of International Cooperation: Transgovernmental Networks and the Future of International Law," *Virginia Journal of International Law* 43 (2002): 4.
57. Mette Eilstrup-Sangiovanni, "Varieties of Cooperation: Government Networks in International Security," in *Networked Politics: Agency, Power, and Governance*, Miles Kahler, ed. (Ithaca, NY: Cornell University Press, 2009), 203.
58. Riedy, "Fact Sheet."

59. United Nations, *A More Secure World: Our Shared Responsibility* (New York: United Nations, December 2, 2004), www.un.org/secureworld/report2.pdf.

60. See, for instance, Uri Dadush and William Shaw, *Juggernaut: How Emerging Markets Are Reshaping Globalization* (Washington, DC: Carnegie Endowment for International Peace, 2011).

61. Randall Schweller, "Ennui Becomes Us," *National Interest* 105 (January–February 2010).

CHAPTER 2

The Character of Conflict

IAN K. ADAM

Adversaries will take the initiative and exploit Alliance vulnerabilities in both the virtual and physical domains of the global
commons, including the realms of sea, air, space, and cyberspace.
—Allied Command Transformation, "Multiple Futures Project"

The nature of conflict is enduring. It can be violent, often uncontrollable, and
unpredictable. Moreover, it has evolved over the centuries because of various factors. Adversaries, be they state or nonstate actors, meet new challenges by
adopting the weaponry and tactics at hand. Lessons are learned after each suc-
cessive war, not least by third parties, and then applied to gain advantage in the
future. The impact of social media on both domestic and international public
opinion is a factor that is shaping conflict and civil unrest in the twenty-first
century, as recent dramatic events in North Africa and the Middle East have
demonstrated.[1]

Although nations once viewed high-end, state-on-state warfare as the greatest military threat, an emerging mix of hybrid threats covering every imaginable
form of commotion is becoming the greatest challenge. The definitions and scope
of hybrid threats are far and wide, but generally they include a mix of irregular,
conventional, and high-end asymmetric tactics and weapons used to maximize
advantage and exploit any actual or perceived vulnerability in an opponent.[2] Even
though these means are neither new nor radical, they are being used by an increasing number of capable state and nonstate actors.

The dawn of the twenty-first century highlighted the various threats posed
by state and nonstate actors, not least those created by sophisticated and highly
adaptive terrorist groups capable of transnational crimes over a prolonged period,
resilient to state countermeasures and able to exploit the latest technologies.

However, such threats, when viewed as risks to the global commons, must be examined in all forms, albeit natural or man-made, state or nonstate. Only by comprehending the full range of threats can measures be taken to preserve the commons as resources over which no group or individual possesses exclusive rights but on which nations of the world rely.

The potential causes of conflict in the global commons are diverse and complex. Unequal treaties, disputed claims of sovereignty, and competing national interests create friction and tension. In particular, commercial access to the natural resources of the commons will become more highly prized as some nations exhaust their own supplies or fail to meet growing demand. Globalization has encouraged formerly unattainable aspirations in developing countries with the effect that increased cooperation is essential for future progress. The physical and virtual networks in the commons that support globalization require various forms of protection and regulation to avoid disorder. Supplies of energy resources, which are the lifeblood of most economies, usually require access to the global commons in order to be transported. Even regional failures in this regard could have far-reaching global consequences.[3]

A RANGE OF THREATS

The threats to the global commons are numerous. Some are new and emerging threats, whereas others have been present in one form or another for time immemorial. The key difference is that today the consequences of some of these threats, exacerbated by advanced information technology coupled with soaring populations, are becoming too large and serious to be ignored by the major nations of the world. The threats emanate from five sources, the first of which is natural disasters. These appear in the form of earthquakes, tsunamis, volcanoes, hurricanes, and falling meteors. None can be easily predicted, and even with warning none can be avoided. Their impact on the global commons will vary, as will their ultimate cost in fiscal, environmental, and human terms.[4] The four remaining sources—state actors, nonstate actors, state proxies, and individuals—respond to the shift in the balance of power, which is driven by globalization as well as the changing character of war.

In an era of multipolar distribution of control, rogue states are viewed with suspicion, although large and economically strong nations often pose the greatest threat to the global commons. Although rogues may ignore international norms and present a greater threat to security, the real danger to the global commons is caused by highly polluting and sizeable resource-consuming nations that use the commons for their own gain. Such advanced nations are often responsible for overfishing, energy consumption that results in pollution and climate change, and disproportionate use of space and cyberspace. Further exacerbating the situation, some nations will publicly condemn abuses or even support policies censuring violators, and then ignore their own populations when acting opportunistically in the commons.[5]

Nonstate actors include a range of organizations from international companies and nongovernmental organizations to transnational terrorist organizations and criminal gangs. The former inevitably operate within international laws and conventions on the domain in which they work but conduct themselves to suit their own purposes. There is a difference between terrorists and criminals.[6] The former use or threaten violence to coerce nations or rivals within a nation for political, religious, and ideological ends. Terrorist organizations exploit the global commons as a safe haven for recruiting, training, and fundraising and as a venue to operate or to strike opponents where they are most vulnerable.[7] By contrast, criminal organizations will utilize the commons for financial gain and usually endeavor to exploit them for the long term. They will attempt inevitably to maintain a low profile and take advantage of the lack of control in the global commons.[8] Their motives for using the commons will range from acts of maritime piracy to global organized crime.

The state proxies that incite violence or commit crimes are the hardest to identify and are not easily defined as terrorists or criminals. Their ability to exist on the margins though comprising large networks makes them hard to locate and counter. As a result of this status they can be well financed and their members can find safe havens under state sponsorship. Moreover, they can shield their criminal acts behind legitimate enterprise, which frustrates effective international policing. Such activities are most rampant in the trafficking of drugs, weapons, and people in the maritime domain.[9] The advantage for state sponsors is that of deniability should the proxy actions become public or simply counterproductive.

The last source of threats is the individual. Lone wolves or madmen are likely to become increasing concerns in cyber security, where the act of one capable and ideologically extreme person can inflict grave worldwide damage.[10] Such individuals might bear a grudge against a particular party or simply want to prove they are capable of such mischief.

FOUR DISTINCT ENVIRONMENTS

Each of the four domains in the global commons faces its own challenges. Although there will inevitably be threats that cross over from one domain to another, they should be considered separately for purposes of highlighting their unique capabilities to interfere in the commons.

The maritime domain, the first of the four, can be exploited with little technological expertise or financial investment. Most nations with access to the coastlines of the world have used this domain for millennia. Threats come in many forms, both legal and illegal. Overfishing and pillaging of resources have led to food shortages and endangered some species.[11] Although these activities can be policed by mutual or universal agreement, self-interest and differing national values make such agreement difficult to achieve. Undersea mining and resource extraction deep below the seabed are also contested and can result in pollution and destruction of marine ecosystems.[12] More common forms of pollution of the oceans by sewage and waste disposal from land and contamination by vessels and offshore platforms have increased in recent decades. Some pollutants in the form of greenhouse gases create global warming, which in turn destroys the arctic ice shelf.[13] Although this provides opportunities for development and increases navigable waters in the extreme north, it exposes this area to exploitation, which exacerbates other risks.

Piracy on the high seas is nothing new, but recently it has become more sophisticated and prevalent in some regions. This form of organized crime has a global impact on distant economies as larger vessels are forced to reroute to avoid danger zones and pay higher rates of insurance.[14] The pirates themselves are well organized and know how to exploit shipping while staying outside the reach of international law. Although coalitions act in the common interest to deter piracy, it becomes difficult to eradicate when failed or weak states provide safe havens. Although the waters around every continent are vulnerable to this threat, it is currently more prevalent off the Horn of Africa and in the straits of Southeast Asia.[15]

Despite the level of attention given to climate change, pollution, and nefarious activities, the disposition of world power and its impact on the maritime domain should not be ignored. Nowhere is this more obvious than in contentious Chinese maritime ambitions in the Western Pacific. China has increased the area of its exclusive economic zone beyond internationally accepted norms and usurped traditionally recognized legal claims by many of its neighbors.[16] Its naval forces have expanded to a point where they pose a challenge to the once dominant US Navy.[17] If left unchecked the Chinese eventually may become the maritime policeman in the region to enforce law and order on the high seas. To most of its neighbors China often is perceived as a bully that seeks to impose illegal maritime claims and threaten freedom of the seas by denying global access to the maritime domain whenever it may suit Beijing.

Airspace, the second domain, was gradually regulated over the last century, which was essential to providing communication around the world. Civil aviation alone carries between two and three billion travelers annually and large amounts of cargo.[18] Both the troposphere and lower stratosphere are heavily used by aircraft and require international cooperation over vast expanses that are not above sovereign territory. In most areas national airspace provides innocent passage but remains a topic of discussion. Although airspace is highly controlled, no universal agreement exists on military aircraft in spite of the fact that they must observe accepted safety practices when operating in recognized air corridors and encountering commercial air traffic.

The issue of crowded airspace has been affected substantially by the rapid development of unmanned aerial vehicles that are expected to increase exponentially in coming decades.[19] Unmanned systems rely on other domains for day-to-day operations, namely, space (satellite communications and global positioning) and cyberspace (control and communication). As new technologies proliferate and become more affordable, some nations seek air superiority by investing in asymmetric means to attack command and control networks on which aircraft depend and in conventional surface-to-air and air-to-air missile systems.[20]

The third domain, space and the upper atmosphere—the top layers of the stratosphere and the mesosphere—has become more contested in recent decades. The range of nations capable of launching satellites has soared, leading to increased congestion and more varied uses, not all of which are benign. Despite agreements including the Outer Space Treaty of 1967, the widespread deionization of space is probably only a few years off.[21] This in itself will create new tensions. For years advanced nations thought nothing of deploying military satellites to spy on their adversaries and yet now are uneasy as this technology proliferates and can be pitted against them by competitors and potential enemies. Defensive measures taken by some nations frequently are perceived as belligerent actions by others.

Although once considered beyond the reach of human destruction, the ozone is listed on environmental agendas as nations tackle issues such as climate change and global warming. Damage to the stratosphere is difficult to blame on individual or group of state or nonstate actors, but collective remedies are needed for the common good of every nation.[22]

Cyberspace, the fourth domain, is characterized by permeable physical, political, and social boundaries and a cyber culture that vigorously resists state control.[23] Although censorship and restricted access to its content have been imposed by some nations, the cyber domain is available to all nations and regarded as part of the global commons.[24] This domain on the electromagnetic spectrum emerged in the latter part of the twentieth century and now has become essential to every instrument of national power. The use of cyberspace requires cooperation among nations that embrace international laws and conventions to safeguard the domain for the common good. Denying access to cyberspace may spell economic disaster and social turmoil in a short period of time, particularly for more advanced nations. Although state and nonstate actors will pursue legitimate and constructive uses for this domain, terrorists and criminals could have catastrophic effects in the commons under various scenarios.

Antarctica is sometimes considered the only part of the global commons on terra firma although many consider it a shared international resource and not part of the commons. As such, threats to Antarctica are not examined in this chapter.[25] However, it should be noted that this area is spared terrorism and criminal activity. Its small, transient population and the difficulties of access and extreme climate are significant advantages. Indeed it is state actors that pose the greatest threat to this huge region and its natural resources, which will become economically and technologically prone to exploitation at some point in the future.

KEY VULNERABILITIES

The geography of the earth and its climate ensure there will always be maritime chokepoints on transport routes on which ships congregate to ply their global trade.[26] Routes around areas such as the Mediterranean and northern Europe likely will remain in, or at least within proximity of, territorial waters. Similarly, most sea-lanes around the Americas, while often less dense and more isolated, generally fall into the same category. This is not so in the Indian Ocean and on many routes in the Atlantic and Pacific Oceans. Commercial vessels are forced deep into the commons, where they lack national protection and become vulnerable to piracy. Although not always isolated from land, some offshore installations and undersea pipelines are beyond the reach of territorial waters.[27] Mass trade and energy supplies depend on seagoing vessels and offshore installations for security. The protection of air travel also has experienced rapid growth and concern in recent years. The last decade has seen a spate of aircraft-related terrorism that resulted in new and expensive security measures being fielded at airports and on board aircraft, which constitute nodes that provide access to global commons.[28]

The world has become reliant on the Internet and the World Wide Web for information, communication, and international trade. Accidental mass failures and deliberate cyber attacks have all resulted in short-term damage to national economies. Although some failures have been attributed to fiber-optic cable damage in international waters, malicious cyber attacks have been instigated within nations.[29] The difficulty is identifying and proving the origin of attacks because cyberspace is borderless, except for servers and hardware that occupy fixed sites. Laws may deter or punish offenders, but sophisticated terrorists and criminals have the know-how to wreak havoc worldwide while remaining unseen.[30] It also would be naïve not to credit some actors for being prepared to exploit this domain when their own interests prevail. Like the maritime domain, operations in cyberspace require only modest resources.

Dependence on satellite communication and global positioning has created vulnerabilities in space. The information age relies on these systems to perform a number of key functions, not least the time signal for global positioning that synchronizes computer networks around the world. Once exclusively state-controlled, high-tech military systems such as computers, satellites, sensors, and information systems are now available commercially on devices operated by millions every day. Even a temporary loss of satellites remains an unimaginable dilemma.[31] Key devices such as the Global Positioning System and weather satellites that were originally developed for military applications have become indispensable to the civil and commercial sectors as well. The development of commercially deployed spacecraft and maneuverable satellites with evident dual-use capabilities compounds the task of controlling this domain.[32]

THE REALITY TODAY

The inhabitants of the world are entering into a more interdependent era where events in one part of the planet can have direct and indirect consequences elsewhere. A recent publication by the British Ministry of Defence titled the "Future Character of Conflict" (FCOC) highlights this phenomenon, and in describing the range of adversaries, discusses the human terrain and its associated linguistic, ideological, tribal, sectarian, and ethnic features. FCOC describes the future battlespace as being more congested, cluttered, contested, connected, and constrained.[33] This concept paper, which describes the world as a whole, has many facets that equally apply to the global commons.

The world is congested by a proliferation of satellites in orbital space, busier shipping lanes, and increased use of cyberspace. These trends show no sign of abating as the world population soars and new technologies become available to emerging nations. As the global commons become cluttered they are harder to monitor and regulate. This enables adversaries to conceal their activities and intentions, especially in cyberspace, where actors can attempt to attack and disrupt targets from a remote location and at a time of their choosing.

Every domain in the commons is contested with an increasing range of anti-access and area denial capabilities that are being developed by state and nonstate actors.[34] This potent mix of threats has the potential to deny even advanced military forces access to large areas of the ocean and to destroy satellites. The recent proliferation of longer-range antiship missiles and more sophisticated cyber attack capabilities only exacerbates this situation.[35]

Realizing that globalization and technology have forged a more connected world, malevolent actors are capable of exploiting this new environment. Some nations will go to great lengths to shield their cyber infrastructures from hostile computer network operations and their communication ports from physical attack, but they remain vulnerable between key nodes, particularly as these links often traverse the globe through the commons. Worse still, in trying to protect this new congested, cluttered, contested, and connected world, most legitimate state and nonstate actors are increasingly constrained. Although legal, moral, and ethical constraints limit many nations in safeguarding the global commons, others will likely feel unconstrained by traditional values and take advantage of any vulnerability.[36]

One major problem is deciding who has the authority to regulate the global commons. Although the United Nations has created a number of internationally accepted conventions, they are invariably linked to nations. Nonstate actors, particularly those with criminal intent, remain unconstrained and often find refuge in either troubled or failed states beyond the reach of international law. Worse are powerful rogue states with high-end technological access as well as significant financial resources, which give them the capabilities to disrupt law-abiding activity in the commons when and where their leadership decides.[37]

Nations generally deal with threats out of self-interest although they may claim other more politically acceptable motives. They may not accede to international treaties and hide under the pretence that they are protecting their inalienable rights or would break their own laws by complying with international regulations. For example, companies that undertake deep-seabed mining and natural resource extraction in the maritime domain are interested primarily in maximizing profits and not in long-term preservation of rare minerals.[38] They would claim that if they did not bring the resources to market then their competitors would step in. To conclude otherwise is naïve. Those state and nonstate actors who champion the protection and regulation of the global commons are invariably those who stand to benefit from instigating such initiatives or who are simply unable to face the competition of others currently exploiting them. This is simply human nature and is unlikely to change.

POTENTIAL SOLUTIONS

An obvious but perhaps simplistic approach is for individual nations to try to take the lead in policing the commons. By default many advanced nations do just that in the cyber world but only as far as protecting their own interests and systems from internal and external attack. The sheer cost, technological complexity, and historically low probability of an attack ensure that most nations will simply rely on international treaties to police both airspace and outer space, leaving major powers to enforce international agreements. Within the maritime domain, nations do not deploy their naval forces to patrol all the oceans, though some larger nations operate worldwide out of self-interest and by so doing help police the global commons.

Both international and regional alliances and coalitions such as the European Union and the North Atlantic Treaty Organization (NATO) often provide the best means of achieving consensus and offering a practical solution to the challenges of enforcement. Their pooled resources and shared goals create an efficient and realistic method of implementing treaties and regulations. For example, these coalitions have proven effective in the space domain by codifying international norms and behavior in concert with voluntary efforts that encourage the collective good with a code of conduct.[39] Their downside is that coalitions can be regionally focused or limited to near-term problems, like areas in the vicinity of war zones or where a failing state is unable to prevent piracy and other forms of maritime crime off its shores.[40] They have negligible mandates or capabilities to monitor pollution, marine stocks, or other vulnerable elements of the commons.

The United Nations is the most appropriate globally accepted international organization to enact treaties and conventions that protect the global commons and articulate measures to enforce them. These arrangements should engender coalitions of state and nonstate actors that are able to assist in enforcement.[41] No other body enjoys as much support or holds the legal mandate to impose necessary remedies on offenders. Current efforts by the United Nations are inadequate because they are spread too thinly on too many problems, thus often relegating its role to that of an ineffectual global monitor or observer to many of the world's ills.

One factor that hampers efforts by the United Nations is that it can take over a decade to negotiate major treaties to secure the commons. This situation is exacerbated by a system that subsequently can take an equal amount of time to achieve substantial changes. The model for treaties is static, requiring years of negotiation to reach agreement that might be obsolescent by the time it was enacted. By contrast, a new model that is more fluid in nature, would allow for intermediate or self-adjusting accords that respond to the evolving circumstances.

Whatever solutions may be adopted, which are likely to be many and varied to deal with an array of possible threats, there must be a unified approach with established priorities and methods and prophylactic measures. This will necessitate developing a grand strategy within the international system for the common good, encompassing a mixture of bilateral, regional, multinational, and international agreements to fulfill the promises made.

Although there is a political need for genuine agreements and long-term commitments in order to safeguard the global commons, there is no real international physical infrastructure to undertake such an endeavor beyond the limited resources of the United Nations. The cost and other requirements for deploying a global police force that is capable of executing a range of protection and enforcement tasks even in one domain would be exorbitant. The security and forcefulness of the instruments needed to defeat a number of threats in the commons would be enormous and almost certainly doomed to failure from the outset. Diverse cultural values would demand consensus on matters of enforcement, and the priority of each effort would be debated meticulously but likely never truly accepted. By contrast, smaller groups of state and nonstate actors, joined by shared goals and a similar ethos, remain the best possible solution to protect unfettered access to every domain and region within the global commons.

The emergence of transnational organized crime during the 1990s was followed by the disconcerting rise of terrorist networks in the next decade. Invariably new, large-scale risks will materialize in the future that will jeopardize, or at least utilize, the global commons. Ignoring such threats, however they manifest themselves, is not an option if the security and freedom of access to the global commons are to be preserved for the benefit of all.

NATIONS tend to act in concert after a catastrophic or decisive event, and thus threats are most likely to be countered only after they materialize. This is understandable given the vast costs associated with preventative measures and the unswerving political will needed to support them. As global terrorism has demonstrated, the true costs in blood and treasure for countering threats is greatest once they arise and come to fruition. Worse still, not every threat will be overcome should it reach the point of no return. Environmental issues such as man-made changes in the composition of the atmosphere and ozone depletion of the stratosphere have the potential for these natural systems not to be able to overcome the current human inputs. As such, state actors must collectively become proactive and regain the initiative, not simply become reactive to future attacks in the global commons.

The future will increasingly blur distinctions between state and nonstate actors. This situation must be addressed by a comprehensive approach in which international actors have a legitimate role to play to counter a minority who attempts to disrupt or damage the long-term common good. The growing needs of some nations for natural or manufactured resources together with the ability to ship or fly them around the world probably will increase tensions and lead to conflicts in future decades. The tendency of nations to take advantage of each other for their own ends must be countered by a more equitable system that advances cooperation and stability wherever and whenever possible. Yet there is no universal defense policy and the sources of instability are growing with alarming speed, particularly in overpopulated and less economically developed nations. Sadly, the reality of security competition is unlikely to yield an egalitarian system as nations continue to seek dominance and survival under the existing international system.

In countering these challenges there must be an acceptance that the range of threats is varied, evolving, and becoming more complex as new technologies emerge. Conventional defense and deterrence policies will not protect the global commons from further exploitation, damage, or even lack of access. Threats in the future will be hybrid in nature, as will the ways in which they are overcome and their consequences mitigated. Without a holistic approach, protecting the commons will be impossible. Failure to act could result in increased terrorism, criminal activity, and conflicts as well as instability and confrontation. For the growing majority of developing and developed nations, ignoring these issues is no longer discretionary.

During the second half of the twentieth century many nations perceived nuclear threats coupled with increased capabilities and proliferation as the greatest single threat to mankind. Although these threats remain, resource scarcity, environmental change, and the security of the commons are likely to present the greatest challenges over the next fifty years.

NOTES

The epigraph appeared in a report issued by Allied Command Transformation titled "Multiple Futures Project: Navigating toward 2030" (Norfolk, VA, April 2009), 7.

1. See Andrea Kavanaugh, Seungwon Yang, Lin Tzy Li, Steve Sheetz, and Ed Fox, "Microblogging in Crisis Situations: Mass Protests in Iran, Tunisia, Egypt" (Blacksburg: Virginia Tech, May 2011).
2. Frank G. Hoffman, "'Hybrid Threats': Neither Omnipresent nor Unbeatable," *Orbis* 54 (Summer 2010): 441–55.
3. Thomas L. Friedman, *The Lexus and the Olive Tree* (New York: Farrar, Straus and Giroux, 1999).
4. Natural disasters are not only unstoppable and unpredictable but also globally disruptive and potentially catastrophic. On the recent tsunami and subsequent nuclear crisis in Japan, see D. K. Matai, "Japan Nuclear: Edge of Chaos and Common Interest," *Business Insider*, March 13, 2011, www.businessinsider.com/japan-nuclear-edge-of-chaos-and -common-interest-2011-3. And on the eruption of the Eyjafjalla volcano in Iceland in 2010, see James Daniell, "CATDAT Damaging Volcanoes Database 2010—The Year in Review," *CEDIM Research Report 2011–2012* (Karlsruhe: Karlsruhe Institute of Technology, January 2011).
5. Alan B. Sielen, "An Oceans Manifesto: The Present Global Crisis," *Fletcher Forum of World Affairs* 32 (Winter 2008): 42–52.
6. Peter Lehr, *Violence at Sea: Piracy in the Age of Global Terrorism* (Abingdon, Oxford: Routledge, 2007).
7. David H. Gray and Albon Head, "The Importance of the Internet to the Post-Modern Terrorist and Its Role as a Form of Safe Haven," *European Journal of Scientific Research* 25, no. 3 (2009): 398, 402–3; Jacqueline Ann Carberry, "Terrorism: A Global Phenomenon Mandating a Unified International Response," *Indiana Journal of Global Legal Studies Journal* 6, no. 2 (1998): 685–88.
8. John Muncie, Deborah Talbot, and Reece Walters, *Crime: Local and Global* (Cullompton, Devon: Willan Publishing, 2010).
9. Kimberley L. Thachuk, *Transnational Threats: Smuggling and Trafficking in Arms, Drugs, and Human Life* (Westport, CT: Praeger Security International, 2007).
10. Raffaello Pantucci, "A Typology of Lone Wolves: Preliminary Analysis of Lone Islamist Terrorists," *Developments in Radicalisation and Political Violence* (London: International Centre for the Study of Radicalisation, March 2011).
11. U. Thara Srinivasan, W. L. Cheung, R. Watson, and U. R. Sumaila, "Overfishing Trends and the Global Food Crisis," *Ocean Science Series* (Washington, DC: Pew Environment Group, September 2010).

12. Jochen Halfar and Rodney M. Fujita, "Danger of Deep-Sea Mining," *Science* 316 (May 18, 2007): 987.
13. Michael Richardson, "Global Warming: The Race to Exploit the Polar Regions," *Viewpoints* (Institute of South East Asia Studies, March 8, 2010), 1–3.
14. Anna Bowden, "The Economic Cost of Maritime Piracy," Ocean Beyond Piracy Project, PowerPoint presentation (London: Chatham House, January 13, 2011), http://oceansbeyondpiracy.org/sites/default/files/documents_old/The_Economic_Cost_of_Piracy_Presentation.pdf.
15. Nigel Cawthorne, *Pirates of the 21st Century: How Modern-Day Buccaneers Are Terrorising the World's Oceans* (London: John Blake, 2010).
16. Peter Dutton, "Military Activities in the EEZ: A US-China Dialogue on Security and International Law in the Maritime Commons" (Newport, RI: China Maritime Studies Institute, Naval War College, December 2010).
17. James Kraska, "China Set for Naval Hegemony," *Diplomat* (Tokyo), May 6, 2010, 1–5.
18. Jane Hupe, "Aviation Outlook," *ICAO Environment Report* (Montreal: International Civil Aviation Organization, 2010), 18.
19. Wendell Minnick, "China Developing Armed, Recon UAVs," *Defense News*, November 29, 2010, 23.
20. Peter Kazimiroff, "Russia to Field More S-400 Air Defence Units," *Jane's Defence Weekly*, February 23, 2011; Robert Hewson, "Air-to-Air Domination," *Jane's Defence Weekly*, March 9, 2011, 32.
21. United Nations, "Treaty on Outer Space" (Vienna: UN Office for Outer Space Affairs, 1967), www.oosa.unvienna.org/oosa/SpaceLaw/outerspt.html. The treaty was reached by the UN General Assembly in 1966, adopted under resolution 2222 (XXI), opened for signature in January 1967, and entered into force in October 1967.
22. For examples of international atmospheric pollution collectives, see Todd Sandler, *Global Collective Action* (Cambridge: Cambridge University Press, 2004), 212–34.
23. David G. Post, "The 'Unsettled Paradox': The Internet, the State, and the Consent of the Governed," *Indiana Journal of Global Legal Studies* 5 (Spring 1998): 521.
24. The status of cyberspace as a domain within the global commons is a topic of continuing debate. See David R. Shedd, remarks presented at the Air Force Association Space and Cyber Warfare Symposium, Keystone Resort, Colorado, June 9, 2010, www.dni.gov/speeches/20100609_speech.
25. Susan J. Buck, *The Global Commons: An Introduction* (Washington, DC: Island Press, 1998).
26. Charles Emmerson and Paul Stevens, "Maritime Choke Points and the Global Energy System" (London: Chatham House, January 2012), 1–12.
27. Laurence Reza Wrathall, "The Vulnerability of Subsea Infrastructure to Underwater Attack: Legal Shortcomings and the Way Forward," *San Diego International Law Journal* 12 (Fall 2010): 223ff.
28. Abraham M. Denmark and James Mulvenon, eds. "The Contested Commons: The Future of American Power in a Multipolar World" (Center for a New American Security, January 2010), 32–33, 98.
29. Iftach Ian Amit, "Cyber [Crime|War]" (Tel Aviv: Security and Innovation, April 2011), 1–7, www.securityandinnovaton.com.
30. Paul Cornish, David Livingstone, Dave Clemente, and Claire Yorke, *On Cyber Warfare* (London: Royal Institute for International Affairs, May 2011).
31. Edward M. Morris, "A Day without Space: Economic and National Security Ramifications," remarks presented at the George Marshall Institute and Space Enterprise Council, Washington, DC, October 16, 2008, www.marshall.org/article.php?id=695.

32. Cesar Jaramillo, ed., *Space Security 2011: Executive Summary* (Kitchener, Ontario: Pandora Press, May 2011), 14–20.

33. Development, Concepts and Doctrine Centre, "Future Character of Conflict" (London: Ministry of Defence, 2010).

34. United States Department of Defense, *Quadrennial Defense Review Report* (Washington, DC: Office of the Secretary of Defense, February 1, 2010), 31–32.

35. Andrew S. Erickson and Gabriel B. Collins, "China Deploys World's First Long-Range, Land-Based 'Carrier Killer,'" *China SignPost*, December 26, 2010, 1. And on the advanced persistent threat kill chain, see Charles Croom, "The Cyber Kill Chain: A Foundation for a New Cyber Security Strategy," *High Frontier* 4 (August 2010): 52–56.

36. Michèle A. Flournoy and Shawn Brimley, "The Contested Commons," *Proceedings* 135 (July 2009): 16–21.

37. The sinking of a South Korean corvette in 2010 was a prime example of the potential for rogue states acting with impunity. See Victor Cha, "The Aftermath of the Cheonan," *Critical Questions*, May 25, 2010. In addition, Iran continues to develop ballistic missiles in the face of international criticism. See Steven A. Hildreth, "Iran's Ballistic Missile Programs: An Overview" (Washington, DC: Congressional Research Service, February 4, 2009).

38. One example is the Nautilus Minerals Solwara 1 project. Its impact statement contrasts sharply with an independent review by the International Union for Conservation of Nature. See Richard Steiner, *Independent Review of the Environmental Impact Statement for the Proposed Nautilus Minerals Solwara 1 Seabed Mining Project, Papua New Guinea* (Madang: International Union for Conservation of Nature, January 10, 2009), which was conducted for the Bismarck-Solomon Seas Indigenous Peoples Council.

39. One initiative is the draft EU code of conduct that "includes transparency and confidence-building measures, as a basis for consultations with key third countries that have activities in outer space or have interests in outer space activities, with the aim of reaching a text that is acceptable to the greatest number of countries." European Union, "Council Conclusions on the Draft Code of Conduct for Outer Space Activities" (Brussels: Council of the European Union, December 17, 2008).

40. For example, see Lauren Gelfand, "Pirates Undeterred by Recent NATO Actions," *Jane's Defence Weekly*, February 23, 2011, 18.

41. An analysis of UN efforts is found in Kauko Aromaa and Terhi Viljanen, eds., *Enhancing International Law Enforcement Co-operation, Including Extradition Measures* (Helsinki: European Institute for Crime Prevention and Control, 2005).

CHAPTER 3

Strategies of Deterrence

SCHUYLER FOERSTER

In early 2011, Secretary of Defense Robert Gates spoke to cadets at the US Military Academy and the US Air Force Academy as part of a farewell tour during which he sought to engage a future generation of officers on the requirements of a twenty-first-century military. He warned them not to view the world "through the prism of the twentieth century . . . oriented towards winning big battles in big wars against nation-states comparably armed and equipped." Neither will the conflicts in Afghanistan and Iraq become templates for military engagements. Instead, the United States and its allies must be prepared to deal with a "range of future threats—from global terrorism to ethnic conflicts; from rogue nations to rising powers with increasingly sophisticated capabilities." Moreover, the future probably will be "complex, unpredictable, and unstructured," according to the secretary, who added, "We have never once gotten it right. . . . From the Mayaguez to Grenada, Panama, Somalia, the Balkans, Haiti, Kuwait, Iraq, and more, we had no idea a year before any of these missions that we would be so engaged."[1]

The challenges to national security are not as easily defined today as they were in the past. The United States is still "the only nation able to project and sustain large-scale operations over extended distances."[2] Nonetheless, given the rapidly changing power dynamics of an increasingly globalized environment, the United States no longer enjoys the supremacy of the post–Cold War unipolar moment.[3] However, it still will "be seen as a much-needed regional balancer in the Middle East and Asia . . . [and] be expected to play a significant role in using its military power to counter global terrorism."[4]

Currently there is no single threat on which to focus, unlike the Cold War when the nation embarked on a strategy of global engagement. But in some critical respects, the challenges of today are similar. First, they are global in scope even if not singular in their perceived source. Second, the United States and its allies must be able to project power effectively to meet these challenges. Third, the capacity to project power is dependent on operating in and communicating through the global commons that include outer space and cyberspace as well as international waters and airspace. Fourth, the primacy of America's power cannot negate fundamental vulnerabilities to military and nonmilitary measures that inflict unacceptable damage on national interests. Fifth, the principal purpose of military power is deterring prospective enemies from threatening the United States and its allies, which includes the integrity of the commons on which that power relies.

TRADITIONAL CONCEPTS OF DETERRENCE

Deterrence is about shaping another's perception of costs and benefits to dissuade threatening behavior.[5] The root of the terms *deterrence* and *terror* suggests exacting severe consequences. Typically acts of deterrence are designed to preserve a behavioral status quo; the behavior that one seeks to avoid has not yet occurred, and the purpose of deterrence is to keep it that way. Thus the success of deterrence only can be inferred by the absence of the behavior one seeks to deter. By contrast, compellence involves motivating another to behave in a certain way; if that desired behavior then occurs, it demonstrates that compellence was successful.[6]

Motivated by the immense power of the atomic bomb, Bernard Brodie penned after World War II, "Thus far, the chief purpose of our military establishment has been to win wars. From now on, its chief purpose must be to *avert* them. It can have almost no other useful purpose."[7] That logic aligned with George Kennan's counsel, which outlined the basis for a Cold War strategy of containment, a defensive geopolitical strategy with which a military strategy of deterrence was totally compatible.[8] Although the United States repeatedly demonstrated its willingness in subsequent decades to use military force to win wars, those conflicts were all limited. Moreover, each occurred within a broader geopolitical context where deterrence—especially deterrence of escalation—remained an overriding consideration.

The ability to deter ultimately depends not only on one's capability to carry out a deterrent threat but also on how the party being deterred perceives both the consequences of action and the credibility of that deterrent threat. Do the prospective costs outweigh the benefits of going through with the provocative behavior? Deterrence during the nuclear standoff of the Cold War was particularly dangerous because it was based on the threat of retaliation that would result in assured destruction, namely, incalculable damage to the party attacked and inevitably to the attacking party. The inescapable dilemma of nuclear deterrence was that the greater the terror associated with the threat, the less credible it became, which arguably weakened the strategy. Launching nuclear weapons to demonstrate the willingness to use them was not an option. Instead, the symbolic tripwire emerged to make deterrence more credible by threatening automatic retaliation, thereby reducing human discretion in the response. Conversely, as the nuclear threat became more credible by making its consequence less terrible and thereby relieving the political pressure on decision makers, the deterrent effect became more tenuous. Fortunately, the Cold War ended before this dilemma was able to play itself out.[9]

Any deterrence strategy is contextual. First, the verb *to deter* is transitive. Deterrence involves a relationship with a potential adversary, so it is essential to specify whom one wants to deter. Second, deterrence involves perception and hence must be clearly communicated for a threat to be effective. In that case it is important to specify not only who is being deterred but also from doing what (behavior to avoid), on whose behalf (oneself or others), and with what (consequences if deterrence fails).

For the United States these questions were easily answered in a bipolar world. The principal object of strategic deterrence was preventing the Soviet Union, and to a lesser extent China, from waging either a major conventional or nuclear war against the United States and its allies. In this regard, deterrence was not only passive—deterring an attack against the United States—but also extended to allied nations. Finally, the threat of deterrence involved nuclear retaliation. Although the United States entertained many flexible options during the Cold War, the underlying premise called for escalation until the hostilities terminated on acceptable terms or culminated in nuclear destruction. However, such alternatives concealed enormous political difficulties, especially as the Unites States sought to manage alliance relations in which reassuring members could prove just as difficult and no less important as deterring the enemy.[10]

DETERRENCE AFTER THE COLD WAR

When the nuclear standoff between the United States and Soviet Union ended, the singular focus of deterrence underwent a major change. A series of crises broadened the problem of deterrence with additional concerns beyond the lingering issue of Russian nuclear arsenals.

The first concern arose when the US-led coalition responded to the invasion of Kuwait and the possible use of chemical weapons by Iraq was confronted. Although public statements were aimed at downplaying the threat of nuclear weapons, President Bush sent a letter to Saddam Hussein that clearly outlined the consequences of any unacceptable behavior: "The United States will not tolerate the use of chemical or biological weapons or the destruction of Kuwait's oil fields and installations. Further, you will be held directly responsible for terrorist actions against any member of the coalition. The American people would demand the strongest possible response. You and your country will pay a terrible price if you order unconscionable acts of this sort."[11]

Five years later, Libya was suspected of building a chemical weapons facility. In comments at the time Secretary of Defense William Perry cautioned that any nation employing chemical weapons would face "the consequences of a response from any weapon in our inventory." Perry went on to suggest that military means were an option to keep the Libyan facility from opening, although he discounted using nuclear weapons.[12] For the next fifteen years US policy in similar contingencies remained ambiguous until the Obama administration ruled out the use of nuclear capabilities against nonnuclear weapons of mass destruction, albeit with some qualifications.[13] The threat of weapons of mass destruction as a deterrent had not diminished, but the enhanced conventional military capabilities available to policymakers offered usable and credible means with which to leverage deterrence without the necessity of threatening nuclear retaliation.

Another crisis arose in 1993 with the discovery of a North Korean nuclear weapons program. The concern was not that another nation sought to join the nuclear club—India and Pakistan tested nuclear weapons before the decade ended without similar alarm—but rather that a hostile nation was intent on acquiring nuclear weapons, and its use of nuclear weapons needed to be deterred. This particular threat posed different problems than deterring the Soviet Union. The number of nuclear devices that Pyongyang had produced and their locations were unknown. Consequently, a preemptive or retaliatory strike could not be planned with any precision, the White House could not be assured this capability could be removed, and devastating conflict on the Korean Peninsula seemed to be more inevitable, even without nuclear use. Whether an enemy had tens of thousands of nuclear weapons or only a handful, their use was fundamentally unacceptable. Although the requirements for deterrence were absolute, there was no assurance that North Korea would behave as rationally or predictably as had the Soviet Union.

A third crisis was reminiscent of the US–Soviet relationship. It was sparked by the Chinese missile tests in 1995–96 designed to communicate determination to extend control over Taiwan by force if required, which prompted the United States to deploy two carrier battle groups in the region. Like earlier tension with Moscow, the incident displayed the type of brinkmanship in which both sides protected their interests by posturing with an implicit threat that nuclear use was not out of the question. Neither side wanted the dispute to result in a conflict or threaten economic relations. Although mutual deterrence that is based on shared interests is an easier proposition, both have been clear that defending key interests is not out of the question.

This so-called Second Nuclear Age includes a shift from a bilateral standoff to a series of conflicts around the world while a US–Russian mutual deterrence relationship persists.[14] The end of the Cold War provoked regional conflicts in which using nuclear weapons was conceivably more rather than less likely. Moreover, threats against the United States and its allies were not limited to nations of comparable strength. Deterrence had become more complex and the issues posed earlier—who is being deterred, from what, on whose behalf, and by what means—had to be answered in different strategic contexts. Just as deterrence was based on relationships during the Cold War, deterrent threat must be targeted at specific nations to dissuade attacks.

The increasing importance of the global commons to allied strategic postures has expanded these post–Cold War problems. At a minimum the growing dependence on the commons creates an expanded set of vulnerabilities that could be targeted by those who threaten international stability. Therefore the problem of deterrence involves not only preventing an attack on the United States and its allies but also dissuading others from attacking the global commons.

THE COMMONS AS STRATEGIC ENVIRONMENTS

Securing strategic interests has traditionally depended on the ability to project power around the world and, in turn, on the ability to transit the commons of international waters and airspace. More recently both outer space and cyberspace have been added as domains or areas that no one nation controls but on which all rely. According to the *Quadrennial Defense Review Report,* the global commons are the connective tissue or fabric that enables "the free flow of goods shipped by air or sea, as well as information transmitted under the ocean or through space.[15]

The significant feature of the global commons is not just wanting to preserve access to them to protect one's own interests. For example, when the United States and the Soviet Union alone had access to space, which was almost exclusively for military and intelligence purposes, it was not considered part of the global commons to be protected for the common good. What has changed, however, is that outer space and cyberspace are no longer the exclusive provinces of superpowers. Today those two domains are indispensable enablers of international order, along with international waters and airspace: "The architecture of the modern international system rests on a foundation of free and fair access to a vibrant global economy that requires stability in the global commons."[16]

The strategic significance of the commons reflects broader international trends, particularly the emergence of new actors in a world where power is increasingly diffused and where wealth relies on active engagement in a global marketplace.[17] Each domain has become increasingly valuable to a variety of international actors—great powers, small powers, nongovernmental and intergovernmental organizations, and the private sector—that have become inextricably dependent on access to physical and virtual resources for their security and prosperity. More-over, the domains are not only indispensable to military operations of a global power but also integral to modern society, especially in regard to communications, transportation, finance, and energy. Today a range of commercial as well as gov-ernmental interests exerts influence on all of the domains of the commons.

As a result, the global commons are congested, contested, and competitive.[18] They are congested because of the growing number of both state and nonstate actors, contested because secure access in some respects is a zero-sum game, and competitive because individual nations do not enjoy unassailable advantages that enable them to dominate the global commons. Neither the United States nor any other nation can control any domain in the commons. Globalization has created a paradox regarding access to and dependency on the commons that shapes the dynamics of security challenges: The more advanced a nation becomes, the more it relies on access to the commons and the more vulnerable it becomes to the loss of access. Technologically advanced nations active in international trade and finance or able to project their political, economic, and military power are more vulner-able to disruptions. Conversely, it is not necessary to be a great power to access the commons, albeit for benign or malign purposes. This democratization of access to the global commons has led to highly asymmetric strategic relationships.

There are various implications of this strategic environment for deterrence. First, deterring attacks on the global commons not only enhances the security of United States and its allies but also preserves the benefits of the commons them-selves, which serve broader interests. In this respect deterrence posture and de-claratory policy do not have to be targeted at a single enemy but can be aimed at disparate state and nonstate actors with the capability to either attack or disrupt the commons. Moreover, the attribution of attacks is problematic because of the nature of the commons as well as the multiplicity of actors. Even when an attack reveals the failure of deterrence, it may not be possible to execute the threatened retaliatory action.

In addition, deterrence establishes an offense-dominant relationship much like the nuclear standoff of the Cold War. Each domain is inherently vulnerable to attacks that can negate some or all of the benefits of the commons, whether in terms of geography or functionality. Defense, denial, and even retaliation within the commons themselves may be counterproductive, if they are possible at all. Piracy on the high seas, for example, denies access to relatively small but poten-tially critical lines of communication, yet mounting concerted defenses against rudimentary pirates appears to be problematic. At the other end of the techno-logical spectrum, disrupting or destroying space and cyberspace assets is simpler than denying or defeating such attacks. However, even when the attacker is known, retaliation within the commons may be prohibitively detrimental to vital US and allied interests.

Finally, unlike the strategic balance during the Cold War, there is no symmetry in either the capabilities or the risks in potential threats to the commons. Like emerging threats in the Second Nuclear Age, less powerful adversaries can inflict unacceptable damage. Moreover, adversaries that are less technologically advanced also tend to be less vulnerable to the loss of access to the global commons whereas damage to advanced nations would be substantial. Coupled with problems of attribution, the likely payoff of an attack could appear quite high although the risks to attackers remain acceptably low. In this respect crisis stability in such an environment would be dangerously low. Thus effective deterrence as applied to the commons is essential.

STRATEGIES FOR DETERRENCE

During the Cold War the strategic debate over how best to deter attack normally was divided into deterrence by punishment and deterrence by denial.[19] With the strategic interdependence that has resulted from contemporary globalization, one might add deterrence by entanglement.[20] However, each of these strategies is prone to the same inherent problem: successful deterrence cannot be empirically demonstrated or validated, only its failure. Although none of these strategies is new, they have assumed different characteristics within the context of the twenty-first-century security environment in the global commons.[21]

Deterrence by Punishment

The first strategy impresses attackers of their inevitable destruction as a punitive consequence of their behavior. During the Cold War the costs of aggression were predictable and understood on all sides as unacceptable, which was known as the crystal ball effect.[22] The basic ingredients of an effective punitive deterrent were the retaliatory capability that would survive to respond and the will to execute that response. As previously seen, the capability to inflict *assured destruction* on the Soviet Union was never really in doubt, although much of the debate over nuclear posture toward the end of the Cold War was focused on surviving under a hypothetical first strike by the Soviet Union. Nevertheless, the greater question was the credibility of the deterrent threat itself. Even a limited nuclear conflict could have possibly escalated out of control. Destruction of the Soviet Union would not change the fact that the United States had been destroyed.

With respect to the commons in the current international security environment, the problem is more difficult. Whether it is an attack on the high seas by pirates, interdiction of air corridors, disrupting computer networks, or disabling satellites in space, the presumption is that attackers are likely to succeed. Therefore a punitive deterrent must threaten an adversary, be it known or unknown, with unacceptable costs that outweighed the strategic benefits of a successful attack.

In the first place the behavior to be deterred must be clear. The threat by the Soviet Union of nuclear warfare and its general aggressiveness toward the United States or its allies became the focus of deterrence in the Cold War. Absent from that strategic equation is the adventurism in the third world on the part of the Soviet Union acting alone or through proxies and the cat-and-mouse games pursued by US and Soviet forces. But what is the objective of deterrence in the global commons? Is it piracy or interdiction of lines of communication? Is it responding to disruptions in space or cyberspace? Where on the conflict spectrum between minor harassment and significant destruction of key assets should an attack trigger punitive action?

And whom does one punish? The range of potential adversaries who might attack is much larger than during the Cold War and it may be impossible to identify a particular attacker with confidence. Moreover, how could the punishment be inflicted? What punitive measures short of capture or death are effective in the combating piracy on the high seas? Will the punishment be cost-effective, that is, less than the harm caused by an attack? Would shutting down a computer network warrant a retaliatory strike that crashes the network? Would an attack on a satellite be sufficient justification for destroying another satellite that increases debris and the volatility of the space domain? Must a punitive response be proportional, and what does that mean? Could such an attack be effective when an attacker is less reliant on the loss of access to space than the United States or its allies?

Finally, how would a conflict be terminated? In the Cold War the real concern was whether any mechanism would survive by which leaders in Washington and Moscow could communicate with one another and cease military operations following a nuclear exchange. In leveraging deterrence in the global commons and the shared benefits of their continued integrity, it would be imperative that a punitive retaliatory attack leave open the possibility of communicating with an adversary to terminate a conflict, assuming its identity is already known or can be determined.

Deterrence by Denial

Throughout the Cold War deterrence by denial was the ideal. Its objective was deterring an attack by denying the confidence of an adversary that its attack would succeed in the first place. Such a posture required the combination of the following four approaches, each of which would enhance the survivability of anticipated targets: hardening, maneuver and deception, redundancy, and active defense. Having denied the possibility of success even if an attack was forthcoming, the decision on whether to retaliate could be taken after careful strategic deliberation, rather than on whether punitive retaliation was established at the heart of the deterrent strategy.

Hardening targets against nuclear weapons was never really achievable. No sooner were ballistic missiles put in underground silos than they became vulnerable to direct strikes by more accurate weapons. In the commons, hardening of respective infrastructure can be prohibitively expensive. Even if governments are prepared to make investments, more numerous commercial actors are less inclined to do so. Hence, although critical assets may become substantially less vulnerable, the broader infrastructure would remain open to attack.

Both Washington and Moscow pursued maneuver and deception to some extent during the Cold War. They invested then and continue to invest in deploying submarine-launched ballistic missiles. The United States considered but ultimately decided against investing in mobile land-based intercontinental ballistic missiles although the Soviet Union fielded them. In the context of the global commons, maneuver and deception are promising strategies, especially in cyberspace and to lesser extent in outer space, which lacks situational awareness. Although no strategy is foolproof, anything that compounds the calculus for attackers enhances deterrence.

Redundancy in the Cold War meant having more warheads than one needed to accomplish the mission, based on the assumption that some would not survive. In the global commons, it is not weaponry but physical and virtual infrastructures for transportation and communication that are at risk. Redundancy means having multiple assets to accomplish the same function, which is more likely as additional actors contribute assets to networks. Moreover, what would be needed is a coordinated capability to facilitate switching among the redundant assets, a mechanism that cannot be presumed given a heterogeneous group of public and private sector actors. The more such coordination can be achieved, the more real redundant capabilities would become.

Finally, active defenses continue to be elusive. With regard to ballistic missile defense, the United States and allies such as Japan have been able to demonstrate limited success, which is more relevant to smaller attacks in the Second Nuclear Age than larger ones in the Cold War. In the global commons, however, active defenses once again confront the economic tyranny of an offense-dominant environment. Simply put, it is easier and less costly to mobilize additional offensive capabilities than to mount effective active defenses. That certainly is true with regard to piracy on the high seas, where the technology is available but the international community is hesitant to provide substantial defenses. In cyberspace, however, technology of active defense remains a challenge even when governments and others are willing to make investments. In outer space, established norms and fear of weaponization as well as economic barriers limit the ability to mount defenses.

It is unlikely the global commons can be defended against attacks by determined enemies. In the culture of the Cold War, the United States focused on ensuring the survivability of assets because every weapon contributed to the mission. Today greater emphasis is placed on mission assurance, which allows for the mission to be accomplished when assets have been destroyed.[23] Even under a strategy of denial, achieving invulnerability will continue to be elusive. Therefore it is prudent to think in terms of managing risks rather than seeking to eliminate them.

Deterrence by Entanglement

The third strategy differs conceptually from deterrence by punishment and denial, both of which are focused on specific actions that the deterring state would take in responding to an attack. Deterrence by entanglement assumes that potential adversaries are stakeholders in the commons, entrenched in the network that they would not attack even in a crisis because of shared interests. Essentially deterrence by entanglement leverages the recognition of those interests to preserve access to and stability in the global commons. The deterrent effect is based on the cost associated with attacks on the commons. It does not require domains to become sanctuaries from military activities, but that serious restraint is exercised to avoid harming the integrity of the environment.

Such restraint is not a new phenomenon. Every domain has a regime of formal and informal rules that govern or regulate behavior at least in peacetime. For example, the United States and Soviet Union exercised restraint in proscribing nuclear weapons testing in the atmosphere and in space, in part motivated by the desire not to endanger manned space flight.[24] In this respect it was the desire to preserve the value of the commons that provided an independent incentive for restraint, separate from bilateral strategic relations. Both superpowers not only shared interests in the commons but also shared vulnerability to the loss of access to the commons for their own purposes.

Therefore strengthening this dimension of deterrence involves a different set of choices than a decision on how to punish or how to deny an attack. These choices include encouraging others, especially potential adversaries, to accept a stake in the integrity of the commons, at a minimum through access to the commons but also by establishing rules and norms for the global commons. Examples include the mechanisms for consultation and rule making that range from maintaining space situational awareness, managing space debris, and developing protocols and procedures to protect against cyber hackers to collaborating on securing sea lanes, protecting against piracy, and cooperating to counter maritime terrorism. Approaches might vary from more formal regimes like binding agreements and codes of conduct to voluntary rules of the road and other restraints. Mechanisms can be state centered or collaborative networks among actors in the private sector who increasingly dominate the commons. Regardless of the means, dependency strengthens these shared values and increases the difficulty and cost of disengaging.

Such an entanglement strategy applies not only to potential adversaries but also to friends and allies as well, especially those who are in transition to more modern societies in an era of globalization. Because global commons are assets shared by virtually all societies, even transitioning and developing societies have a stake in ensuring continued access to the benefits of the commons and can be encouraged to share the burdens of securing them. For example, US security assistance policies—once an important Cold War strategy to bolster friends in the developing world against Communist influence—have evolved, especially in the wake of conflicts in Afghanistan and Iraq, as essential elements of a strategy of counterterrorism and conflict prevention. Whether as an aid to fighting terrorism and piracy in and around Africa or as a way to build allied capacity to protect air and sea (and potentially cyber) lines of communication, security assistance is ultimately a way to increase a network of countries with shared interests and entangled commitments in protecting the global commons.[25]

THE growing importance of the global commons is a two-edged sword. On the one hand, relying on the domains exposes vulnerabilities to would-be attackers. Actors who may lack an ability to attack the interests of the United States and its allies could potentially inflict substantial harm on the homeland as well as military forces by disrupting or destroying their access to operate in and through the commons. National vulnerability is inevitable, and the potential for asymmetric attacks from disparate quarters is high. Thus the United States and its allies must be capable of deterring attacks on the commons on which they depend as well as on themselves.

On the other hand, the global commons represent a potential network of shared values that may complicate decisions by adversaries on the benefits versus the costs of launching an attack. As nations modernize, it is likely that they will join an interdependent network in the commons and at some level share political, economic, commercial, and strategic interests as well as some degree of vulnerability, which any loss of access to the global commons would imply.

Deterrence became more stable during the Cold War when the two superpowers developed a so-called essentially equivalent posture and less stable when one side believed the other had acquired a strategic advantage.[26] That type of balanced relationship is unlikely today because the potential adversaries do not and probably will never have similar military capabilities. However, a more symmetrical relationship may evolve with respect to the commons whereby nations with disparate military capabilities share dependency on them. To the extent shared dependency and vulnerability can be cultivated, they will contribute to deterrence in the global commons.

As in the Cold War, no single deterrence strategy will suffice in the twenty-first century. Although a strategy of entanglement may provide a complementary route to stability in deterrent relationships, traditional strategies of punishment and denial also will remain essential. Punitive threats require the capability and will to inflict unacceptable damage on adversaries, whether by weapons, sanctions, or virtual targeting in cyberspace. And deterrence by denial will require sober recognition of existing vulnerabilities and an effective strategy for mission assurance.

The world is a paradoxical and nuanced place where the United States and its allies cannot control the commons and find themselves perilously vulnerable to their loss or disruption. Thus, with respect to the global commons, any strategy of deterrence cannot simply involve unilateral exercise of punitive threats and denial measures. Such a strategy must take advantage of the increasingly shared interests and vulnerabilities that accompany globalization in the twenty-first century.

NOTES

The views expressed are those of the author and do not necessarily reflect the official positions of the US Department of Defense, the US Air Force, or the US Air Force Academy.

1. The speeches were presented at West Point on February 25, 2011, and in Colorado Springs on March 4, 2011. See the texts at www.defense.gov/speeches/speech.aspx?speechid=1539 and www.defense.gov/speeches/speech.aspx?speechid=1543, respectively.
2. United States Department of Defense, *Quadrennial Defense Review Report* (Washington, DC: Office of the Secretary of Defense, February 2010), iv.
3. Charles Krauthammer, "The Unipolar Moment," *Foreign Affairs* 70, no. 1 (1991): 23–33.
4. *Global Trends 2025: A Transformed World* (Washington, DC: National Intelligence Council, December 2008), xi.
5. For a further discussion of traditional deterrence theory, see Schuyler Foerster, "Theoretical Foundations: Deterrence in the Nuclear Age," in *American Defense Policy*, 6th ed., Schuyler Foerster and Edward Wright, eds. (Baltimore, MD: Johns Hopkins University Press, 1990), 42–54.
6. On deterrence as manipulation of risk and the differences between deterrence and compellence, see Thomas C. Schelling, *Arms and Influence* (New Haven, CT: Yale University Press, 1966), especially 69–125.
7. Bernard Brodie, ed., *The Absolute Weapon* (New York: Harcourt Brace, 1946), 76.
8. George F. Kennan, "The Sources of Soviet Conduct," *Foreign Affairs* 25, no. 4 (1947): 566–82.
9. For a discussion of nuclear policy during the Cold War, see Lawrence Freedman, *The Evolution of Nuclear Strategy*, 3rd ed. (London: Palgrave Macmillan, 2003).
10. See Michael Howard, "Reassurance and Deterrence: Western Defense in the 1980s," *Foreign Affairs* 61 (Winter 1982–83): 309–24.
11. "Statement by Press Secretary Fitzwater on President Bush's Letter to President Saddam Hussein of Iraq" (Washington, DC: The White House, January 12, 1991), http://bushlibrary.tamu.edu/research/public_papers.php?id=2617&year=1991&month=01.
12. See United States Department of Defense, press briefing, May 8, 1996, www.fas.org/news/libya/960508-436361.htm.
13. United States Department of Defense, *Nuclear Posture Review Report* (Washington, DC: Office of the Secretary of Defense, April 2010), viii.

14. See Keith B. Payne, *Deterrence in the Second Nuclear Age* (Lexington: University Press of Kentucky, 1996). See also Paul Bracken, "The Second Nuclear Age," *Foreign Affairs* 79 (January–February 2000): 146–56.

15. Department of Defense, *Quadrennial Defense Review Report*, 31.

16. Michèle A. Flournoy and Shawn Brimley, "The Contested Commons," *Proceedings* 135 (July 2009): 16–21.

17. *Global Trends 2025*, 28–37.

18. United States Department of Defense and Director of National Intelligence, *National Security Space Strategy* (Washington, DC: Office of the Secretary of Defense and Office of the Director of National Intelligence, January 2011), 1–3.

19. For a discussion of this debate, see Foerster, "Theoretical Foundations," 47–51.

20. Roger Harrison, Collins G. Shackelford, and Deron R. Jackson, "Space Deterrence: The Delicate Balance of Risk," *Space and Defense* 3 (Summer 2009), 1–30. The authors view entanglement as one of four elements of layered deterrence, the others being retaliation (akin to punishment), denial, and international norms.

21. See Forrest Morgan, "Deterrence and First Strike Stability in Space: A Preliminary Assessment" (Santa Monica, CA: Rand Corporation, 2010), on the difficulties of punishment- and denial-based deterrent strategies related to space.

22. Albert Carnesale, Paul Doty, Stanley Hoffmann, Samuel P. Huntington, Joseph S. Nye Jr., Scott D. Sagan, and Derek Bok, *Living with Nuclear Weapons*, 5th ed. (Cambridge, MA: Harvard University Press, 1983).

23. See, for example, United States, Executive Office of the President, *National Space Policy of the United States* (Washington, DC: The White House, June 28, 2010), 9.

24. James Clay Moltz, *The Politics of Space Security: Strategic Restraint and the Pursuit of National Interests* (Stanford, CA: Stanford University Press, 2008), 124–75, especially the discussion of cooperative restraint.

25. For a detailed discussion of this role for the US military, see Derek S. Reveron, *Exporting Security: International Engagement, Security Cooperation, and the Changing Face of the U.S. Military* (Washington, DC: Georgetown University Press, 2010).

26. The term *essential equivalence* was used not only by the Nixon administration to describe the rationale for strategic arms control but also in the Jackson amendment as a precondition for such agreements. See Richard Smoke, *National Security and the Nuclear Dilemma*, 2nd ed. (New York: Random House, 1987), 160–61.

PART II

CONFLICT METHODS

CHAPTER 4

The Maritime Commons
and Military Power

SAM J. TANGREDI

Oceans and the airspace above them were the first internationally recognized global commons and the model for analyzing the emerging space and cyberspace domains. The role of the commons in developing and facilitating international trade is indisputable. Mitigating security threats to the maritime commons benefited all nations, even noncoastal states. Piracy, terrorism, and other criminal acts at sea must be countered to protect free trade and international commerce. Respect for freedom of navigation must be maintained by all nations, particularly through nonterritorial waters illegally claimed by coastal states and international straits. Other threats to the oceans are major concerns including resource exploitation through overfishing in proscribed areas, pollution, and other acts of ecological and environmental degradation.[1]

The navies and coast guards around the world are responsible for securing the maritime commons.[2] For those nations that do not perceive a direct military threat to their national security from the maritime domain, policing the commons represents the primary mission of their naval forces.[3] International naval forces often combine for the common good by providing commons security. One recent example is cooperation by many navies including nonmember nations of the North Atlantic Treaty Organization (NATO) to suppress piracy along the Somali coast.[4] Even when operating unilaterally on the high seas, navies are empowered under international law to protect access to the commons including thwarting piracy against vessels of all nations.[5] As a friction-reduced surface for transporting heavy loads, the maritime commons provide one of the best mediums for protecting commerce and facilitating humanitarian assistance, functions that many navies of the world have long performed in support of strategic objectives.[6]

For island nations such as Britain, Japan, and Australia as well as continental nations like the United States and Canada, access to the global commons is more than a matter of security. Historically oceans provide barriers against enemies and means to transport forces in defense of national interests and in support of allies in crises. Moreover, the concept of freedom of the seas takes on another important meaning. Traditionally, oceans are the prime medium by which states act militarily. Although military power is projected by long-range aircraft and missiles and from bases in the region, only the oceans can sustain it. Power projection requires forces with combat vehicles and heavy equipment, much of which cannot be transported by air. Sustaining military operations depends on the maritime commons, even in the case of a landlocked country such as Afghanistan, which depends on access to the seaport of Karachi in Pakistan.[7]

DUAL USE OF THE MARITIME COMMONS

For major maritime nations the maritime commons is a dual-use environment. The term *dual-use* describes technology and products with civilian and military uses. This is particularly true for powers intent on shaping the international security environment. Force projection would be impossible if nations lack the means to gain access to the maritime commons. Military uses of the seas require more economic resources than their commercial use.

Because there is a legal component in maritime power projection, it is important to think in terms of the maritime commons and not simply the maritime domain. Access of naval vessels to the commons is guaranteed under international law including transit through international waters and straits. In peacetime there are no constraints on stationing naval or other forces anywhere on the high seas, which are navigable waters more than twelve miles from sovereign land territory. For nations with global navies, the oceans provide unfettered access in peacetime, and all nations have the legal right to deploy forces wherever they choose on the high seas.

The right to operate on the high seas is one reason there never has been major opposition to the principle of freedom of the seas for warships under international law. In effect, there is no distinction between the dual uses of the commons; the peaceful transit of commercial vessels and that of warships have legal equivalency.[8] But warships (and other government-operated vessels) have the right or protection of immunity. With the exception of malignant acts such as terrorism, flagged vessels on the high seas remain under national authority and require governmental permission to interfere with their transit, but they do not possess absolute immunity.

The right to transit the high seas, however, is a practical right, which can be exercised only when a nation uses vessels for military and commercial purposes. Oceangoing and joint forces sustained from the maritime environment can operate in a dual-use mode that provides a globe-spanning base (the sea) to exercise defense in depth, power projection, and influence.[9]

DOMAINS VERSUS COMMONS

The term *domain* frequently is used to delineate the physical areas in which joint forces operate. In the *Department of Defense Dictionary* there are definitions of *air domain*, *maritime domain*, and *cyberspace*, as well as references to the *air, land, maritime,* and *space domains* in conjunction with full-spectrum superiority.[10] This has led some military planners to utilize the terms *domains* and *commons* interchangeably.[11] But *maritime domain* does not capture the legal aspects of *maritime commons* or the interdependence of the maritime and air domains. In the airspace over oceans, freedom of the high seas applies to aircraft as well as ships. By contrast, airspace over land is considered to be territorial and belonging to a nation, which gives it the same legal status as land.

The term *maritime domain* also does not convey economic dependence on ocean trade and interdependence of that trade and security. Although military victories often are considered the outcome of battles, in many cases they result from the economic strangulation of the enemy. For example, the defeat of the Confederacy during the Civil War depended on a naval blockade to prevent matériel reaching the South. The military response to German unrestricted submarine attacks on convoys supplying Britain was waged in every domain: the high seas, air, land, and undersea (the last distinct enough to qualify as a separate domain). In addition, unrestricted submarine warfare by the US Navy prevented resources from reaching Imperial Japan.

The role of naval forces in preventing and protecting international trade is best exemplified by the concept of the commons because access to the commons in peace and war requires similar resources. In peacetime pre-hostilities and phase-zero operations, global/power projection naval forces operate in the maritime domain and maritime-air domain in a similar fashion: conducting forward operations within striking range or responding to land-centered contingencies or hostile shores. Naval forces that use the commons can deter conflicts, influence or intervene in regional crises, or cut off military or economic access of an enemy to the commons.

Advocates of the use of the term *maritime domain* over the term *maritime commons* maintain that in a war the concept of the commons becomes irrelevant. They argue belligerents would disregard legal rights and requirements that define the commons, as demonstrated by the actions taken by the Royal Navy against neutrals including American vessels that led in the War of 1812.[12] However, conflicts no longer involve declarations of war, and actions such as enforcing maritime sanctions often occur in supposed peacetime. It has become difficult to delineate between war and peace. As demonstrated in the Cold War, forward operations by naval and joint forces were conducted under peacetime laws in the commons, despite being critical to a strategy of deterrence.

Violations of the maritime commons boundaries have occurred in connection with covert near-shore intelligence-gathering missions. However, the fact that such missions are covert and the nations involved go to lengths to establish plausible deniability is indicative of the effort to seemingly respect the rules of the maritime commons. Thus the concept of the commons cannot be easily dismissed from the analysis and planning that go into military operations.

THE GEO-ECONOMIC PURPOSE
OF NAVAL POWER

The term *commons* remains relevant to joint military planning because naval power cannot be separated from its geo-economic purpose.[13] Navies exist not only to fight but also to ensure access to the commons. Given a global economy reliant on international trade, maritime forces may be more important in providing access to the commons than in performing a counterforce role. As guarantors of maritime trade, navies must not allow access to be threatened by a hostile power. Conversely, maritime forces can be used to deny similar access by an enemy.

Alfred Thayer Mahan, the American who is credited with developing the modern concept of the commons, stressed the role of navies in providing secure access for international trade.[14] He referred to oceans as "a wide common" and the role of navies in denying access to the globe-spanning "great highway."[15] Mahan summarized this geo-economic idea as follows: "It is not the taking of individual ships or convoys, be they few or many, that strikes down the money power of a nation; it is the possession of that overbearing power on the sea which drives the enemy's flag from it, or allows it to appear only as a fugitive; and by controlling the great common, closes the highway by which commerce moves to and from the enemy's shore."[16]

Military planners may not consider the relevance of naval control in the maritime commons because it does not involve combat operations by great fleets. It is somewhat ironic that critics of Mahan cite his alleged fixation on decisive battle as the objective of naval warfare as influencing the Royal Navy during World War I to seek fleet-on-fleet engagements like the Battle of Jutland while being unprepared to counter U-boats. Jutland may have decided nothing; but Mahan, who gained experience of blockades during naval operations in the Civil War, was a far more nuanced analyst. But only the existence of great fleets, or joint forces in current parlance, can guarantee control of the commons, which provides economic strength to generate military power.

FORCES . . . *FROM THE SEA*

The control of the commons, which in a conflict may involve naval forces, is a prerequisite for another meaning of dual use: projecting power from the sea on land.[17] Although the maritime commons are a fluid medium for both international commerce and resource exploitation, it is uninhabited by humankind. Moreover, outcomes of war are ultimately decided on land.[18] As one historian described this reality in the interwar years: "The supreme test of the naval strategist is the depth of his comprehension of the intimate relationship between seapower and land power, and of the truth that basically all effort afloat should be directed at an effect ashore."[19]

Projecting military force by sea requires the capabilities of what formerly were regarded as superpowers or major multinational alliances. One reason the United States remains the primary global power is because it has the military forces to command the commons—at least at the time and place that it chooses.[20] In fact the strategy of forward defense—intended to keep the oceans as protective barriers—originates in and arguably depends on control of the commons.[21]

In the past decade, seabasing has been the focus of analysis and incremental improvements. Seabasing is described as utilization of the maritime commons by joint military forces in roughly the same way as overseas land bases.[22] Although largely associated with naval expeditionary and amphibious warfare operations, the concept of seabasing also can be applied to missions such as territorial ballistic missile defense. In fact, the Obama administration has selected a seabased antiballistic missile system (Aegis with the Standard SM-3 missile)—augmented by radars on ships and launchers on land—for the defense of European members of the NATO alliance.[23] This plan is an alternative to the exclusive land-based approach of the previous administration.[24]

A working definition of seabasing includes various missions conducted by joint forces with peacetime freedom to operate globally, which relies on the political-legal status of the maritime commons. To establish a general definition of seabasing, the Office of Force Transformation in the Department of Defense during the Rumsfeld years described sea-base as "a noun; the sea and not the things on it."[25] Although that description is not officially accepted, it accurately points to the maritime commons as the environment that makes the concept of seabasing possible.

Except under difficult circumstances it is impossible to establish seabases that can deter or influence regional crises without the rights afforded by the commons. Without such rights—for example, under a regime in which the high seas were divided into territories of coastal states—it would be hard to gain diplomatic permission to base forces close to a potential enemy just as it is to obtain overseas land bases.

Open access of the maritime commons allows forces from the sea to rapidly intervene in crises on land. As a liberal democracy with national interests that usually correspond to those of the global community regarding acts of aggression, genocide, the proliferation of weapons of mass destruction, and others, the United States in its role as international hegemon may be considered as delivering the common good of global security to other nations.[26] This is thus a common good derived, at least in part, by military forces operating within the commons.

FORWARD PRESENCE AND ANTI-ACCESS STRATEGIES

As previously noted, the rights of the commons are held as practical rights. But without means to guarantee access to the maritime commons, rights cannot be exercised. This is true of projecting military power and influence from the sea by deploying US and allied forces. Forward presence describes peacetime operations by naval forces in the maritime commons within range of crises or threats. It can deter war, reassure our allies and partners to preclude hostilities, position naval forces to respond in a crisis, and gain access to enemy territory in a conflict to mount a decisive campaign.[27] Embedded in this logic is the idea that the forward presence of maritime forces can be a substitute for overseas land bases—a strategy made explicit by the term *seabasing*.

To conduct routine naval forward presence deployments on a global basis requires more than warships; it requires an alliance and logistics network capable of supporting far-flung and diverse forces. The United States gained this capability through alliances during World War II and the Cold War. Allied forces maintain naval forward presence on a limited or regional basis, notably in Britain and France. In the Cold War, the Soviet Union attempted to create a network to support naval forward presence. Although the Soviet Navy was successful in obtaining friendly port facilities in Cuba, Libya, and elsewhere in Africa, it was unable to build more than a basic network and relied on submarines and long-range naval aircraft to realize temporary presence in parts of the maritime commons. In the wake of the Cold War both Russia and China are seeking to replicate US capabilities in what each regards as its respective sphere of influence.

Unable to restrict naval forward presence, potential enemies are seeking anti-access or area denial capabilities to keep US and allied forces as far away as possible from their coastal waters as well as land territory and airspace instead of engaging in a force-against-force battle on their territory.[28] This approach is a lesson of Operation Desert Storm: allowing the United States and its coalition partners to assemble forces in a region either ends in defeat or compels an enemy to use nuclear weapons if they are available. The People's Republic of China (PRC) is committed to this approach by keeping US forces out of the Taiwan

Strait in the event Taiwan is forcibly annexed (or reunified from the perspective of Beijing).[29] Iran also appears to be preparing to respond to US and other forces in the Persian Gulf by closing the Strait of Hormuz.[30] An anti-access strategy inevitably involves restricting use of part of the maritime commons.

US concern over the expanding reach of anti-access capabilities to the maritime commons is reflected in the flurry of articles on the development of a terminally guided antiship ballistic missile designed to target US aircraft carriers and other vessels at distances over 810 miles.[31] Although this technology was developed originally by the Soviet Union in the 1980s, China is the only nation to actively pursue it in recent years.

TACTICAL AND DIPLOMATIC CONSTRAINTS

In addition to closing regional or near high-seas and littoral approaches by means of anti-access systems, tactical constraints on the use of the maritime commons can be achieved through naval blockade, *guerre de course* (armed raids on commerce), or the threat of such actions.

Blockading ports is the most decisive means of denying access to the maritime commons in a conflict. Its objectives can range from preventing military equipment and manufactured goods or raw materials from reaching an enemy to decisively cutting off maritime commerce. However, the term *blockade* signifies an act of war under customary international law and the law of war.[32] The more nuanced activities of maritime sanctions enforcement (particularly when backed up by UN resolutions) are a modern variant of blockade that does not constitute a direct act of war, although it can achieve the same objectives. Sanctions have been applied in recent years by the United Nations and coalitions to oppose the belligerent posturing of Saddam Hussein and prevent the flow of arms to warring factions in the Balkans with varying degrees of success.

Guerre de course was commonplace when limited hostilities were conducted by European nations against rival or opposing navies because they were too strong to engage in force-on-force combat, although enemy merchant fleets were vulnerable. The origin of the term reflects periods when French navies were unable to confront or blockade Britain yet could capture or sink unescorted or unprotected merchant ships. Guerre de course ranged from state-sponsored piracy during the Elizabethan age to German submarine attacks on shipping along the US coast during World War II. Neither of these activities constituted full blockades, but both were destructive to maritime commerce.

The threat of such activities can restrict access to the global commons by leading nations to acquiesce or limit trade while driving up insurance rates on commercial shipping. Threats are more credible when backed by historical precedent and unpredictable or bizarre action by nations like North Korea, which gives them advantages in a confrontation.[33] Obviously tactical methods of denying access involve considerable violence. But there are also diplomatic and legal measures that can be taken to constrain or restrict access to the maritime environment.

Customary international law holds that acquiescence to restrictions on access over time establishes a legal regime. Nations that do not challenge such claims in effect reinforce them. This principle was key to a decision by the International Court of Justice in 1992 on claims to islands in the Gulf of Fonseca, which involved El Salvador, Honduras, and Nicaragua.[34] Freedom of the seas also is threatened in areas claimed beyond the provisions of the UN Convention on the Law of the Sea (UNCLOS) if they go unchallenged. Many claims are based on historical situations in which a nation or predecessor state declared ownership or had jurisdiction over some contested area in the past, which frequently are exaggerated. Preventing acquiescence to restrictions on access is the purpose of freedom of navigation exercises by the US Navy.

The potential for international legal constraints on the use of the maritime commons has been suggested to curb military power and contribute to a more peaceful world. Such proposals that would sacrifice freedom of the seas to prevent conflict arose during and after World War I, then subsided in the wake of World War II, and later became a minor cause of the arms control movement in the Cold War era.[35] Such proposals would assign jurisdiction over the maritime commons to an international committee or sections of the commons to coastal states to prevent conflicts at sea instead of the customary freedom of the seas regime as codified by the UNCLOS. There is little evidence to support these proposals that retain the cachet of peacemaking, and thus should be regarded as a threat to the traditional reliance on freedom of the seas.

Support for tighter control of the maritime commons by international organizations is based on the concept of the "common heritage of all mankind" advanced in the UN General Assembly and codified in the undersea mining provisions of the UNCLOS. Rather than approach this common heritage in terms of existing freedoms in the maritime commons, this proposal requires forming international committees to control profits from nonterritorial undersea mining and diverting revenue to lesser-developed states without the infrastructure to mine the seabed. This course of action would forfeit national sovereignty to a collective of free riders and prompt nonratification of the UNCLOS agreement, although the United States has pledged to adhere to its other provisions, which are largely based on the customary laws of the sea.

Nongovernmental organizations (NGOs) have tried to control activities in the maritime commons. Greenpeace has taken aggressive action involving blockades and deliberate collisions at sea that its leaders opposed. Known for interfering in the last remaining vestiges of the whaling industry, Greenpeace has conducted protests against nuclear-powered vessels and naval deployments that have been largely American. Such actions are intended to heighten awareness of its agenda and provoke overreaction by governments and generate public support for legal restrictions.[36]

COMMONS AND COMMON SECURITY TODAY

Two major disputes over the maritime commons could result in conflict. The first involves the Chinese claims in the South China Sea, the East China Sea, and nearby high seas, and efforts to prevent the transit of US military vessels through waters adjacent to PRC territory (see map 4.1). The second involves the Russian claims to control of the seabed and the waters of the Arctic Ocean.

Claims by Beijing in the South China Sea directly affect the interests of Vietnam and at least four other members of the Association of Southeast Asian Nations, which border the sea, utilize its resources, and have their own claims to largely uninhabited islands and periodically uncovered shoals of the Spratly and Paracel Islands. These islets and outcroppings are believed to sit on top of undersea oil deposits, hence the regional interest in otherwise desolate territory. The Spratleys are roughly 310 miles from the Philippines, Malaysia, Brunei, and Vietnam, and 620 miles from China. Beijing regards the South China Sea as one of its core national interests, which is the same term used to describe Tibet and Taiwan.[37] As one source notes: "Beijing's unwelcome intent appears to give notice that China is opting out of the Global Commons, and that the Western Pacific [of which the South China Sea has always been an indivisible part] is not to be accessible to all, but instead increasingly part of China's exclusive sphere of influence."[38]

China supports this position with two claims: first, its territorial waters historically have reached into the South China Sea, and second, its right to control navigation and research—including military presence—extends throughout the 200-nautical-mile Exclusive Economic Zone. Both claims violate the UNCLOS and are vigorously protested by neighboring albeit militarily weaker nations.[39] It is also difficult not to conclude that the challenge by China to the principles that define the maritime commons "puts it at direct odds with the United States."[40]

The PRC has made maritime claims that conflict with other nations, particularly with Japan over the East China Sea and Senkaku Islands and with South Korea over the Yellow Sea.[41] Beijing also objects to American naval exercises with its regional allies.[42]

Claims to control over high seas by the Chinese led to harassment of USNS *Impeccable* and USNS *Victorious* in 2009, USNS *Sumner* in 2002, and USNS *Bowditch* in 2001, plus the collision of a People's Liberation Army (PLA) fighter with a US Navy EP-3 surveillance plane more than seventy-five nautical miles off the coast in 2001.[43] After the American crew made an emergency landing on

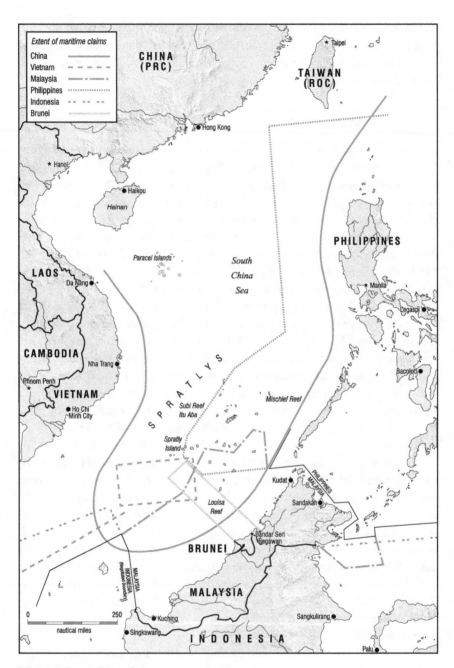

Map 4.1 South China Sea

Hainan Island, the Chinese refused to repatriate them until the United States expressed its sorrow for the death of a PLA pilot and apologized for landing on Chinese territory without permission.[44]

The second major dispute involves escalating claims by the Russian Federation to parts of the Arctic Ocean. These claims are fueled by the possibility that global warming may create ice-free passages, which would greatly reduce the shipping distances between Western Europe and the Far East, and lead to exploitation of undersea resources such as natural gas and oil.[45]

Claiming that the Lomonosov Ridge under the North Pole is an extension of the continental shelf of Russia, a member of the Duma planted a titanium flag on the ocean floor at the Pole via a submersible in 2007. This claim by Moscow includes waterspace as well as the seabed and is expansive enough for the daily government newspaper *Rossiiskaya Gazeta* to report that efforts to divide "the Arctic [are] the start of a new redistribution of the world."[46]

The United States, Canada, Norway, and Denmark (Greenland), which constitute the other Arctic coastal states, have challenged claims by Moscow. Responding belligerently, the Russian national security strategy of 2009 asserted: "In a competition for resources it cannot be ruled out that military force could be used to resolve emerging problems that would destroy the balance of forces near the borders of Russia and her allies." In addition, the Russian Federation has criticized Norway for conducting military exercises that are motivated by "a conflict over access to resources," and has warned the NATO alliance "not to meddle in the Arctic."[47]

It is likely that a conflict over resources of the Arctic would involve high seas transit and whether the passage through the Canadian archipelago actually constitutes international straits.[48] Ironically, China has invoked the principle of the "common heritage of all mankind" in claiming that it should share the natural resources of the region although it is a non-Arctic nation.[49]

IMPLICATIONS AND RECOMMENDATIONS FOR SECURITY

Given the dual use of the maritime commons for the global economy and the forward defense of the United States, NATO members, and other partners, any constraint on the freedom of transit challenges international security and warrants a collective response. Actions could involve appeals to the International Court of Justice, diplomatic pressure, or military suasion. But to prevent the need for such reactive responses, the United States and like-minded nations should adopt or maintain four critical policies concerning the maritime commons.

First, the legal status of the maritime commons should be maintained and any attempts to constrain the free passage on the high seas and through international straits should be opposed. Although the United States and its partners support agreements on pollution, fishing, safety, and other cooperative measures, they must insist on the irrevocable right of all vessels (except those engaged in piracy and other criminal acts) to operate on the high seas, including their warships. Moreover, the US Senate should ratify the UNCLOS to prevent the erosion of rights on the high seas.[50] The treaty has been modified in part to address earlier objections to its deep-sea mining provisions. There is no reason why the Senate cannot add caveats during the formal ratification process to any provisions that it finds objectionable, thus allowing the United States to participate as a full member of UNCLOS forums.[51]

Second, freedom of navigation should be continued in areas claimed illegally or subject to state-imposed conditions, including the East and South China Seas and the Arctic.[52] An incident might occur, however, that interferes with operations or damages vessels and aircraft exercising their rights of passage. Yet the chance of a major conflict erupting over rights on the high seas remains low.[53] One can point to the EP-3 incident when neither of the parties took steps toward open conflict. Threats by China to exclude US vessels from its nearby seas have resulted in acts of harassment, but overall economic relations appear to preclude military reactions. One region that could precipitate hostilities in the region is Taiwan. Although the maritime commons in the Western Pacific could become a battle zone, Taiwan does not pose a challenge to the maritime commons regime itself. By contrast, acceding to exclusion by a coastal state and later attempting to reverse that de facto accession by operating in the area are more likely to cause conflict.

Third, the United States and its partners should seek to preserve their capabilities to utilize the maritime commons for defense and potential power projection. Having a fixed number of ships is not as important as maintaining capabilities on which forces can be built as required by global trends. Constructing warships takes years, which focuses attention on numbers rather than capabilities. However, this slowness is partly caused by regulations designed to make acquisition more efficient and partly due to a general lack of urgency. If greater importance were placed on the upgrading of existing vessels rather than new construction, the numbers problem might be mitigated. Of course, the issue of retaining the industrial capacity to build ships is also a concern that requires trade-offs. Prior to the 1970s the US government operated shipyards in addition to purchasing vessels from the private sector. This sector is worth revisiting as part of the trend to in-source advocated by the Pentagon. Other areas such as deep–seabed mining that rarely garner attention should be developed to levels that provide enough capacity for times of crisis.

No tools that preserve the use of the maritime commons should be forsaken because they remain a hedge in the event of unexpected requirements. Capabilities that require high levels of training are much easier to reconstitute when required if experienced personnel can be retained and systems are updated and improved. When capabilities have been entirely shut down in the past, it has taken years of reinventing the wheel and huge investments to reconstitute them.

Fourth, investments should be made to determine the requirements for joint seabasing as an alternative to overseas land bases. The legal standing of the maritime commons gives seabasing the ultimate security advantage to provide access. When supported by intelligence, surveillance, reconnaissance, and targeting systems, anti-access weapons can threaten seabasing in a conflict. Through maneuver and dispersed operations, however, seabasing units become more survivable than forces that utilize other basing alternatives.

Whether through altruism or self-interest (or a combination of both), the United States as the world's dominant seapower traditionally has opted to support an open commons approach to the high seas. In addition to furthering international trade and economic globalization, this has allowed other nations to have dual-use access to the maritime commons.

Critics may point out that maintaining an open regime greatly favors relative US military dominance because it faces no global naval challenger and that maintaining freedom of access for all states has become a cynical method to preserve American hegemony. This was not true when Mahan expounded the concept of the maritime commons; at the time, US naval power was considered to be inferior to that of Europe. Mahan conceived of the "great highway" before the US Navy destroyed the Spanish fleet in 1898, which is interpreted as the prelude to the American rise to global power. It also was not true during the Cold War when the Soviets sought to challenge US predominance. Support for open seas appears to be as much a result of liberal democratic beliefs and free trade as a long tradition of military predominance.

Protecting a commons approach to the high seas remains a vital interest for economic growth as well as national security. The *National Security Strategy* declares that "safeguarding the global commons . . . [including] keeping strategic straits and vital sea lanes open" is a "key global challenge" that requires the United States to "sustain broad cooperation" throughout the world.[53] As the most powerful and influential champion of that ideal, America should continue to protect the heritage of the maritime commons today and in the future.

NOTES

1. On maritime security and the commons, see Jeff Kline, "Maritime Security," in *Securing Freedom in the Global Commons*, Scott Jasper, ed. (Stanford, CA: Stanford University Press, 2010), 67–82. The same volume considers sea control as the focus of navies in the maritime commons. See Thomas Bowditch, "Sea Control," in Jasper, *Securing Freedom*, 144–56.

2. The US Navy and US Marine Corps are known collectively as naval services and as the sea services when the US Coast Guard is added. Any coast guard is really a navy with domestic law enforcement authority. For the purposes of this chapter, which does not treat law enforcement, coast guards are included under the rubric of naval forces. This is not meant to denigrate coast guards in general or the US Coast Guard in particular, which perform a range of maritime and riverine responsibilities, from enforcing public safety to maintaining aids to navigation.

3. The tradition of navies acting as constabularies to defend "good order at sea" is discussed by Geoffrey Till in *Seapower: A Guide for the Twenty-First Century* (London: Frank Cass, 2004), 358–61. See also James Cable, *Navies in Violent Peace* (London: Macmillan, 1989).

4. Gary Roughhead, James T. Conway, and Thad W. Allen, "A Cooperative Strategy for 21st Century Seapower," remarks presented at the International Seapower Symposium at the Naval War College, Newport, Rhode Island, October 17, 2007, www.navy.mil /maritime/MaritimeStrategy.pdf; reprinted in *Naval War College Review* 61 (Winter 2008), www.usnwc.edu/press.

5. Some observers claim that modern laws against piracy are nonexistent and that it is difficult to prosecute pirates because there are incentives for not applying the existing law in a commonsense manner. See article 104, part 7, "High Seas," in the preamble to the UN Convention on the Law of the Sea, www.un.org/Depts/los/convention_agreements /texts/unclos/part7.htm.

6. Jessica Piombo and Michael S. Malley, "Beyond Protecting the Land and the Sea: The Role of the US Navy in Reconstruction," in *Naval Peacekeeping and Humanitarian Operations: Stability from the Sea*, James J. Wirtz and Jeffrey A. Larsen, eds. (New York: Routledge, 2009), 61–80.

7. Although other ports could be used, they would entail longer timelines and greater expense.

8. James Kraska, "Indistinct Legal Regimes," in *Securing Freedom in the Global Commons*, Scott Jasper, ed. (Stanford, CA: Stanford University Press, 2010), 56–57.

9. The military advantage of the commons was recorded by Francis Bacon: "He that commands the sea is at great liberty, and may take as much and as little of the war as he will; whereas those that be strongest by land are many times nevertheless in great straits." From "On the greatness of kingdoms," in Bacon, *Works*, vol. 12 (Cambridge, MA, 1867–73), 186.

10. See *Department of Defense Dictionary of Military and Associated Terms*, Joint Publication 1-02, as amended through November 15, 2011 (Washington, DC: Joint Chiefs of Staff, November 8, 2010), 11, 86, 138, 209, www.dtic.mil/doctrine/dod_dictionary.

11. For example, see Mark E. Redden and Michael P. Hughes, "Global Commons and Domain Interrelationships: Time for a New Conceptual Framework?" *Strategic Forum* 259 (Washington, DC: National Defense University Press, October 2010), which states "no distinction is made between the broader notion of domain interrelationships and, as a subset of that, commons interrelationships. . . . The terms *domain interrelationships* and *commons interrelationships* may be used interchangeably."

12. The conflict between Britain and America over the rights of neutrals was addressed by Theodore Roosevelt in *The Naval War of 1812* (New York: G. P. Putnam's Sons, 1882; Annapolis, MD: Naval Institute Press, 1987), 31–38.

13. Sam J. Tangredi, "Seapower: Theory and Practice," in *Strategy in the Contemporary World: An Introduction to Strategic Studies*, John Baylis, James J. Wirtz, and Colin S. Gray, eds. (Oxford: Oxford University Press, 2002), 114, 130–33.

14. Some argue Mahan and not Clausewitz provides the exemplar for US defense planners. See Ralph Peters, *New Glory: Expanding America's Global Supremacy* (New York: Senti-

nel, 2005), 266–67; and Peters, *Never Quit the Fight* (Mechanicsburg, PA: Stackpole, 2006), 69–70.

15. See Michèle A. Flournoy and Shawn Brimley, "The Contested Commons," *Proceedings* 135 (July 2009): 17.

16. Alfred Thayer Mahan, *Lessons of the War with Spain and Other Articles* (Boston: Little, Brown, 1899), 106.

17. The first post–Cold War strategic vision issued by the navy was titled . . . *From the Sea*, which was followed by *Forward . . . From the Sea*. With the collapse of the Soviet Union, the focus of American naval planning shifted from war *for command of the sea* to war *from the sea* to command the land. See Sean O'Keefe, Frank B. Kelso, and Carl E. Mundy Jr, . . . *From the Sea: Preparing the Naval Service for the 21st Century* (Washington, DC: Department of the Navy, 1992), and John H. Dalton, Jeremy M. Boorda, and Carl E. Mundy Jr., *Forward . . . From the Sea* (Washington, DC: Department of the Navy, 1994); Bowditch, "Sea Control," 144–56.

18. On fluid mediums, see Sam J. Tangredi, "Beyond the Sea and Jointness," *Proceedings* 127 (September 2001): 60–63.

19. Dudley W. Knox, *The Naval Genius of George Washington* (Boston: Houghton Mifflin, 1932).

20. In a speech known as "The Few" to the House of Commons on August 20, 1940, Winston Churchill said: "When we speak of command of the seas, it does not mean command of every part of the sea at the same moment, or at every moment. It only means that we can make our will prevail ultimately in any part of the seas which may be selected for operations, and thus indirectly make our will prevail in every part of the sea."

21. This is the conclusion reached by Barry Posen in "Command of the Commons: The Military Foundation of US Hegemony," *International Security* 28 (Summer 2003): 5–46.

22. Sam J. Tangredi, "Seabasing: Concept, Issues and Recommendations," *Foreign Policy Research Institute*, November 2010, www.fpri.org/enotes/201011.tangredi.seabasing.html.

23. Ronald O'Rourke, "Navy Aegis Ballistic Missile Defense (BMD) Program: Background and Issues for Congress" (Washington, DC: Congressional Research Service, June 10, 2010).

24. On differences between the Bush and Obama plans, see Brian Weeden, "The Space Security Implications of Missile Defense," *The Space Review*, September 29, 2009, www.thespacereview.com/article/1474/1.

25. Robert O. Work, *Thinking about Seabasing: All Ahead, Slow* (Washington, DC: Center for Strategic and Budgetary Assessments, 2006), 8.

26. This construct has been popularized by Thomas L. Friedman and Thomas P. M. Barnett.

27. See Sam J. Tangredi, "The Fall and Rise of Naval Forward Presence," *Proceedings* 126 (May 2000): 28–32.

28. An introduction to anti-access strategies can be found in Sam J. Tangredi, *Futures of War: Toward a Consensus View of the Future Strategic Environment, 2010–2035* (Newport, RI: Alidade Press, 2008), 105–9. See also Kenneth F. McKenzie, *The Revenge of the Melians: Asymmetric Threats and the 2001 Quadrennial Defense Review* (Washington, DC: National Defense University Press, 2000).

29. The Pentagon published details on the Chinese anti-access systems in its *Annual Report to Congress on Military and Security Developments Involving the People's Republic of China 2010* (Washington, DC: Department of Defense, 2010), 29–33. The potential for conflict over Taiwan is discussed in Richard C. Bush and Michael O'Hanlon, *A War Like No Other: The Truth about China's Challenge to America* (Hoboken, NJ: John Wiley and Sons, 2007).

30. Anti-access or area denial strategy is discussed in Andrew J. Krepinevich, *Why AirSea Battle?* (Washington, DC: Center for Strategic and Budgetary Assessments, 2010).
31. See Andrew S. Erickson and David D. Yang, "Using the Land to Control the Seas: Chinese Analysts Consider the Antiship Ballistic Missile," *Naval War College Review* 62 (Autumn 2009): 53–86; Andrew S. Erickson and David D. Yang, "On the Verge of a Game Changer," *Proceedings* 135 (May 2009): 26–32; Sam J. Tangredi, "No Game Changer for China," *Proceedings* 136 (February 2010): 24–29; and Craig Hooper and Christopher Albon, "Get Off the Fainting Couch," *Proceedings* 136 (April 2010): 42–46.
32. One of the first efforts to regulate blockades appeared in 1856 with the promulgation of the *Declaration Respecting Maritime Law*, which remains part of customary law. It established that blockades must be effective in order to be lawful. Although the United States is not a signatory to this declaration, it was applied to the Union blockades during the American Civil War. See International Committee of the Red Cross, *International Humanitarian Law—Treaties and Documents, Declaration Respecting Maritime Law, Paris, 16 April 1856,* www.icrc.org/ihl.nsf/FULL/105?OpenDocument.
33. "11 Reasons Why North Korea Is the Most Bizarre Nation on Earth," *Economic Collapse,* November 24, 2010, http://theeconomiccollapseblog.com/archives/11-reasons-why-north-korea-is-the-most-bizarre-nation-on-earth.
34. Mark J. Valencia, Jon M. Van Dyke, and Noel A. Ludwig, *Sharing the Resources of the South China Sea* (The Hague: Kluwer Law International, 1997), 19.
35. An early proposal was made by Norman Angell in *The World's Highway: Some Notes on America's Relation to Seapower and Non-Military Sanctions for the Law of Nations* (New York: George H. Doran, 1915), who faulted Mahan as a dangerous imperialist. He is best remembered for *The Great Illusion*, a treatise published in 1910 that postulated the impossibility of war given international trade and the destructiveness of weapons. World War I disproved his contention.
36. Sam J. Tangredi, "Seapower: Overview and Context," in *Globalization and Maritime Power*, Sam J. Tangredi, ed. (Washington, DC: National Defense University Press, 2002), 11.
37. Patrick M. Cronin and Paul S. Giarra, "China's Dangerous Arrogance," *Diplomat* (Tokyo), July 23, 2010, http://the-diplomat.com/2010/07/23/china%e2%80%99s-dangerous-arrogance/.
38. Ibid.
39. *Annual Report to Congress on Military and Security Developments Involving the People's Republic of China 2010* submitted by the Secretary of Defense references the claim made by China in 2009 that it has "indisputable sovereignty over the islands in the South China Sea and the adjacent waters and enjoys sovereign rights and jurisdiction over the relevant waters as well as the seabed and subsoil thereof." See Peter A. Dutton, "Through a Chinese Lens," *Proceedings* 136 (April 2010): 24–29.
40. Cronin and Giarra, "China's Dangerous Arrogance."
41. On the Senkaku Islands, see Andrew T. H. Tan, *The Politics of Maritime Power* (London: Routledge, 2007), 226–27.
42. PRC threats apparently dissuaded the United States from deploying USS *George Washington* in the Yellow Sea for joint exercises after North Korea sank the South Korean warship *Cheonan*. See Patrick J. Buchanan, "The Message of Tokyo's Kowtow," *Human Events*, September 28, 2010, http://humanevents.com/article.php?id=39174. Moreover, Beijing criticized South Korean exercises after North Korea shelled Yeonpyeong Island because they were located in what China termed its exclusive economic zone. See "China Appears to Criticize US-South Korean Military Exercise," *CNN World*, November 26, 2010,

http://articles.cnn.com/2010-11-26/world/koreas.crisis_1_military-exercise-north-korea-kcna?_s=PM:WORLD.

43. James Kraska, "China Set for Naval Hegemony," *Diplomat* (Tokyo), May 6, 2010, http://the-diplomat.com/2010/05/06/china-ready-to-dominate-seas/. The PLA has harassed unarmed naval auxiliary ships and patrol aircraft but so far has not interfered with US warships, something that the Soviet Navy undertook during the Cold War.

44. See Marc Lacey and Steven Lee Myers, "Collision with China: The Overview; with Crew in US, Bush Sharpens Tone toward China," *New York Times*, April 13, 2001, www.nytimes.com/2001/04/13/world/collision-with-china-overview-with-crew-us-bush-sharpens-tone-toward-china.html.

45. On the military implications of global warming, see Jessie C. Carman, "Economic and Strategic Implications of Ice-Free Arctic Seas," in *Globalization and Maritime Power*, Sam J. Tangredi, ed. (Washington, DC: National Defense University Press, 2002), 171–86.

46. Ed Struzik, "Dawn of a New Arctic," *Edmonton Journal* (Alberta), May 3, 2009, www.edmontonjournal.com/news/Dawn+Arctic/1558738/story.html.

47. Tony Halpin, "Russia Warns of War within a Decade over Arctic Oil and Gas Riches," *Times* (London), May 14, 2009.

48. On transit disputes, see Donna J. Nincic, "Sea Lane Security and US Maritime Trade: Chokepoints as Scarce Resources," in *Globalization and Maritime Power*, Sam J. Tangredi, ed. (Washington, DC: National Defense University Press, 2002), 143–70.

49. Gordon Chiang, "China's Arctic Play: An Admiral Stakes a Territorial Claim—And It Looks Like There's More to Come," *Diplomat* (Tokyo), March 9, 2010, 1–3.

50. Doug Bandow has made the case against ratification in *The Law of the Sea Treaty: Impeding American Entrepreneurship and Investment* (Washington, DC: Competitive Enterprise Institute, September 2007).

51. The Obama administration urged ratification of the treaty in the *National Security Strategy* (Washington, DC: The White House, May 2010), 50.

52. See George Galdorisi, "The US Freedom of Navigation Program Preserving the Law of the Sea," *Oceans and Coastal Management* 25, no. 3 (1994): 179–88.

53. *National Security Strategy*, 47, 49–50.

CHAPTER 5

Coercive Aerospace
Campaigns

MARK A. STOKES and IAN EASTON

No country has won a war in the face of enemy air superiority,
no major offensive has succeeded against an opponent who
controlled the air, and no defense has sustained itself against
an enemy who had air superiority.

—John A. Warden, "The Enemy as a System"

Aerospace power is the key to gaining strategic advantages in any theater by
the application of military force via platforms either operating in or passing
through air and space. Control of the skies is a critical enabler in dominating the
earth's surface and a major determinant of victory. Air superiority provides leaders with the operational freedom to coerce other nations to make concessions in
an international dispute or gain a decisive edge on the land in the event of war.

Aerospace power uses the integrated application of force and information operations on the strategic and operational levels to compel enemies to act in a given
way. Therefore, air strikes are mounted or threatened not only against infrastructure but also to change the policy and behavior of intended targets. Hence the
effectiveness of coercive air campaigns is measured by strategic outcomes that
achieve political objectives rather than unleash violence on an enemy.

Coercive aerospace campaigns will almost certainly affect future conflicts.
Nowhere is this trend more apparent than in the Asia-Pacific region, where strategic shifts are under way that will reverberate in the future and be manifest in
problematic ways that will have implications for the global commons. Although
the militaries in North Korea and Iran are working to develop limited systems

for coercive aerospace campaigns, numerous technological challenges make their primary strike capabilities, cruise and ballistic missile systems, instruments of terror rather than precision.[1] Of all potential competitors, only China is acquiring the means to fully apply the concept of coercive aerospace campaigns.

Enabled by air campaign theory and the diffusion of technology, the People's Republic of China (PRC) is exploiting asymmetries in developing traditional and untraditional capabilities, which may alter the strategic landscape on China's periphery and beyond. This chapter explores the concern over coercive aerospace campaigns in PRC strategy, doctrine, and modernization to exploit weaknesses in regional air defenses. It provides details on both short- and medium-range ballistic missiles, ground-launched cruise missiles, antiship ballistic missiles (ASBMs), and antisatellite (ASAT) weapons and looks at conventional modernization, sensor architecture, and integrated air and space defense. Finally, it presents alternatives for countering the aerospace power of the People's Liberation Army (PLA) including cooperative threat-reduction initiatives.

AEROSPACE CAMPAIGN THEORY

China is rapidly advancing its capacity to leverage aerospace power to defend against perceived threats to national sovereignty and territorial integrity. Constrained by an underdeveloped aviation sector, the PLA is investing in capabilities to offset the advantages of technologically advanced militaries. Whoever dominates the skies over Taiwan, disputed territories in northern India, and the South China Sea will have a decisive military advantage on the surface.

The drivers shaping Chinese aerospace power as instruments of national power include the ability to enforce territorial claims and resolve sovereignty disputes. Threat perceptions also influence PLA operational concepts and force modernization. An efficient and effective system of leveraging military-related technologies is also influencing operational and organizational concepts that accommodate capabilities such as long-range precision-strike and counterspace systems. In the long term, developing and deploying intermediate- and intercontinental-range conventional ballistic missiles and other precision-strike capabilities will provide PRC leaders with a flexible deterrent to achieve strategic and operational effects in a crisis.

Given the difficulty of fielding effective countermeasures, Chinese conventional theater missiles—specifically short- and medium-range ballistic and extended-range land attack cruise missiles (LACMs)—may offer a decisive advantage in a future conflict on China's periphery. Ballistic missiles and ground- and air-launched LACMs present a means to deliver lethal payloads because of their inherent advantage on the offense-to-defense scale. Ballistic missiles and LACMs have coercive effects because potential enemies on China's periphery have limited defensive countermeasures, which are prohibitively costly to deploy in numbers when available.

China is developing the means to deny or complicate the capability of the United States and its allies to intervene in a crisis. PRC sources indicate research and development on accurate and longer-range conventional strategic strike systems that could be launched against both land- and seabased targets in crisis situations throughout the Asia-Pacific region. During the next five to ten years the extended range of conventional precision-strike assets could suppress attacks from Japan, aircraft battle groups in the Western Pacific, and Guam. The deployment of an ASBM will grant that capability. In addition, China has been expanding its regional maritime surveillance. Most noteworthy is the development of a network of integrated sensors in space and near-space for real-time tracking and precision strikes on ships.

PLA FORCE MODERNIZATION

Beijing has characterized its modernization efforts as defensive in nature. To that end, aerospace power is regarded as vital for territorial air defense with offensive air operations as a key asset. Over the years China has made advances in developing a force capable of applying aerospace power.[2] Chinese analysts view aerospace campaigns as integral to firepower warfare, which involves the coordinated use of the People's Liberation Army Air Force (PLAAF) strike aviation assets, Second Artillery conventional theater missiles, and information warfare assets.

China depends on its ballistic missile and ground-launched cruise missile (GLCM) force known as the Second Artillery to deter potential adversaries and defend against threats to national sovereignty and territorial integrity. Increasingly, accurate ballistic and cruise missiles are optimal in suppressing enemy air defense and creating a more permissive environment for conventional air operations because of their relative immunity to defense systems. In addition, space-based, airborne, and ground-based sensors facilitate command and control and provide crucial strategic intelligence, theater awareness, targeting, and battle damage assessment. This combined application of aerospace forces creates a synergy with political-military significance. Beyond ballistic and cruise missiles, China considers the zone between the atmosphere and space a new area of global competition, which has led its research and development community to conduct feasibility studies on a new generation of flight vehicles and sensor systems.

BALLISTIC AND LAND ATTACK MISSILES

Growing arsenals of conventional ballistic missiles and LACMs have emerged as a cornerstone of PLA warfighting capability. With the formation in 1993 of the first brigade of short-range ballistic missiles (SRBMs), these weapons became an instrument of psychological and political intimidation with devastating effects. In the last two decades conventional ballistic missiles and LACMs of the Second Artillery have emerged as the form of aerospace power for leveraging information dominance and air superiority in the opening phase of a conflict. The headquarters of the Second Artillery reports directly to the Central Military Commission and oversees the central nuclear warhead storage base and six missile bases across China.

The Second Artillery headquarters exercises direct control over operational support such as a regiment-sized unit north of Beijing, which specializes in all-source intelligence and could be deployed to a theater command center.[3] In addition, one or two electronic countermeasure units could support the Second Artillery component commander within a joint theater. The principal regiment is based in Dingxing and a second unit appears to have been organized in Nanchang. Moreover, a central depot north of Beijing stores non–mission-essential supplies.[4]

The SRBM force is key to a coercive political and military strategy. In 2000 it was limited to one regimental-sized unit in southeastern China. The force of seven brigades has five brigades subordinate to Second Artillery 52 Base and two reporting to military regions, one to Nanjing in Xianyou and the other to Puning in Guangdong Province. The number of their missiles, which is thought to exceed 13,000 (including tactical missiles assigned to ground forces), may be less relevant than how they are organized and prepared for deployment in a crisis.

A standard SRBM brigade consists of six battalions with two companies that each has two or three launchers. Thus five brigades could leverage between 120 and 180 mobile launchers and fire salvos to saturate missile defenses, paralyze airbases, and destroy infrastructure. In addition to the six battalions, there is a brigade headquarters consisting of a command post, technical and communications battalions, an electronic countermeasures group, and a rail transfer point. Some five ballistic missile brigades under the Second Artillery have been arrayed against Taiwan.[5]

Deployment of conventional SRBMs has expanded the war-fighting capability of the Second Artillery. The centerpiece of its regional mission is the two-stage solid-fuel DF-21 medium-range ballistic missile (MRBM). The first DF-21s with a dedicated nuclear mission became operational in the Second Artillery in 1991 and gradually replaced older liquid-fueled DF-3A intermediate-range ballistic missile systems.

Within the next five to ten years the centerpiece of the extended-range conventional strike capability of the Second Artillery will be DF-21C MRBMs. Capable of both conventional and nuclear missions, its guidance, navigation, and control system is modeled after the Pershing II. Terminally guided DF-21Cs can fire a 2,000-kilogram warhead to a range of 1,750 kilometers with a circular error probability (CEP) of less than fifty meters. The systems could be used for conventional strikes against targets throughout Japan from east and northeast China, New Delhi from bases located in Xinjiang, and western India from sites in Yunnan.[6]

The Second Artillery has an operational force structure of eight or possibly as many as ten brigades equipped with DF-21s. Conventionally capable variants are gradually replacing some DF-21A systems. The standard organizational structure resembles the SRBM brigades with each unit having six launch battalions with two companies. Assuming that each company has a single launcher, a DF-21C brigade may be armed initially with a force of twelve launchers.

GROUND-LAUNCHED CRUISE MISSILES

To augment its ballistic missiles, the Second Artillery is expanding its ground-launched LACM infrastructure. GLCMs are powerful instruments with political and military utility because of the difficulty in defending against them. The Chinese possess the largest inventory of extended-range GLCMs, only a few years after its initial deployment, in the world. Able to penetrate defenses and strike targets on land to a range of 2,000 kilometers, the Second Artillery DH-10 LACMs enjoy a relatively high acquisition priority. Based in south-central and southwestern China and highly mobile via rail, cruise missiles can strike from any direction, challenging defenders with low-altitude trajectories. DH-10s are deployed on a three-tube road mobile launcher. Because it began operational deployments in the 2007–8 timeframe, the PLA has deployed somewhere between 200 and 500 GLCMs.[7]

The Second Artillery established a regimental-level GLCM unit under 53 Base in the Liuzhou area of Guangxi Province in 2000. After final testing in 2003, the regiment conducted operational testing and by 2006 had achieved brigade status. Identified as a rapid reaction unit for cross-country deployment and trained in concealment, the brigade organized in a fashion similar to SRBM and MRBM units—six launch battalions with two companies each.[8] New units have appeared in Guiyang, Guizhou Province, and Yichun City in Jiangxi Province.

Beijing has developed the fastest-growing and most sophisticated extended-range ground-launched LACM infrastructure. Based in south-central and southwestern China, two or even three Second Artillery GLCM brigades could forward deploy rapidly during a crisis.

ANTISHIP BALLISTIC MISSILES

Chinese sources have indicated that research and development are being conducted on long-range conventional strategic strike systems that could be launched against seabased targets throughout the Asia-Pacific. The deployment of conventional MRBMs capable of engaging naval combatants including aircraft carrier strike groups located in the Western Pacific would signal the long-term strategic intentions of the PLA.[9]

The technology for a rudimentary ASBM capability has been developed in the last twenty years. At its core is an advanced missile-borne sensing and data processing system supported by strategic cueing from a dual-use maritime surveillance network. Building on the successes of the terminally guided DF-21C and DF-15C programs, the ASBM program is centered on advanced microelectronics and an upgraded guidance, navigation, and control package.[10]

Technical studies address a range of guidance, navigation, and control issues, including the need for midcourse update, missile-borne synthetic aperture radar, automated target recognition, terminal guidance, thermal protection, and radio-frequency blackout associated with a flight vehicle traveling at hypersonic speeds in the upper atmosphere. Manufacturing facilities for solid rocket motors involving an initial ASBM variant, designated as the DF-21D, appear to have been constructed in 2009. Moreover, some form of basic testing of a new motor and airframe probably is under way.[11] Integrated flight-testing of the airframe, motor, guidance, navigation, and control systems against targets at sea will be the final step in the design certification process.[12]

Barring deployment of effective defenses, an initial ASBM would provide the Chinese with precision-strike capability against carriers and other ships within 1,500 to 2,000 kilometers from the coast. Over the longer term, PLA technical writings indicate the conceptual development of conventional global precision-strike capability. The accuracy and range of conventional ballistic missiles are likely to improve in the next ten to fifteen years with advanced inertial and satellite-aided navigation, terminal guidance systems, and more powerful solid rocket motors.

ANTISATELLITE WEAPONS

China is developing a range of ASAT capabilities that threaten assured US and allied access to space in the Asia-Pacific region in times of crisis and conflict. The contested nature of the space domain has been highlighted by repeated tests of missile-borne kinetic-kill, high-powered laser, and co-orbital ASAT capabilities. China is also developing other ASAT weapons that could be difficult to detect and defend against such as high-powered microwave and particle beam weapons, high-performance radar and electronic jammers, and cyber attack and precision-strike capabilities that could be directed against satellite tracking and control stations. What is more, Beijing has conducted cyber intrusions in power grids and tested other capabilities that could mount attacks on power grids supporting space command and control centers.[13]

The growth of the ASAT program is due in no small part to the overall space program, which is inherently military.[14] China launched twenty satellites in 2010 and intends to launch another twenty per year over the next two years.[15] In 2008 it launched more satellites than the United States.[16] Benefiting from increased resources, a large pool of talented engineers, and backing by party leaders, the Second Artillery and PLAAF counterspace units will play a key role in waging successful aerospace campaigns at the outset of conflict.

CONVENTIONAL MODERNIZATION

Although the Second Artillery has been expanding, PLAAF modernization has progressed more modestly.[17] The latter service has diversified its roles and missions, moving away from a force exclusively responsible for air defense, interdiction, and close air support for land forces to adopt a primary mission of deterrence and strategic attack. This diversification stems from a theory that a firepower warfare campaign could support national objectives independently. The focus is denial by paralyzing enemy capabilities to the extent that further resistance appears futile.

Given resource constraints and overlap in the core strategic strike mission, the rise of the Second Artillery may have slowed the pace of PLAAF modernization. Deployment of ballistic and cruise missiles dampened requirements for offensive airpower. Another possible constraint can be attributed to the limitations of the aviation sector and corresponding reliance on foreign procurement. Nevertheless, a technologically advanced industrial base might be able to support the PLAAF vision of conducting air campaigns independently of the Second Artillery.

To close the gap between doctrine and capabilities, senior PLAAF officials have outlined the requirements to meet anticipated strategic challenges. Guided by a strategy of integrated air and space assets and combined offense and defense assets, they noted the requirements for long-range precision strike, local air superiority, stealth, full-spectrum air and missile defenses, new trump card weapons systems, long-range airlift, and unmanned aerial vehicles.[18]

Conventional platforms include Su-27 air superiority fighters procured from Russia in the 1990s, the Su-27 variant known as the J-11 assembled in Shenyang, and the indigenous J-10 fourth-generation fighter made in Chengdu, which eventually will form the bulk of the fighter force.[19] The backbone of the long-range precision-strike capability is the Russian Su-30MKK. Three regiments of JH-7As replacing older Q-5s augment these aircraft and reportedly fire YJ-91/Kh-31P high-speed antiradiation missiles, which indicates their role is suppressing air defenses. The bomber fleet is equipped with H-6s that are likely to be upgraded to launch DH-10 LACMs.[20] With aerial refueling, supporting firepower, and early warning assets from the Second Artillery, China is improving its capabilities to fly interdiction missions beyond the periphery.[21]

PLAAF capabilities are likely to increase more rapidly than in the past. For example, one Chinese source outlined the intent to procure a next-generation fighter within eight to ten years.[22] Investments are being made to deploy an advanced active electronically scanned array radar, and the General Armaments Department has experts working on achieving breakthroughs in stealth technology.[23] China has begun flight tests of the J-20, one early prototype of the fifth-generation combat aircraft with stealth characteristics.[24] According to an assessment by Taiwan, the PLAAF had set a goal of conducting an air campaign within a 1,000-kilometer radius of the periphery of China by 2010, which has not occurred to date, and extending the range to 3,000 kilometers by 2030.[25] The PLA ability to conduct strategic and operational strike missions will be limited by the range of its persistent surveillance. To expand battle space awareness, China is investing in the capabilities to monitor the Western Pacific, South China Sea, and Indian Ocean.

ADVANCED PLA CAPABILITIES

Chinese analysts view the zone between the atmosphere and space (or near space) as a potential dimension of strategic competition.[26] Within a decade, near-space flight vehicles could emerge as a dominant platform for a persistent region-wide surveillance capability in a crisis. Near space is characterized as the region between 20 and 100 kilometers above the earth's surface.[27]

Although challenges exist, the Second Artillery and research and development community have become interested in near-space flight vehicles for reconnaissance, communications relay, electronic countermeasures, and precision-strike operations.[28] To address the technical demands in this advanced field, the aerospace sector established research institutes to design, develop, and produce near-space flight vehicles. In leveraging the unique features of near-space vehicles, these dedicated entities have shown the importance China attaches to this domain.[29]

Increasingly sophisticated space-based systems would expand PLA battlespace awareness and support strike operations farther from China's shores.[30] Space assets monitor naval activity in surrounding waters and track air force deployments in the region. Space-based reconnaissance systems also provide imagery for mission planning such as navigation and terminal guidance in the case of LACMs. In addition, satellite communications provide survivable transmission that will become particularly important as the PLA operates farther from its home territory.

A regional strike capability would depend partly on high-resolution, dual-use, space-based, synthetic aperture radar, electro-optical, and electronic intelligence satellites. The Chinese are completing second-generation synthetic aperture radar satellites and electro-optical capabilities. In addition, there are signs funding has been dedicated to developing a space-based electronic intelligence capability.[31] From late 2009 to 2010 China launched six military space platforms composed of single and co-orbital satellite systems, substantially augmenting its space-based C4ISR infrastructure.[32] In a crisis, China may have the option of augmenting existing space-based assets with microsatellites launched on solid-fueled launch vehicles. Existing and future data relay satellites and beyond line of sight communications systems could transmit targeting data to and from the theater and/or the Second Artillery operational command center.[33]

In addition to space-based, near-space, and airborne sensors, over-the-horizon backscatter radars are key to extended-range air and maritime surveillance.[34] Under the PLAAF such radars could determine the range of maritime precision-strike capabilities. Skywave over-the-horizon radar emits a pulse that bounces off the ionosphere and illuminates the target from the top down. As a result, detection by wide-area surveillance reaches 1,000 to 4,000 kilometers.[35]

The expanding PLA sensor architecture is integral to its evolving concept for integrated air and space defense. In the last fifteen years China has invested significant resources in enhanced air defenses with the acquisition of advanced Russian double-digit surface-to-air missile systems including the SA-10B, SA-20PMU1, and SA-20PMU2 as well as the SA-15. The PLA also has developed indigenous systems such as the HQ-9. With a reported intercept range of 200 kilometers, the effectiveness of the PLA air defense network has been extended into the Western Pacific. Moreover, the Chinese electronics sector has been conducting research and development to produce bistatic, multistatic, and ultra-wideband radar systems with capability of reducing the effectiveness of older US stealth aircraft such as F-117 attack fighters and B-2 bombers.

The PLA aerospace campaign intended to coerce an enemy would emphasize preemption, surprise, and concentration of advanced capabilities to achieve shock. Although technologically behind the US and other militaries, the PLAAF is becoming capable of dominating the skies on the periphery with the support of the Second Artillery and information warfare assets.

AEROSPACE MODERNIZATION AND
REGIONAL STABILITY

The Asia-Pacific region is undergoing fundamental change that has implications for long-term stability in the region. The growth of PLA precision-strike capabilities, especially sophisticated conventional ballistic and cruise missiles, is altering the strategic environment. Because of their speed, precision, and difficulties in fielding viable defenses, the deployment of these systems in adequate numbers could provide China with a decisive advantage in a conflict over territorial or sovereignty claims. Reliance on both ballistic and extended-range LACMs also encourages other nations to develop similar capabilities. In addition to force modernization programs in India and Taiwan, the PLA expansion of its aerospace capabilities is responsible at least in part for causing a modest shift in overall US defense policies.[36]

The expanding PLA capacity to deny the United States access to bases and project power in the region figured prominently in the latest Quadrennial Defense Review.[37] In addition, a number of analyses outlining ways to manage dynamic shifts in the region have appeared. With concerns mounting over anti-access in the Western Pacific and area denial capabilities to restrict US naval operations, the pressure to reduce the American footprint in Japan and elsewhere could increase. Noting an emerging arms race, one observer predicted that US bases will be moved to Guam and the South Pacific Islands and that US naval presence in the Indian Ocean will grow.[38]

To counter the PLA capacity to carry out an extended-range aerospace campaign, one study proposes ways of withstanding initial strikes and limiting damage while neutralizing command and control networks and suppressing theater sensor architecture and strike systems to sustain initiatives in the air, on the sea, in space, and within the cyber domain.[39] Another study outlined operational advantages of forward-based conventional ballistic missiles and other global strike systems launched from Japan or Guam and the need for survivability in that event.[40]

A NUCLEAR FORCE TREATY

The expanding aerospace capabilities of the PRC influence other defense establishments including the United States. However, they may have another effect. PLA successes in fielding advanced long-range precision-strike systems dilute international efforts to stem proliferation of the means of delivery for weapons of mass destruction. This may encourage other countries to follow suit, especially as China's global leadership and standing increase. In particular, GLCMs have emerged as another proliferation concern. In light of Russia's threats of withdrawal, partially because of proliferation of short- and medium-range ballistic missiles and GLCMs, the selection of PLA systems to defend its territorial claims could also undermine the enduring value of the Intermediate-Range Nuclear-Forces (INF) Treaty.

In 1987 the INF Treaty called for the United States and the Soviet Union to eliminate land-based ballistic and cruise missiles with ranges of 500 to 5,500 kilometers within three years. By 1991 both parties dismantled the last of more than 2,500 GLCMs and ballistic missiles in their inventories with support equipment as required by the treaty.

In part because of the PRC buildup of theater missiles, Russia has expressed its concern over the bilateral INF Treaty as well as the advocates of a ballistic missile and flight test ban.[41] Both Washington and Moscow have encouraged other nations to join the accord, and President Vladimir Putin has informed senior American officials that his nation would find it difficult to comply with the terms of the treaty unless other nations also ratified the agreement.[42]

A withdrawal of the SRBM infrastructure could enable China to join the global initiative to roll back land-based ballistic and cruise missiles because its emphasis on these weapons provides an impetus for other nations to develop similar capabilities. Restraint on the part of Beijing in deploying conventional ballistic and cruise missiles could build confidence among its neighbors and reduce incentives to develop and field countermeasures.

THE Chinese capacity to conduct a coercive aerospace campaign is surpassing defenses that its neighbors, including Taiwan, Japan, perhaps India, and even US forces operating in the Western Pacific, can field. Among the most significant capabilities that are contributing toward an imbalance are PLA long-range precision-strike systems, primarily its conventional ballistic missiles and LACMs. Perhaps equally important, however, is an expanding counterspace program and an evolving sensor network that would be needed to cue strike assets and offer situation awareness around China's periphery. Another factor is China's growing ability to defend its strike assets from interdiction on the ground.

With the growth of theater missile infrastructure, counterspace capabilities, conventional airpower, and sensor systems, China could gain a decisive edge in the skies on its periphery in the event of a war over territorial disputes. The ability to dominate airspace in a given region might create instability in political disagreements. As one becomes more confident of military success, the greater the chance that force will be applied to coercive aerospace campaigns. The Chinese may become more assertive in coming years by challenging other nations in the region. A strategic shift in the aerospace balance could unravel the system of US alliances and prompt some nations to consider weapons of mass destruction as a means of defense.

Addressing these challenges to regional stability requires maintaining or developing the means to undercut the political and military utility of Chinese theater missile-centric strategy and striving for a balance that could deter recourse to force or other means of coercion. However, alternative approaches could offer initiatives for moderating PLA force postures and address underlying security dilemmas through cooperative threat-reduction programs.

NOTES

The epigraph by John A. Warden appeared in an article titled "The Enemy as a System," *Airpower Journal* 9 (Spring 1995): 40–45.

1. Technological challenges include lack of battlefield awareness, command and control system weaknesses, and missile guidance troubles. Examples of North Korean deployments include the October 2010 parade in Pyongyang that unveiled Musudan intermediate-range ballistic missiles, No Dong intermediate-range ballistic missiles with triconic nose cones, and canistered surface-to-air missiles, similar to Russian S-300 and Chinese HQ-9 air-defense systems. See Sebastien Falletti, Duncan Lennox, and Ted Parsons, "Pyongyang Shows Off Hardware and New Heir," *Jane's Defence Weekly*, October 20, 2010, 4–7. On Iranian systems and their limitations, see Scott Peterson, "Iranian Missile System Tested, Rhetoric Sharpened on Eve of NATO Summit," *Christian Science Monitor*, November 18, 2010, www.csmonitor.com/World/Middle-East/2010/1118/Iran-missile-system-tested-rhetoric-sharpened-on-eve-of-NATO-summit. Also note that an unclassified technical analysis estimates the No Dong missile, which forms the basis for Iran's Shahab-3 and Shahab-4 missiles, has an estimated CEP of 3 to 4 kilometers. Therefore, half of all missiles fired would land outside a 3- to 4-kilometer radius from the target point. See Jeffery Lewis, "Iran and the Bomb 2: Iran's Missiles," *Arms Control Wonk*, January 22, 2006, http://lewis.armscontrolwonk.com/archive/948/iran-the-bomb-2-irans-missile-capabilities.

2. Mark A. Stokes, "The Chinese Joint Aerospace Campaign: Strategy, Doctrine, and Force Modernization," in *China's Revolution in Doctrinal Affairs: Emerging Trends in the Operational Art of the Chinese People's Liberation Army*, James C. Mulvenon and David M. Finklestein, eds. (Alexandria, VA: CNA Corporation, 2005), www.cna.org/documents/DoctrineBook.pdf.

3. See, for example, Liu Feng and Wang Bingjun, "Di Erpao Bing 9667 Budui Ying Zao 'Shangwu' Wenhua" [Second Artillery 96637 Unit Establishes 'Warrior Culture'], *Gongren Ribao* [Worker's Daily] (Beijing), August 3, 2006, http://news.sina.com.cn/c/2006-08-03/01009640261s.shtml.

4. See "Di Erpao Bing Houqinbu Mou Zonghe Cangku Yu Ren Jingyan Tan" [Experience in Personnel Education in the Second Artillery Logistics Department Integrated Depot], *Zhongguo Qingnian Bao* [China Youth Daily] (Beijing), November 30, 2000, www.chinayouthdaily.com.cn/gb/djysd/2000-11/30/content_120940.htm.

5. On the Second Artillery, see Kenneth Allen and Maryanne Kivlehan-Wise, "Implementing the Second Artillery's Doctrinal Reforms," in *China's Revolution in Doctrinal Affairs*, James C. Mulvenon and David Finkelstein, eds. (Alexandria, VA: Center for Naval Analyses, 2005), 159–219.

6. See "The DF-21 Series Medium Range Ballistic Missile," *KKTT Blog*, August 23, 2009, http://liuqiankktt.blog.163.com/blog/static/121264211200972375114290/.

7. The Pentagon reported in 2007 that the PRC would deploy first- and second-generation LACMs; in 2008 that it had deployed 50 to 250 LACMs and 20 to 30 launchers; in 2009 that it had 150 to 350 LACMs and 40 to 55 launchers in the inventory; and in 2010 and 2011 that it had 200 to 500 LACMs and 40 to 55 launchers. See annual reports published by the United States Department of Defense, *Military and Security Developments Involving the People's Republic of China* (Washington, DC: Office of the Secretary of Defense, 2007–2011).

8. See "Luji Xunhang Daodan Fang Duizhang Gou Yi" [Ground Launched Cruise Missile Group Commander Gou Yi], *Xinhua* (Beijing), October 1, 2009, http://news.xinhuanet .com/mil/2009-10/01/content_12133327.htm; "Jinri Changying Zaishou" [Taking the Spear into Battle], *Liberation Army Daily* (Beijing), May 26, 2005, http://uclibs.org /PID/133469. See also "Erpao Xin Xunhang Daodan Yanlian Liangci Duobi 'Zhencha Weixing'" [New Second Artillery Cruise Missile Exercises Twice to Avoid 'Satellites'], *Zhongguo Qingnian Bao* [China Youth Daily] (Beijing), January 15, 2010, http://news .xinhuanet.com/mil/2010-01/15/content_12813545.htm.

9. See Andrew S. Erickson and David D. Yang, "On the Verge of a Game-Changer: A Chinese Antiship Ballistic Missile Could Alter the Rules in the Pacific and Place US Navy Carrier Strike Groups in Jeopardy," *Proceedings* 135 (May 2009): 26–32. See also Andrew S. Erickson, "Chinese ASBM Development: Knowns and Unknowns," Jamestown Foundation *China Brief* 9 (June 24, 2009): 4–8. For a summary, see Andrew S. Erickson and David D. Yang, "Using the Land to Control the Sea? Chinese Analysts Consider the Antiship Ballistic Missile," *Naval War College Review* 62 (Autumn 2009): 53–86. Additionally, see Eric Hagt and Matthew Durnin, "China's Antiship Ballistic Missile: Developments and Missing Links," *Naval War College Review* 62 (Autumn 2009): 87–115; Mark A. Stokes, "China's Evolving Conventional Strategic Strike Capability: The Anti-Ship Ballistic Missile Challenge to US Maritime Operations in the Western Pacific and Beyond" (Arlington, VA: Project 2049 Institute, September 14, 2009).

10. See "New Chinese Missiles Target the Greater Asian Region," *International Assessment and Strategy Center*, July 24, 2007; Zhang Yiguang and Zhou Chengping, "Didi Dandao Daodan Shixian Yuancheng Jingque Dajide Jishu Tujing" [Technological Trends Associated with Surface-to-Surface Ballistic Missile Precision Guidance], *Zhanshu Daodan Kongzhi Jishu* [Tactical Missile Control Technology] 4 (2004): 58–60.

11. Robert F. Willard, testimony before the House Armed Services Committee, 111th Cong., 2nd Sess., March 23, 2010.

12. See "Guanyu 2009 Nian Diwupi Jianshe Xiangmu Huanjing Baohu Sheshi Jungong Yanshou Gongzhong Canyu de Gongshi" [Fifth Announcement of 2009 for Completion and Acceptance of Construction Projects for Environmental Protection], Hohhot City Government Environmental Protection Bureau, August 20, 2009.

13. Ian Easton, "The Great Game in Space: China's Evolving ASAT Weapons Programs and Their Implications for Future US Strategy" (Arlington, VA: Project 2049 Institute, June 24, 2009), http://project2049.net/documents/china_asat_weapons_the_great_ game_in_space.pdf.

14. US-China Economic and Security Review Commission, *2008 Report to Congress* (Washington, DC: US-China Economic and Security Review Commission, November 2008), 160, www.uscc.gov/annual_report/2008/annual_report_full_08.pdf.

15. Chen Zewei, "Zhongguo Weilai Liangnian Yuji Meinian Jiang Fashe Yu 20 Ge Hangtianqi" [China Plans to Launch More than 20 Spacecraft Each Year for the

Next Two Years], *Huanqiu* (Beijing), April 26, 2010, http://mil.huanqiu.com/china/2010 -04/793060.html.

16. Rob Chambers, *China's Space Program: A New Tool for PRC "Soft Power" in International Relations?* unpublished thesis (Monterey, CA: Naval Postgraduate School, March 2009), 17.

17. John Wilson Lewis and Xue Litai, "China's Search for a Modern Air Force," *International Security* 24 (Summer 1999): 64–94, http://iis-db.stanford.edu/pubs/20614 /China's_search_for_a_modern_air_force.pdf; Kevin M. Lanzit and Kenneth Allen, "Right-Sizing the PLA Air Force: New Operational Concepts Define a Smaller, More Capable Force," in *Right Sizing the People's Liberation Army: Exploring the Contours of China's Military*, Roy Kamphausen and Andrew Scobell, eds. (Carlisle, PA: US Army War College, 2007), 437–78; Phillip C. Saunders and Erik Quam, "Future Force Structure of the Chinese Air Force," in *Right Sizing the People's Liberation Army*, Kamphausen and Scobell, eds., 377–436; Xiaoming Zhang and Sean D. McClung, "The Art of Military Discovery: Chinese Air and Space Power Implications for the USAF," *Strategic Studies Quarterly* 4 (Spring 2010): 36–62.

18. See Liu Yalou, "Zaixin de Lishi Qidianshang Tuijin Kongjun Xiandaihua Jianshe" [New Historical Starting Point in Modernizing the Air Force], *Qiushi* [Seeking Truth] (Beijing), January 17, 2008, www.chinavalue.net/Article/Archive/2008/9/18/135542 .html.

19. See Richard D. Fisher Jr., "Chinese Chengdu J-10 Emerges," *Aviation Week*, January 14, 2010, www.aviationweek.com.

20. See US-China Economic and Security Review Commission, *2011 Report to Congress* 112th Cong., 1st Sess. (Washington, DC: US Government Printing Office, November 2011), 190.

21. Phillip C. Saunders and Eric R. Quam, "China's Air Force Modernization," *Joint Force Quarterly* 47 (2007): 28–33.

22. "Duihua He Weirong: Zhongguo Zhengzai Yanzhi Disidai Zhanji" [Discussion with He Weirong: China Conducting R&D on Fourth-Generation Aircraft], *Xinhua Network*, November 9, 2009, http://news.xinhuanet.com/mil/2009-11/09/content_12416003.htm.

23. The leading Chinese specialist in applied research on stealth is Wu Zhe of Beijing University of Aeronautics and Astronautics, who also serves on the Stealth Technology Working Group of the PLA General Armaments Department S&T Committee. See Harbin Institute of Technology, "Changjiang Xuezhe Tepin Jiaoshou Wu Zhe Xiaoyou" [Changjiang University Alumni and Scholar Wu Zhe], May 7, 2010, http://90.hit.edu .cn/news/Showfc.asp?id=1827.

24. Reuben F. Johnson, "China's J-20 Clocks Up 18-Minute Maiden Flight," *Jane's Defence Weekly*, January 19, 2011, 4.

25. Wang Changhe, "Zhonggong Kongjun 20 Nian de Huigu Yu Zhanwang" [PLA Air Force 20-Year Review and Outlook], in Li Chentong, Zhu Chuanzhi, and Le Yijun, *Zhanzheng Zhexue Yu Zhonggong Zhanlue Yanjiu* [The Philosophy of War and the Study on PRC's Strategy] (Taipei: National Defense University War Academy, 2008), 96–97.

26. See Li Yiyong and Shen Huairong, "Fazhan Jinkongjian Feihangqi Xitong de Guanjian Jishu" [Key Technologies for Developing Near Space Flight Vehicles], *Journal of the Academy of Equipment Command and Technology* (October 2006): 52–55.

27. Guo Weimin, Si Wanbing, Gui Qishan, and He Jiafan, "Daodan Zuozhanzhong Linjin Kongjian Feihangqi Yu Hangtianqi de Xietong Yingyong" [Coordination and Applicability of Near Space Flight Vehicles in Missile Warfare], *Feihang Daodan* [Winged Missiles Journal], (May 2008): 19–21.

28. On the Second Artillery, see Li Chao, Luo Chuanyong, and Wang Hongli, "Aerodynamic Modeling and Design of Sensors on Stratospheric Airship," *Journal of Engineering*

Design 13, no. 5 (2006): 307–16: Tang Jiapeng, Guan Shixi, Ling Guilong, and Duan Na, "Study on Propulsion System of Near Space Vehicles," *Journal of Projectiles, Rockets, Missiles, and Guidance* (June 2009): 145–48.

29. Yang Jian, "Hangtian Yiyuan 10 Suo Jiepai Chengli" [China Aerospace Science and Technology Corporation First Academy 10th Research Institute Established], *China Space News* (Beijing), October 24, 2008, www.china-spacenews.com/n435777/n435778 /n435783/49822.html.

30. For American views of Chinese space modernization, see Andrew S. Erickson, "Eyes in the Sky," *Proceedings* 136 (April 2010): 36–41; Gregory Kulacki and Jeffrey G. Lewis, *A Place for One's Mat: China's Space Program, 1956–2003* (Cambridge, MA: American Academy of Arts and Sciences, 2009), www.amacad.org/publications/spaceChina.pdf; Kevin Pollpeter, "The Chinese Vision of Space Military Operations," in *China's Revolution in Doctrinal Affairs: Emerging Trends in the Operational Art of the Chinese People's Liberation Army*, James C. Mulvenon and David Finklestein, eds. (Alexandria, VA: CNA Corporation, December 2005), 329–69, www.defensegroupinc.com/cira/pdf/doctrine-book_ch9.pdf; Larry M. Wortzel, *The Chinese People's Liberation Army and Space Warfare: Emerging United States–China Military Competition* (Washington, DC: American Enterprise Institute, 2007), www.aei.org/paper/26977.

31. Wang Huilin, Huang Wei, Ma Manhao, and Zhu Xiaomin,"Mianxiang Quyu de Dianzi Zhencha Weixing Guihua Xitong Sheji Yu Shixian" [Design and Implementation of Area-Covering Electronic Reconnaissance Satellite Planning System], *Jisuanji Gongcheng Yu Yingyong* [*Computer Engineering and Applications*] 46, no. 26 (2010): 209–13. See also Yuan Xiaokang, "Satellite Electronic Reconnaissance, Anti-Jamming," *Shanghai Hangtian*, October 9, 1996, 32–37, in FBIS-CST-97-011 (Reston, VA: Foreign Broadcast Information Service, 1996).

32. The platforms included at least eleven satellites as part of *Yaogan*-7, *Yaogan*-8, *Yaogan*-9, *Yaogan*-10, *Yaogan*-11, and *Shijian*-6 missions, which launched two electro-optical and two SAR satellites, a co-orbital naval ocean surveillance system satellite formation, and a dual satellite co-orbital electronic intelligence payload.

33. "China Blasts Off First Data Relay Satellite," *Xinhua News Agency*, April 26, 2008.

34. Sean O'Connor, "OTH Radar and the ASBM Threat," *IMINT & Analysis*, November 11, 2008, http://geimint.blogspot.com/2008/11/oth-radar-and-asbm-threat.html.

35. See Tang Xiaodong, Han Yunjie, and Zhou Wenyu, "Skywave over the Horizon Backscatter Radar," CIE International Radar Conference Proceedings, January 2, 2001.

36. Erickson and Yang, "On the Verge," 26–32; Paul S. Giarra, "A Chinese Anti-Ship Ballistic Missile: Implications for the USN," testimony before the US-China Economic and Security Commission, June 11, 2009, www.uscc.gov/hearings/2009hear ings/written_testimonies/09_06_11_wrts/09_06_11_giarra_statement.pdf; Andrew F. Krepinevich, *Why AirSea Battle?* (Washington, DC: Center for Strategic and Budgetary Assessments, 2010), www.csbaonline.org/4Publications/PubLibrary/R.20100219 .Why_AirSea_Battle/R.20100219.Why_AirSea_Battle.pdf; Roger Cliff, Mark Burles, Michael S. Chase, Derek Eaton, and Kevin L. Pollpeter, *Entering the Dragon's Lair: Chinese Anti-Access Strategies and Their Implications for the United States* (Arlington, VA: RAND Corporation, 2007), www.rand.org/pubs/monographs/2007/RAND_MG524.pdf.

37. United States Department of Defense, *Quadrennial Defense Review Report* (Washington, DC: Office of the Secretary of Defense, February 2010), www.defense.gov/qdr /images/QDR_as_of_12Feb10_1000.pdf.

38. Robert D. Kaplan, "The Geography of Chinese Power," *Foreign Affairs* 89 (May–June 2010): 22–41.

39. Jan van Tol, Mark Gunzinger, Andrew F. Krepinevich, and Jim Thomas, *AirSea Battle: A Point-of-Departure Operational Concept* (Washington, DC: Center for Strategic and Budgetary Assessments, 2010), xiii.
40. On prompt global strike, see Bruce M. Sugden, "Speed Kills: Analyzing the Deployment of Conventional Ballistic Missiles," *International Security* 34 (Summer 2009): 113–46.
41. See Thomas Graham and Dinshaw Mistry, "Two Treaties to Contain Missile Proliferation," *Disarmament Diplomacy* 82 (Spring 2006), www.acronym.org.uk/dd/dd82/82tgdm.htm; J. Jerome Holton, Lora Lumpe, and Jeremy J. Stone, "Proposal for a Zero Ballistic Missile Regime" (Washington, DC: American Association for the Advancement of Science, 1993), 379–96.
42. Luke Harding, "Putin Threatens Withdrawal from Cold War Nuclear Treaty," *Guardian* (London), October 12, 2007. See also the joint statement on the treaty to eliminate intermediate- and shorter-range missiles, 62nd session of the UN General Assembly, October 25, 2007, http://moscow.usembassy.gov/st_10252007.html.

CHAPTER 6

Aggression in Cyberspace

KEVIN G. COLEMAN

We are now in a world in which cyber warfare is very real. . . .
It could paralyze this country, and I think that's an area we have
to pay a lot more attention to.
—Leon Panetta, *This Week* (ABC Television News)

Computer intrusions and attacks have become methods for aggression. The frequency of incidents coupled with their implications has driven the Pentagon to formally recognize cyberspace as a domain for military activities for the purposes of organizing, training, equipping, and when directed, operating our forces.[1] Technological advances continue to influence the art of war. Perhaps the greatest technological impact came when attacks moved from being physical to being digital. Given that reality, cyberspace now has joined the other traditional conflict domains. However, cyber represents a primary form of attack as well as a support role for other domains. Over the years as technology has matured, advanced traditional domains have become more reliant on microprocessors, computers, and digital networks, and in many cases on the Internet for offensive capabilities, defensive measures, and intelligence collection. Although computer intrusions have been around for decades, recent intrusions are dangerous and have escalated to the point where military leaders have expressed concern.[2] Many nations of the world are busy developing, advancing, and implementing computer intrusion and attack strategies and digital weaponry designed to disrupt or destroy hostile military systems as well as critical infrastructure. Today cyber warfare is viewed as a critical component of national security strategy rather than a stand-alone option. The policies, doctrine, strategies, and operational models for conducting cyber warfare are emerging and will change as new weaponry evolves and the lessons from cyber attacks are learned. As Deputy Secretary of Defense

William Lynn remarked: "There's no agreed-on definition of what constitutes a cyberattack. It's really a range of things that can happen—from exploitation and exfiltration of data to degradation of networks or even physical equipment, physical property."[3]

The Pentagon established US Cyber Command with dedicated service components and began to define cyber warfare.[4] It is paramount that the government leadership and the defense, intelligence, and homeland security communities develop the appropriate doctrine to systematically and appropriately counter the threat of cyber warfare. More than 100 nations are actively developing cyber weapons. Nations such as China, Russia, Iran, India, and North Korea are actively increasing offensive, defensive, and intelligence cyber capabilities. It is important to note that acts of cyber aggression are not restricted to states. Thieves, criminals, activists, and terrorists have perpetrated computer intrusions and participated in cyber attacks. Another important point is that the private sector, in particular owners and operators of critical infrastructure assets, are highly susceptible to becoming targets of cyber attacks. Cyber warfare is a real high-tech threat with the potential of becoming one of the most dangerous and damaging weapons for nations of all sizes and economic standing to employ in gaining the upper hand in modern international conflict. The winners in the cyber domain will be innovative actors with superior technical staffs.

CYBER ATTACK PROCESS

The North Atlantic Treaty Organization has initiated strategic planning for the next generation of warfare, which includes the cyber dimension of conflict.[5] Following large-scale denial-of-service attacks on Estonia in 2007 and Georgia in 2008, the alliance established the Cooperative Cyber Defence Centre of Excellence in Tallinn, staffed by international personnel conducting research and training on cyber warfare.[6] Those two assaults on sovereign nations made militaries around the world recognize that they lacked a common language and decision-making framework to effectively respond to threats in the area of cyber aggression.

Although many organizations and individuals perceive a cyber attack as an event, they are wrong. It is a process composed of five components: reconnaissance, scanning, system access, malicious activity, and exploitation (see figure 6.1).[7] In addition, there are four subprocesses: cyber attack planning, cyber attack design, cyber attack initiation, and attack, which operate in concert to achieve the stated objectives of cyber attack strategy.

Reconnaissance deals with acquiring targeting information during the planning phase. If the target is a cell phone, then the first step is to obtain its number and usage patterns when the device is normally on the air. The second step is scan-

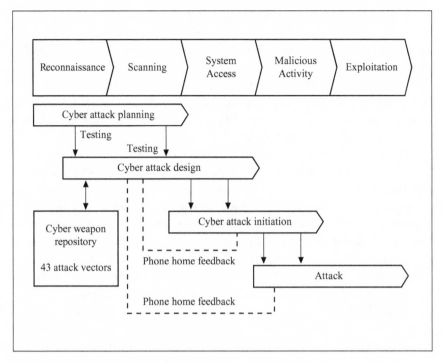

Figure 6.1 Cyber Attack Process Framework
Source: Technolytics Lecture Series (200 and 300 Cyber Warfare Programs), Air Force Institute of Technology.

ning the device that will be the point of attack. By obtaining specific information about the device, its operating system software including the version, patches, and security software and other information are collected on the target, the service provider, and even the manufacturer. Then cyber attack planning begins using all information that has been gathered. During this phase a list of unpatched vulnerabilities in targeted systems identified during scanning becomes the basis of the attack. Additionally, the zero-day vulnerabilities identified during the vulnerability research phase that have not been reported to the vendor, National Institute of Standards and Technology, and other organizations are examined to locate flaws that can be exploited to gain system access. Once this has been completed and an exploitation method identified, the cyber weapons repository is reviewed to determine if weapons exist to exploit unpatched holes and unknown vulnerabilities that are believed to exist in the targeted systems.

> FACT In the 2010 Stuxnet incident, four unreported vulnerabilities were used to carry out the intrusive cyber attack on Iranian systems that allowed an attacker to access the target systems rather than simply to disrupt processing.

If no cyber weapon matches the exact need of the mission, a cyber weapon is custom designed and produced or acquired on the black market. Weapons developed in the design phase normally undergo a formal process that includes quality assurance and testing. When the appropriate exploit is readied, attackers may decide to conduct a low-intensity test against similarly configured systems to verify operational abilities as well as to obscure their intentions. Once the test shot is complete, its results are reviewed and necessary adjustments made. Only then is the cyber weapon finally assembled.

Developers of cyber weapons recognize that despite their best efforts, attack code artifacts may be left in compromised systems. This explains why the decision is made on whether to include comments in the malware code base for disinformation and misdirecting. Purposefully embedding phrases or references in the comments of the code that are specific to a group tend to distract forensic investigators and point them in the wrong direction. Embedding encrypted areas of the code or comments is another technique that often consumes scarce investigative time and resources. Forensic investigators attempting to crack the encryption key and discover what has been hidden experience the same misdirection and delays.

> FACT The Stuxnet malware had encrypted capabilities embedded deep inside the code base. This encrypted code has unknown functions and capabilities. In addition, many believe the religious references embedded in the comments were for misdirection.[8]

The next phase initiates the cyber attack. At this point malicious software that makes up the cyber weapons may be pre-positioned either through a staging location or within the confines of an intermediary. A pre-staging area could be a compromised piece of equipment in a targeted supply chain or simply an infected thumb drive. Many cyber attack planners use an intermediary, typically in a hostile nation, to impede the ability of forensic investigators to trace the origin of the attack and who was actually responsible. Whether pre-staged or conducted through an intermediary, the target is infiltrated. The infiltration or compromise is often done on a time delay that ranges from minutes or hours to days or even months in some rare cases.

When triggered by specific times, events, or actions, the malicious activities of cyber weapons enter the attack phase. There are five typical activities. The previously identified vulnerability is engaged to gain system access and the status of system access that is fed back through an intermediary as indicated in figure 6.1. With system access achieved, one or more of the following malicious activities are conducted to meet the objectives of an attack as defined back in the planning stage:

- Delete information.
- Copy and steal information.
- Change information.
- Disrupt system operations.
- Change system operations.

As malicious activities progress, a dynamic feedback loop is established with a compromised machine in a physical or virtual location. The status and progress of malicious activity are reported to an additional intermediary to isolate and cloak the identity of an attacker. At the same time, critical information is often collected and packaged. Packaging can be encryption or stenography specifically designed to hide the specifics of the data being taken from the target. The feedback about the performance of a cyber weapon is returned to those in exploit development and vulnerability research to achieve continuous improvement. Mission-specific information obtained from a target for exploitation, namely, a compromised system, is sent to exfiltration staging in order that an attacker can collect it at a specific time and date. Like with previous activities, a bidirectional feedback line may be established through an intermediary that is unaware of their participation in the cyber attack.

A cyber attack is really a complex and sophisticated process. Deceptive, misdirecting, and misleading functionality are becoming common in advanced cyber weapons. The cyber offensive intelligence collected during reconnaissance, scanning, and vulnerability research enables successful cyber attacks. Almost every cyber attack, even those that leverage antiforensics techniques, leaves digital evidence that can assess the capabilities and identity of an attacker. Analysis of this evidence creates a digital DNA signature that can help investigators determine attribution. This signature depicts and classifies multiple aspects of the attack and malicious code and is analogous to the genetic instructions in human DNA. The term *ASDF* is used to represent four digital DNA characteristic sets that are spelled out below.[9]

- A = attributes, abilities, abstraction, architecture, assembly, adaptation
- S = style, signatures, syntax, structure, source, specification, scope
- D = demographics, delivery, development, discipline, data, design
- F = functions, features, faults, formidability, fields, forms, factors

CYBER WEAPONRY CHARACTERISTICS

The topic of cyber weapons recently has moved from behind closed doors in classified sources to the private sector and mainstream media. This new class of weaponry has been discussed in the same context as weapons of mass destruction.[10]

That association suggests how dangerous cyber weapons can become and the risks they pose. Even more troubling is the fact that such weapons have moved from being the projects of hackers to hostile code that is generated within a formal development process with quality assurance that includes testing and evaluation.

The characteristics of this new class of weaponry combine to create a substantial challenge for governments and military forces around the world. What is the difference between a security testing tool and a cyber weapon? The answer is simple: intent. Cyber weapons can be activated instantaneously and the identity of an attacker is quite difficult to discern. All that are needed to develop a cyber weapon are an Internet connection, a few computers, technical manuals, and one or more smart people. These characteristics make this new class of weapons a very attractive addition to the arsenals of clandestine operations. They also make controlling the proliferation of cyber arms nearly impossible. Supporting that observation is their adaptation by terrorist groups such as al-Qaeda, Hamas, and Hezbollah. They are recruiting new, younger members who are more knowledgeable and have computer technology skills. Although self-development of cyber weapons is clearly the method of choice for states and terrorist and criminal groups, the ability to purchase cyber arms or to contract with dealers to mount cyber attacks on selected targets has made such capabilities economically available to just about any individual, group, or nation.

FACT The Iranian Cyber Army, whoever attacked Twitter, and the Chinese search engine Baidu run networks of computers for rent to distribute malware known as botnets.[11]

The term *cyber power projection* used by military and political strategists refers to the capability of a government to intimidate other nations and implement policy by means of force from cyber actions or the threat thereof. Such use of cyber weapons and highly targeted attacks as an instrument of national power is becoming increasingly more common. What is even more concerning is keeping abreast of the advances being made in this relatively new method of power projection. This is problematic because of the likelihood of escalation between the party that projects power through intermediaries and its intended target. Solid attribution of an attack is quite elusive and requires the cooperation of all intermediaries involved. The applicability and relationship of the laws of war to cyber operations are immature and untested. The unique functions and features of cyber weapons coupled with the lack of distinction between civilian and military targets hinder the alignment of the rules of cyber engagement with the law of armed conflict. The ability to evolve international cyber warfare doctrine to keep up to date with rapid technological changes will require a Herculean effort and cooperation among nations connected to the Internet. Although

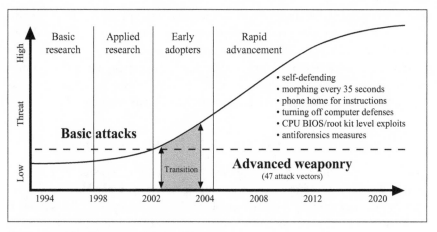

Figure 6.2 The Evolution of Cyber Weapons
Source: Technolytics Lecture Series (Cyber Conflict Program), US Army War College.

efforts are under way, it is unlikely that this will be happening anytime soon, and the proliferation and the use of cyber weapons will continue to advance unchecked.

CYBER WEAPONRY EVOLUTION

The origin of cyber weapons can be traced to the emergence of the Internet. Figure 6.2 illustrates the evolution of cyber weaponry. What have become known as malware were computer viruses—programs, scripts, or macros—designed to infect, destroy, modify, and harm computers. Criminals who sought profit in their malicious activities initiated many early computer attacks. These activities continue with organized criminal enterprises selling advanced cyber weapons and even offering their services to launch cyber attacks. Viruses and other malicious software have become complex threats. This rapid evolution has led law enforcement agencies to ask whether it is possible to keep up with cyber crime or face an unwinnable crusade. The defense and intelligence communities also are raising this question.

Between 1994 and 2002, cyber weapons continuously evolved at a moderate rate as indicated in figure 6.2.[12] A transition between 2002 and 2004 occurred in which cyber weapons went from being produced by individuals with basic know-how to being professionally developed by teams that used advanced architecture in the context of a cyber attack process. In fact, comments made by quality assurance analysts were embedded throughout the malicious code. The formalization of this process coupled with a structured development and strategic approach to attacks combine to thrust the weapons into the advanced category. The six attributes represent only a few of the capabilities of such cyber weapons. Nontraditional computers are being compromised and utilized as weapons. Industrial controllers, smart or cell phones, and microprocessors and chips are being exploited as platforms for cyber weapons. In June of 2010, the website Dark Reading claimed there was "more than twice the number of malware and spy ware hitting Black-Berry, Windows Mobile, and Android phones than six months ago."[13]

COMPUTER CHIPS

One of the most troubling cyber threats arises from the insertion of malicious code in firmware of computer or computerized devices or embedded throughout application software developed and supported by foreign suppliers. This threat is perhaps the most difficult to detect or defend against given that attacks could be hidden in the circuitry, firmware, and software within chips. Foreign suppliers of microprocessors could easily slip harmful code into the tens of millions of lines of code embedded in microprocessors or microcontrollers as well as basic input/ output systems, which are the programs that start up every computer.

Computer chips perform critical functions in both military and commercial products and systems. Malicious code or circuitry embedded inside microprocessors and microcontrollers during the manufacturing process is the nightmare scenario for cyber defenders because those changes are almost impossible to detect. A deluge of foreign counterfeit chips poses a growing threat to civilian and military systems and infrastructure. Studies have concluded that US military forces—"which use chips in everything from communication and radar systems to aircraft and missiles—is alarmingly vulnerable to fakes."[14] Counterfeit chips have been found in the computers of F-15 fighter jets, SH-60 helicopters, and E-2C surveillance planes, and in the long-range radar for the aircraft carrier USS *Ronald Reagan*.[15]

The US Government Accountability Office has concluded the "DOD is limited in its ability to determine the extent to which counterfeit parts exist in its supply chain" because it "does not currently have a policy or specific processes for detecting and preventing counterfeit parts."[16] Moreover, a report by the US Department of Commerce stated that "all elements of the supply chain have been directly impacted by counterfeit electronics."[17] Two American citizens recently have admitted to importing more than 13,000 bogus chips from China that were altered to resemble items produced by legitimate companies including Intel, National Semiconductor, and others.[18] Additionally, a two-year investigation called Operation Cisco Raider disrupted a large effort to distribute counterfeit Cisco network hardware that was manufactured in China.[19] As a source of counterfeit chips, the Chinese share of global sales of microprocessors and microcontrollers continues to experience double-digit growth.

KEVIN G. COLEMAN

CELL PHONES

Although malicious chips are among the main concerns of cyber defense experts, advances in the application of malicious code that targets other devices are near the top of the list. Every day more than 1.5 billion people use the Internet and 4.5 billion rely on cell phones, which create attractive targets for malicious cyber activities.[20] Attackers perceive huge value in subverting phones, knowing that they have sensitive information including location and financial data. Phones offer different gateways of attack through e-mail, internal applications, text messaging, and even call fraud. Botnets (an autonomous group of software agents that flood and overload targeted computers with malicious traffic), root kits, and other means to exploit the vulnerabilities of smart phones or their applications have increased dramatically as the devices have become more affordable and popular.

CONTROLLERS

Cyber attack modalities that target traditional computers are being repurposed and used against nontraditional computing devices such as supervisory control and data acquisition (SCADA) systems including hardware, software, and sensors that gather and analyze data in real time on an industrial process. The industrial systems in question monitor and control physical plants and equipment in various sectors. SCADA systems range from simple heating, ventilating, and air conditioning units for office buildings to highly complex systems that control and monitor nuclear power plants.[21]

The unclassified list of advanced cyber weapon capabilities indicates the nature of threats that transcend devices and platforms used to access the Internet (see figure 6.2). In June 2010 several of these advanced features were found in a state-of-the art Stuxnet cyber attack against nontraditional targets deep inside the Iranian nuclear program. *Computerworld* reported that the worm is a groundbreaking piece of malware so devious in its use of unknown vulnerabilities, so sophisticated in its multipronged approach, that the security researchers who tore it apart believe it may be the work of state-backed professionals.[22] Its use of encryption is inhibiting cyber forensic specialists from understanding the totality of the Stuxnet malware capabilities. There has been speculation that this section is a digital time-bomb that would take the SCADA system completely down. Our ability to collect insight and knowledge from the cyber incidents through detailed investigations of the digital DNA provides knowledge that is of critical importance to those in the global cyber conflict environment.[23]

At the end of September 2010 Iran blocked the website Ars Technica that provided detailed reporting on the Stuxnet attack in what appeared to be an attempt to control the spread of information on the extent and impact of the attack. Tehran has a history of censoring Internet content deemed offensive or critical of the government. This was far more than spin control or a public relations stunt. When commenting on Western media claims that the Stuxnet worm had attacked nuclear plant systems, Iranian Defense Minister Ahmad Vahidi proclaimed, "We had no problem in this regard because officials had taken necessary precautions." This is seen as an effort to save face on the global stage after this significant compromise and reinforce the perception of Iran's ability to produce nuclear materials. He went on to call the Stuxnet incident "computer terrorism," carried out by the domineering powers.[24]

The true impact of the Stuxnet malware on the Iranian operations is not fully known. Intelligence sources have stated that several of the centrifuges used in the enrichment process went offline and others operated at a significantly reduced pace.

> FACT Inspectors from the International Atomic Energy Agency were able to detect that 984 Iranian centrifuges were taken offline.

Other intelligence sources report that an industrial incident at the nuclear plant claimed at least one life while one senior official stepped down as a result of these events. There is speculation that this action was due to problems encountered at the nuclear facility and failure to meet agreed-upon milestones and dates. The delays are thought to be associated with the Stuxnet malware attack on critical systems within the nuclear facility. As the Stuxnet saga continues, some believe that in our lifetime we will not know who was behind the creation and distribution of the malware or their true intent.

CYBER ARMS CONTROL

The world has yet to come to grips with the fact that cyber weapons exist, and due to their unique characteristics, it would be next to impossible to control their development, spread, and use. Unlike weapons of mass destruction, these cyber weapons require no controlled materials, special manufacturing facilities—they can be produced in a garage or apartment—or restricted skills and expertise. Moreover, existing mental models of intelligence are inadequate at best when applied to cyberspace. A fundamental and radical rethinking of intelligence sources and collection techniques is just beginning. The threat of cyber aggression has risen to unprecedented levels and triggered the need to accelerate cyber intelligence collection by security companies, government agencies, military organizations, and traditional intelligence agencies. The culmination of their efforts has increased our defenses and expanded our understanding of the current state of cyber arms globally.

An online poll on cyber arms control conducted in 2009 by DefenseTech and Technolytics surveyed a wide international audience to determine if an international cyber arms control treaty would help halt a cyber war. More than 80 percent of respondents felt any such agreement would be unsuccessful. The respondents said the inability to verify whether nations have or are building cyber weapons would render any such treaty ineffective—the old issue of trust but verify. In addition, they indicated that if a cyber arms control treaty were negotiated, only criminals, terrorists, and rogue states would have the weapons. Both Russia and China have called for advancing international disarmament, arms control, and a nonproliferation process that include conventional and cyber weapons. One senior Chinese delegate to the UN General Assembly said, "Cyberspace constitutes a new dimension of multilateral arms control diplomacy."[25] At this point it is unlikely cyber arms control will become a reality anytime soon. Even if it did, the chances that any international treaty can be enforced or have a profound impact on the development, sale, and use of cyber weapons for criminal acts, acts of espionage, or acts of aggression or war are very slim. According to one DefenseTech cyber warfare blog respondent, "Trying to negotiate Cyber Arms Control is like trying to negotiate the spread of the common cold."[26]

The proliferation of cyber attack capabilities goes unchecked around the world. Alternative devices and nontraditional systems are being compromised and turned into platforms for cyber weapons with alarming speed. Cyber attacks continue to evolve in the area of attack strategy as well as the design, codification, and processes used in cyber attacks. Make no mistake about it: We are in an offensive and defensive cyber arms race that has no end in sight. Creativity, innovation, and human intelligence are key components in the development of a cyber weapon, and currently there does not appear to be any shortage of those capabilities. Civilian and military leaders are seeking solutions to this threat, which is becoming uncontrollable.

The Chinese stress the importance of education and technological advancement.[27] Beijing has made significant progress in space, computer, and military technologies. Between 2006 and 2009 China had an annual growth rate of more than 21 percent in patents as compared to 5.5 percent for the United States.[28] In 2010, a Chinese research center demonstrated the fastest supercomputer ever manufactured, thereby surpassing the United States as the leader in supercomputer technology. The Chinese supercomputer named Tianhe-1A is 1.4 times faster than the previous leader, which is located in Tennessee at a national laboratory.[29] When we look at current and forecasted economic conditions and the corresponding investment in research and development for advance technology, the ability of China to outpace the United States is apparent. This wake-up call came years ago but has gone unanswered. This gap is the single most critical issue when it comes to cyber warfare supremacy as well as overall military power.

FACT The full extent and capabilities of the US arsenal of cyber weapons are among the most tightly guarded secrets. Some experts believe cyber capabilities are more closely guarded than strategic nuclear capabilities.

DIPLOMATIC SOLUTION

The reality that any country with an Internet connection can engage in acts of cyber aggression indicates the complexity of the issue facing world leaders. Many individuals and organizations believe a diplomatic solution can be found to mitigate the threat being posed by cyber weapons. In July 2010 the United States, Britain, China, Russia, and fifteen other nations agreed to work together on reducing the threat of cyber attacks. An agreement was signed at the United Nations that represented a shift in the American position on the cyber domain. It recommended that the United Nations establish norms for acceptable behavior in cyberspace, which suggests a trust-but-verify-style agreement. But it raises the question of how the United Nations will be able to verify whether any state has cyber weapons. Although the United States and other nations have agreed to control nuclear, biological, and chemical weapons, the success of such an agreement on cyberspace is highly doubtful. In addition, the United Nations is seeking an agreement that would require collaboration and assistance with international cyber attack investigations and attribution. The openness required for UN cyber investigations will be the greatest challenge. Cooperation will be key in attribution of cyber attacks that will undoubtedly stretch around the world. It is difficult to imagine a nation opening its digital infrastructure to a level that would allow investigators to determine who was behind an attack. Just consider the situation in the United States, where much of the digital infrastructure is privately owned and privately operated. Competitive secrets, proprietary hardware, software, and techniques would be potentially exposed. Even if UN cyber arms control and attribution initiatives were successful, an attack could be routed through compromised systems in states that do not accede to the agreements.

The militarization of cyberspace is no longer a theoretical question; it has become a reality. Many nations have begun to develop cyber warfare rules of engagement, but that appears to be a premature response. In light of that, four critical issues must be addressed:

- What constitutes an act of cyber war?
- What is considered a proportional response to a cyber attack?
- Whether we need a Geneva Convention on cyberspace to establish a framework.
- What separates cyber crime, cyber terrorism, and cyber war?

As more nation-states create legal frameworks to address the plethora of issues in cyberspace, the more difficult the issue becomes. The issue of law and cyber conflict, while relatively new, has been a discussion that people, nation-states, and military organizations have been having for more than a decade with still no agreed-upon standard definitions or laws.

THE chief technology officer of the US Cyber Consequences Unit, John Bumgarner, remarked that "all military conflicts in the future will include a cyber component."[30] As nations develop offensive, defensive, and intelligence collection capabilities in cyberspace, militarization will become more pronounced. Many know that cyber weapons together with well-designed cyber attack strategies can become a force multiplier and potential equalizer when confronting much larger and better-financed adversaries. At present more than 150 nations are thought to have cyber capabilities programs under development, and many possess moderately effective cyber weapons. In addition, several terrorist organizations including al-Qaeda, Hezbollah, and Hamas have developed moderately advanced cyber attack capabilities.

The use of cyber weapons and the cyber attack process combine to create the most modern platform to launch or support attacks that cut across conflict domains and the global commons. Although discussions of cyber weapons have taken place behind closed doors, experts on defense and foreign affairs doubt the ability to control their development, spread, and use. A presentation given at the Cyber Security Forum Initiative–Cyber Warfare Division Conference held in Miami raised the unresolved question on the dissemination and containment of cyber weapons: How can the spread of cyber weapons be controlled when the only difference between attacks by cyber weapons and legitimate security testing tools are the intent behind their use?

It is clear that the advancement of cyber weapons and their use as a means of projecting soft and hard power will continue for the foreseeable future. At present the cyber conflict domain in the global commons is making rapid advances, though it is still quite immature. The attempt to force-fit cyber conflicts into existing domain or commons models must be abandoned and a new hybrid mental model developed to operate advantageously in cyberspace. Progress on this hybrid model is not limited by money, technology, or interest. If anything it is constrained by the availability of skilled resources as well as creativity and innovation of those resources.

Cyber aggression poses the second most significant threat to international security bested only by weapons of mass destruction. Governments are racing to protect digital infrastructures from would-be attackers who hold the upper hand. Leaders must promote cooperation between military research and development labs and efforts in the private sector to create the great majority of security products used in defense of computers, networks, and alternative devices. In fact, the current situation may be likened to an arms race on steroids. The threat can be mitigated only through mutual cooperation.

NOTES

The epigraph by Leon Panetta was broadcast in an interview on June 27, 2010 with *This Week* (ABC Television News), http://blogs.abcnews.com/politicalpunch/2010/06/cia-cyber-warfare-could-paralyze-us.html.

1. James N. Miller, testimony before the House Committee on Armed Services, March 16, 2011.
2. Ben Bain, "Military Wrestles with Cyber War Battle Planning," *Federal Computer Week*, July 26, 2010, http://fcw.com/articles/2010/07/26/feat-cyber-command-tackles-cyber-war.aspx.
3. See Cheryl Pellerin, "Lynn: Cyberspace Is the New Domain of Warfare," American Forces Press Service, October 18, 2010, www.defense.gov/news/newsarticle.aspx?id=61310.
4. Amber Corrin, "Military Readies Its Cyber Forces," *Federal Computer Week*, July 26, 2010, http://fcw.com/articles/2010/07/26/feat-cyber-command-launch-timeline.aspx.
5. "Lisbon Summit Declaration" issued by the heads of state and government participating in the meeting of the North Atlantic Council, paragraph 36, November 20, 2010, www.nato.int/cps/en/natolive/official_texts_68828.htm.
6. Eleanor Keymer, "The Cyber-War," *Jane's Defence Weekly*, September 29, 2010, 19–24.
7. Lectures delivered to the 200 and 300 cyber warfare programs at the Air Force Institute of Technology, Wright-Patterson Air Force Base, Dayton, Ohio, on various dates.
8. John Markoff and David E. Sanger, "In a Computer Worm, a Possible Biblical Clue," *New York Times*, September 29, 2010, www.nytimes.com/2010/09/30/world/middleeast/30worm.html.
9. Kevin G. Coleman and Randy Favero, *Cyber Commander's Handbook: The Weaponry and Strategies of Digital Conflict* (McMurray, PA: Technolytics, December 15, 2009), 25–26.
10. George W. Foresman, "The Complexities of America's National Security: Enabling a New Generation of Leadership," *High Frontier* 7 (November 2010): 5.
11. Jeremy Kirk, "Iranian Cyber Army Running Botnets, Researchers Say," *Computerworld*, October 25, 2010, www.computerworld.com/s/article/9192800/Iranian_Cyber_Army_running_botnets_researchers_say.
12. Technolytics lectures delivered in the cyber conflict program at the US Army War College, Carlisle Barracks, Pennsylvania, on various dates.
13. See Kelly Jackson, "Smartphone Malware Multiplies," *Dark Reading*, June 7, 2010, www.darkreading.com/insiderthreat/security/attacks/showArticle.jhtml?articleID=225402185. See also John E. Dunn, "Smartphone Users Clueless of Malware Risks," *PCWorld*, March 7, 2011, www.pcworld.com/article/221375/smartphone_users_clueless_of_malware_risks.html.
14. Steve Johnson, "Fake Computer Chips Threaten US Military," McClatchy-Tribune News Service, *Providence*, September 27, 2010, www.theprovince.com/technology/tech-biz/Fake+computer+chips+threaten+military/3528425/story.html?id=3528425.
15. Brian Grow, Chi-Chu Tschang, Cliff Edwards, Brian Burnsed, and Keith Epstein, "Dangerous Fakes," *Business Week*, October 2, 2008, 34–44, www.businessweek.com/magazine/content/08_41/b4103034193886.htm.
16. Belva Martin, "Defense Supplier Base: DOD Should Leverage Ongoing Initiatives in Developing Its Program to Mitigate Risk of Counterfeit Parts" (Washington, DC: US Government Accounting Office, March 29, 2010), 1–20.

17. United States Department of Commerce, "Defense Industrial Base Assessment: Counterfeit Electronics" (Washington, DC: Bureau of Industry and Security, January 2010), ii.

18. Johnson, "Fake Computer Chips."

19. Brian Grow, "Fake Cisco, Real Threat," *Business Week*, October 2, 2008, 38, www.businessweek.com/magazine/content/08_41/b4103038201037.htm.

20. Georgia Tech Information Security Center, "Emerging Cyber Threats Report 2011," October 7, 2010, 6–7, www.gtiscsecuritysummit.com/.

21. On SCADA devices, see William Matthews, "Attack on Reactor Hints at Future of Cyberwar," *Defense News*, October 4, 2010, 14.

22. Gregg Keizer, "Is Stuxnet the 'Best' Malware Ever?" *Computerworld*, September 16, 2010, www.computerworld.com/s/article/9185919/Is_Stuxnet_the_best_malware_ever_.

23. Kevin G. Coleman, "A Big Pot of Money," *Defense Tech*, June 13, 2008, http://defensetech.org/2008/06/13/a-big-pot-of-money.

24. "Iran: Stuxnet Worm, Computer Terrorism," *Press TV*, October 13, 2010, www.presstv.ir/detail/146567.html.

25. Statement by Wang Qun, Chinese delegate to the 65th session of UN General Assembly, October 7, 2010, http://mu.china-embassy.org/eng/zgxw/t759455.htm.

26. Kevin G. Coleman, "Stuxnet—Game Changer," *DefenseTech*, comments in blog response, October 4, 2010, http://defensetech.org/2010/10/04/stuxnet-game-changer.

27. United States Department of Defense, *Military and Security Developments Involving the People's Republic of China* (Washington, DC: Office of the Secretary of Defense, August 2010), 47, www.defense.gov/pubs/pdfs/2010_CMPR_Final.pdf.

28. Thomson Reuters, "China to Be Number One in Patents," *Managing Intellectual Property*, October 6, 2010, www.managingip.com/Article/2682996/China-to-be-number-one-in-patents.html.

29. Ashlee Vance, "China Wrests Supercomputer Title from US," *New York Times*, October 28, 2010, www.nytimes.com/2010/10/28/technology/28compute.html.

30. Eleanor Keymer, "Interview," *Jane's Defence Weekly*, September 29, 2010, 34.

PART III

COOPERATIVE OPPORTUNITIES

CHAPTER 7

Building Collaborative Capacity for Maritime Security

SUSAN PAGE HOCEVAR

T he global commons facilitate the movement of people, goods, information, and technology via air, sea, space, and cyberspace.[1] International security and economic competitiveness depend on open access to the commons. The UN Convention on the Law of the Sea has established rules for activity on the seas, including rights and duties of coastal states regarding territorial seas and rights and duties of ships in innocent or transit passage on the oceans of the world. This treaty was signed in 1982 by more than 155 nations and demonstrates global commitment to maritime security.

SECURITY OF THE COMMONS

The introduction to this book argues that maintaining access, safety, and security in the global commons requires cooperation by diverse organizations.[2] It proposes a comprehensive approach to identify interests and establish policies, incentives, and mechanisms for cooperative behavior. A similar multistakeholder approach is addressed by Schuyler Foerster in chapter 3 on deterrence strategies.[3] One of the identified strategies is entanglement that emphasizes benefits to stakeholders of linkages based on shared interests, vulnerabilities, and rewards.[4] The author encourages greater use of relationships among nations rather than appeals to international law.

The various threats to collaboration include mistrust based on competition over interests, nationalism, lack of resources, and technocratic obstacles to information sharing. But there are virtues in overcoming some of these obstacles: "The foundations for mutual trust can be built through the development symposia for communities of interest, bilateral agreements, regional partnership, and international standards."[5] Examples of the various collaborative approaches to security in the maritime domain, which encompasses "oceans, seas, bays, estuaries, islands, coastal areas, littorals, and the airspace above them,"[6] are outlined below in detail.

Australia and the Netherlands display best practices in organizational collaboration for maritime security.[7] Examples of multinational and multi-organizational collaboration also are found in the Malacca Strait Patrols (MSP) and Regional Cooperation Agreement on Combating Piracy and Armed Robbery against Ships in Asia (ReCAAP). In addition, both the Joint Harbor Operations Center (JHOC) and Maritime Unified Command (MUC) in San Diego present two examples of interorganizational collaboration. These examples demonstrate collaboration among multiple agencies with shared interests and complementary capabilities. In this chapter the Interorganizational Collaborative Capacity (ICC) model is used to analyze the three cases based on available sources.[8]

INTERORGANIZATIONAL COLLABORATION

Collaborating across boundaries promotes both national and international security.[9] Given the complexities of aligned and competing interests, collaboration is a demanding exercise.[10] The ICC model was developed using data from US homeland security agencies at the federal, state, and local levels.[11] It identifies the factors that influence interorganizational collaboration, which is defined as the capacity "of organizations (or a set of organizations) to enter, develop, and sustain interorganizational systems in pursuit of collective outcomes."[12] One assumption of the model is that building capacity requires both leadership and alignment of organizational design elements. The model and related diagnostic can guide leadership action to improve collaboration by organizations and systems of organizations.[13] This approach is based on the notion that a security community constitutes a learning process that facilitates multiparty maritime arrangements.[14]

The ICC model provides a means of assessing factors that contribute to the ability of organizations to collaborate and includes the following domains: purpose and strategy, structure, incentives and reward systems, lateral mechanisms, and people.[15] Thirteen factors are measured by the diagnostic shown in figure 7.1.[16]

There are three factors in the purpose and strategy domain: felt need, strategic actions, and resource investment. Felt need indicates recognized interdependence and a requirement for organizational collaboration. It can be derived from a perceived threat that emphasizes a response capability or an opportunity for pro-action or prevention. The next factor, strategic actions, includes the goals for collaboration, the demonstrated commitment by senior leaders, and the willingness to weigh the interests of other organizations in planning. The third factor, resource investment, gauges the extent to which organizations provide adequate

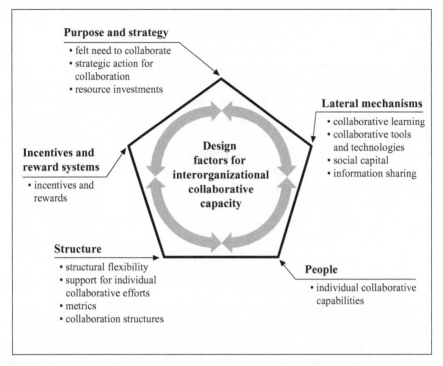

Figure 7.1 Interorganizational Collaborative Capacity Model

Source: Susan Page Hocevar, "Inter-Organizational Collaborative Capacity: A Conceptual Model and Measurement Tool," presented at the 4th Annual Homeland Defense and Security Education Summit, Georgetown University, Washington, DC, February 24–25, 2010.

budgets and personnel for successful collaboration. Felt need is typically the initiating factor. Yet without the addition of leadership, planning, and resources, there is inadequate strategic focus on building collaborative capacity.

The structure domain includes collaboration structures, structural flexibility, metrics, and support for individual collaboration efforts. Collaboration structures include liaison roles, participation in interagency teams and task forces, clearly established roles of participating organizations, and internal processes to enable effective interorganizational collaboration. Structural flexibility permits the adaptation of partnerships as requirements change, demonstrates willingness to adjust procedures to facilitate coordination, and responds to requirements of other organizations. Metrics include established criteria and performance standards for evaluating interorganizational efforts, and routine mechanisms for assessing outcomes. Support for individual collaboration efforts is provided by structuring individual collaborative work in terms of goals, constraints, and authorities. It is also demonstrated by the strength of links between the personnel who span boundaries to work with other organizations and the strategic leadership of their own organization. This is manifested in the extent to which organizations follow up on recommendations of boundary spanners.

Because the ICC model is aimed at organizational efforts to align internal design elements to improve collaboration, the incentives and reward systems domain considers its impact on personnel. Are employees rewarded for successful collaborative efforts? Does talent for collaboration figure in promotion systems? External factors that mandate an organization to collaborate or offer financial rewards can inspire collaboration, but these incentives come from the organization's external environment and hence are not reflected in the ICC model.

Four factors constitute the lateral mechanisms domain and include hard and soft aspects of lateral coordination: social capital, collaborative tools and technologies, information sharing, and collaborative learning. Counterpart relationships produce social capital, mutual awareness, and trust. Collaborative tools include interoperable information, planning, and decision systems; and information sharing represents norms, values, and adequacy of access. Finally, collaborative learning promotes joint training, knowledge of partner organizations, and systematic efforts to improve collaboration.

Individual collaborative capabilities are the single factor in the people domain and include attitudes, skills, knowledge, and behaviors that impact on the ability to collaborate. Examples are conflict management skill, shared decision making, respect for the expertise of members of other organizations, and understanding of how partner organizations work.

THREE NATIONAL APPROACHES

The first case to analyze using the Interorganizational Collaborative Capacity model is based on a study of the approaches to national maritime security policy by Australia, the Netherlands, and Norway to inform the Canadian government on best practices. The study found that a response to maritime security involves domain awareness, safeguarding, responsiveness, and collaboration. The first category of domain awareness comprises surveillance, intelligence, and information analysis "to collectively build a comprehensible picture of a nation's maritime zones and interests—both domestic and international."[17] Safeguarding addresses physical protection of ports, vessels, offshore platforms, and people. Responsiveness deals with law enforcement or military action to assure security. Finally, collaboration differs qualitatively from other categories as "an enabler for all parts of maritime security. Collaboration includes elements of information sharing, coordination, cooperation, and unified action."[18]

The study describes the maritime security approaches and priorities of the three nations using the above categories. For two nations, collaboration was seen to represent the priority approach to maritime security. The priority for collab-

Table 7.1 Priorities in Approaches to Maritime Security

Key Activities	
Australia	collaboration, domain awareness, safeguarding, responsiveness
Netherlands	collaboration, safeguarding, responsiveness, domain awareness
Norway	responsiveness, domain awareness, safeguarding, collaboration

Source: Peter Avis, "Best Practices for Canadian Maritime Security: A Comparison of Three National Approaches," *Canadian Military Journal* 7, no. 4 (2008): table 1.

orative approaches in Australia is based on a strong perceived need for maritime security preparedness and prevention in relation to potential terrorist threats. The priority for collaboration by the Netherlands is based on critical interdependencies given the complex geopolitical context of the European Union and economic dependence on maritime commerce. According to this study, Norway does not consider its maritime security to be directly threatened and thus emphasizes maintaining independence through governmental policies and prioritizing response capabilities (table 7.1).

The study identified seven best practices from the three national cases and attributed each practice to one of the four categories. The first of three collaborative best practices was from Australia, which reported the successful use of a whole-of-government approach to maritime security. "Through timely, wide-ranging legislation and steadfast government leadership, the Australian security structure was rebuilt" emphasizing horizontal information sharing, establishing intelligence coordination with law enforcement, and creating horizontal and vertical interdepartmental linkages.[19] Australia also presented a second best practice regarded as collaborative. Australia uses a Common Risk Assessment Methodology to bring together risk assessment input from different regional offices. This information is compared and evaluated against established risk criteria (economic, social, and environmental) to generate comparable risk scores. This analysis is used to determine the appropriate action and allocation of resources. The third best practice specifically identified as collaborative is the Netherlands International Deliberations over North Sea Governance, which is described as a twenty-five-year-old strategic mechanism with a permanent committee of decision makers from relevant government departments, which is convened to "debate maritime-related laws and policies, in which political issues of economy, environment, security, and society overlap."[20]

There is evidence in the three collaborative best practices of several domains and factors from the ICC model. The purpose and strategy domain reveals the felt need to collaborate in addressing perceived threats to Australia and the Netherlands and the significance of risks to maritime security. Both nations demonstrate strategic actions in governmental leadership and acknowledge the importance of multiple stakeholder involvement. Finally, the best practices evidenced both budgetary and personnel resource investments in collaboration. In the structure domain Australia demonstrates flexibility in the legislative, structural, and process changes required for the whole-of-government approach to maritime security.

The Common Risk Assessment Methodology provides a model for a metrics process that uses multiple-source data and criteria to allocate security resources. The International Deliberations over North Sea Governance collaborative structure conducts effective national planning and provides the Netherlands a unified voice in the European Community and other forums. Australian information sharing and intelligence coordination demonstrate lateral mechanisms between defense and law enforcement. Finally, the two Australian best practices and the North Sea initiative represent collaborative learning systems where organizations learn from each other to improve plans, policies, and resource allocation decisions.

REGIONAL COLLABORATION

The second case examines efforts to reduce piracy in the critical passages in Southeast Asia between the Indian and Pacific Oceans through the waters of Malaysia, Singapore, and Indonesia.[21] The Straits of Malacca and Singapore extend for 435 miles with the narrowest channel only one and a half miles wide.[22] About one-fourth of all the traded goods in the world, including oil, pass through this region each year. In 2008, for instance, more than 75,000 ships transited these waters. The importance of maritime safety and security in this area is obvious as is the threat of piracy and robbery. Between 2001 and 2004 there were more than 160 attacks attempted or carried out by pirates annually; in 2004 there were 46 attacks off the Malay Peninsula alone.[23] In 2005 the Joint War Committee of the Lloyd's Market Association declared the Strait of Malacca to be a high-risk zone. This led insurance underwriters to raise premiums on ships transiting the straits and increased the calls for greater law enforcement by the littoral states.[24] In response two collaborative initiatives were undertaken: the Malacca Strait Patrols and the Regional Cooperation Agreement on Combating Piracy and Armed Robbery against Ships in Asia.

The Malacca Strait Patrols include coordinated sea and air patrols, intelligence exchanges, a shared information system, and the Joint Coordinating Committee.[25] In 2004 Malaysia, Singapore, and Indonesia instituted a trilateral agreement to coordinate sea patrols and facilitate information sharing. In 2005 the patrols were reinforced by aerial surveillance and in 2006 the Intelligence Exchange Group was established to support patrols; this led to the development of the MSP Information System.[26] Thailand joined this effort in 2008 with coordinated sea patrols and in 2009 with air patrols (map 7.1).[27]

Map 7.1 Strait of Malacca

The four participating nations commit to operating a specific number of Eyes-in-the-Sky sorties each week. Aircraft are permitted to fly over the waters of the participating nations by embarking a Combined Maritime Patrol Team composed of one officer from each nation. Team members establish a comprehensive surface picture of the patrol area and report any suspicious activities to ground-based monitoring agencies in each nation.[28] The Intelligence Exchange Group meets regularly to share information, analyze security incidents, and recommend improvements in air and sea patrols. The MSP Intelligence System shares data on commercial shipping, vessels of interest, and specific incidents. It also provides data on more than 150,000 vessels and identifies suspicious anomalies. A combined exercise in 2008 led to enhancements in intelligence gathering including the Open and Analyzed Shipping Information System; Sense-Making, Analysis, and Research Tool; and chat functions. Finally, the Joint Coordinating Committee serves as the key MSP decision-making body and provides communication opportunities among top officials.[29] It has developed standard operating procedures, oversees patrols, and reinforces existing bilateral arrangements for cross-border pursuit.[30]

In addition to the Malacca Strait Patrols, collaboration has been established at the strategic level. In 2006 the International Maritime Organization held a tripartite ministerial meeting in Kuala Lumpur that proposed a Cooperative Mechanism among littoral and user nations, which was officially launched the following year in Singapore. The organization established terms of reference and procedures for three components of the Cooperative Mechanism: the Forum for Cooperation comprising senior officials and technical experts from the littoral states, the Project Coordination Committee to facilitate participation and funding for projects proposed by the littoral states, and the Aids to Navigation Fund to extend best practices in financial affairs to promote greater transparency and accountability.[31]

Concern over the increasing regional trend in crimes at sea led Japan to organize the Asia Challenge Conference in 2000 to lay the foundation for the Regional Cooperation Agreement on Combating Piracy and Armed Robbery against Ships in Asia.[32] The terms of the agreement were finalized in 2004 and came into effect in 2006 after ratification by fourteen member nations.[33] The agreement established the Information Sharing Centre (ISC) in Singapore with the status of an international organization. Currently there are seventeen members, each of which has a designated focal point for coordination and information sharing, all linked via a secure web-based network.[34] A governing council of member nations administers a consensus decision process to oversee ISC activities.

The three pillars of the multilateral ReCAAP agreement are information sharing, capacity building by sharing best practices, and engaging in cooperative arrangements with members and organizations to strengthen the ability to manage incidents at sea.[35] A number of strengths in this agreement have been identified. First, to meet the responsibilities and expectations of their focal point, member nations identify and examine interagency processes. Next, the capacity-building program has initiated exercises, training, and technical assistance that share best practices. Finally, the agreement engages governments, international organizations, and research institutes that are interested in maritime security to broaden awareness and increase information sharing.

Nonetheless, limitations have been identified in the Regional Cooperation Agreement on Combating Piracy and Armed Robbery against Ships in Asia. For one, Malaysia and Indonesia have not ratified it. The Information Sharing Centre also does not have an operational role and ships are not required to alert it when an incident occurs, only their respective flag nation or designee. The ISC subsequently is informed by the focal point, but this affects the timeliness of the response. Another limitation is the missed opportunity to improve maritime security by addressing shipping practices and the security at hub ports.[36]

There is strong evidence in this case of felt need to collaborate in the purpose and strategy domain of the ICC model. Both the Malacca Strait Patrols and the Information Sharing Centre of the Regional Cooperation Agreement on Combating Piracy and Armed Robbery against Ships in Asia demonstrate that participants recognize the importance of collaboration in improving maritime security and have made resource investments in structures, systems, and technologies. Strategic actions for collaboration are evident in the involvement of leadership in initiating these efforts and senior representation serving as designated focal points and on the governing council. Although it is impossible to evaluate the adequacy of resource commitments and strategic actions from reports, increased emphases may be required to address ReCAAP limitations and proposed projects.

Within the structure domain of the ICC model there is strong evidence of the collaboration structure factor. The Joint Coordinating Committee provides a senior-level MSP decision-making mechanism. At the operational level the Combined Maritime Patrol Team enables surveillance in what otherwise would be considered sovereign airspace. The Forum for Cooperation and Project Coordination Committee were established as part of the Cooperative Mechanism to provide strategic-level three-party structures. The Information Sharing Centre provides a structure with defined roles for the focal points and governance processes for collaborative decision making. Structural flexibility is offered by involving different parties in cooperative arrangements. However, it is limited by the lack of a formal commitment by Malaysia and Indonesia to ReCAAP and the MSP cross-border pursuit arrangements that are bilateral rather than multilateral. Some metrics relating to incident rates appear in annual reports on the ReCAAP website; but neither the reports nor documentation on the Malacca Strait Patrols discusses the systematic use of metrics to assess or improve collaboration.

Finally, the reports do not describe how leaders support individual collaborative efforts by operational and tactical personnel. Yet one can infer that the achievements described in this case could not have occurred without collaborative leadership guidance, encouragement, and support.

There is strong evidence of collaborative capacity in the domain of lateral mechanisms. The MSP and ReCAAP Information Sharing Centre utilize technologies for information sharing, data collection, and analysis. The participating organizations illustrate the value of information sharing not just in technical systems but also in their structural, governance, and decision-making processes. In addition, there are systematic mechanisms for collaborative learning. The Re-CAAP Information Sharing Centre disseminates best practices and the MSP nations routinely collaborate in analyzing security incidents to improve patrols, and both Regional Cooperation Agreement on Combating Piracy and Armed Robbery against Ships in Asia and Malacca Strait Patrols use combined exercises to build collaborative capacity. Although developing social capital is not explicitly discussed, one can assume that as both the combined patrol teams and strategic-level representatives work together, they are building increased awareness and trust that will improve future collaboration.

INTERAGENCY OPERATIONS CENTERS

Project SeaHawk was organized in 2003 as a test site for an operations center to identify and close gaps in port security in Charleston, South Carolina.[37] In 2004 another center was established in San Diego, California. These Joint Harbor Operations Centers address tactical-level weaknesses found in intelligence fusion by the 9/11 Commission and yield several benefits. First, they provide a central locale to bring together equipment, employees, sensors, and data to improve information sharing, situational awareness, and response time. Second, they disseminate information through an interoperable system for data sharing and intelligence gathering. Third, they provide awareness of the assets possessed by each agency (both capabilities and locations) to identify proximate resources and reduce duplication as well as increase the efficiency and effectiveness of the responses. Finally, they furnish a test bed for the innovation of concepts, procedures, and equipment.[38]

The US Coast Guard serves as lead agent in both operations centers working with federal, state, and local partners in port security. Most of the time, on-site agency representatives function independently using information systems linked to their headquarters.[39] These representatives are connected to smart technologies that provide mechanisms for unified responses when security situations require.[40] The presence of the onsite agency partner watch standers enables joint manning of the organization. This system not only allows for real-time coordination but also increases knowledge of other agencies' procedures and practices.[41]

One US Coast Guard officer involved in the development of the Joint Harbor Operations Center in San Diego has described the value of interagency partnerships as follows: "Regular one-on-one contact with representatives from an organization and periodic evaluations of common procedures through interoperability exercises and other training evolutions must be included within the business practices of a successful [Joint Harbor Operations Center]."[42] Memoranda of understanding or standard operating procedures are useful in clarifying responsibilities and authorities; tactics, techniques, and procedures; and lines of communication. These strategic-level initiatives reduce uncertainty and facilitate engagement by multiple agencies in planned events as well as effective responses to unplanned events. Exercise debriefings are used to identify lessons learned for improving interagency procedures and training protocols.[43]

Recognizing the importance of adding strategic and proactive planning mechanisms to the more tactical orientation of the Operations Centers, the Maritime Unified Command was formed in San Diego in 2008. Five components of the Department of Homeland Security are involved in supporting its activities: the US Coast Guard, three activities of Customs and Border Protection, and Immigration and Customs Enforcement, plus federal, state, and local agencies.[44]

The participating organizations establish strategic objectives and meet on a weekly basis to review operations and develop action plans that include resource commitments for port security activities. They use both the National Incident Management System and the Incident Command Structure to provide a common format and shared website (Homeport) to update plans. The Maritime Unified Command has created a single database to capture metrics of interest to all participating organizations; these metrics are regularly reviewed and revised. The benefits of the Command include the formal collaboration processes, a systemic tactical to strategic approach, willingness to share credit for missions accomplished through collaboration, and the support of strategic leadership. Finally, the Command has been acknowledged as a best practice and a model for use in other regions.[45]

Following the purpose and strategy domain of the ICC model, the events of September 11, 2001 increased the felt need to collaborate to improve information sharing, intelligence analysis, and coordinated planning and response related to port security. The strategic actions for collaboration initially emphasized the development of tactical and operational capabilities at the JHOC pilot ventures in Charleston and San Diego. The subsequent establishment of the Maritime Unified Command in San Diego recognized the need for a stronger strategic emphasis. Indicators of strategic actions include leadership involvement, goals for collaboration, and a willingness to consider interests of other organizations. The last factor in this domain, resource investment, is evident in the initial commitment of personnel and other assets as well as a subsequent increase in both number of participating organizations and their overall levels of involvement.

All of the factors in the structure domain are evident in the case data. Both the Joint Harbor Operations Center and the Maritime Unified Command are structures that provide mechanisms to link organizations through defined roles and modes of operation. Their structural flexibility is demonstrated by proactive and reactive JHOC activities. The different organizations' capabilities are combined depending on requirements and available assets. The Maritime Unified Command in San Diego recognizes the value of identifying and tracking metrics and provides resources to maintaining a database that can be accessed by all organizations. Its strategic guidance stresses the importance of supporting individual collaborative efforts. Personnel are encouraged to take the initiative by working with counterparts to identify ways to improve collaborations and ultimately improve port and maritime security.

The lateral mechanisms domain offers evidence of collaborative capacity. At the core of interagency operations centers are tools and technologies to aggregate data from various sensors as well as solve problems through integrated agency perspectives. Shared situational awareness, better understanding of the interests and capabilities of other organizations, and interpersonal trust are benefits of JHOC and MUC collaboration. Information sharing is fundamental to the purpose of the Joint Harbor Operations Center and Maritime Unified Command and is facilitated by their collaborative systems that create necessary mechanisms and norms. It is also supported by social capital accrued by representatives who work together on a daily or weekly basis. Periodic evaluations of procedures through training and exercises also demonstrate collaborative learning capabilities.[46] The Joint Harbor Operations Centers began as pilot efforts to test innovative concepts, procedures, and equipment, which provide further evidence of the collaborative learning factor.

The last two domains, incentives and reward systems and people, are noteworthy but less quantifiable from the open literature documents used in the first two cases. Interviews at the Joint Harbor Operations Center in San Diego discovered that no formal rewards were given for collaboration but significant intrinsic rewards for collaboration did exist in port security and law enforcement. The individual collaborative capabilities include better understanding of how organizations operate and their interests and capabilities in port security, mutual respect among members of diverse organizations, and an ability to engage in shared problem solving and decision making.

The thirteen factors of the ICC model are all demonstrated in the Joint Harbor Operations Center and the Maritime Unified Command. Not all of them were evident initially, and some like formal rewards may lag behind as an institutionalized mechanism. But the importance of building collaborative capacity for port security is seen in these cases and more importantly in the passage of the

Security and Accountability for Every Port Act of 2006 that directed creation of interagency operation centers in twenty-two US ports considered to be high risk.[47]

A model based on Interorganizational Collaborative Capacity was used as the conceptual framework to define organizational design strategies that enable multi-organizational and multinational efforts for maritime security. The most consistent finding in the three cases is that felt need compels organizations to make commitments to build collaborative capacity. Without strategic actions such as explicit goals and resource investments for collaboration, a perceived need could motivate impassioned words yet prove insufficient in achieving effective outcomes. Research has found that organizations often depend on the strength of individual collaborative capacity and social capital in lieu of the more challenging development of collaborative structures and technologies.[48] The former allow ad hoc and informal collaboration, but to improve maritime security more formalized institutional support is necessary.

Furthermore, collaboration structures clarify the roles, processes, and authorities of organizations engaged in partnerships. Because structures are subject to change, there is evidence of structural flexibility. In the second and third cases, metrics document successful outcomes and provide data for improvement. Information sharing is a central purpose and benefit of collaboration, and achieving collaboration requires organizational norms as well as accessible information systems. The latter are evident in the collaborative tools featured in the three cases. Details are not provided on the adequacy of information access from the perspective of different partners, which often presents challenges for collaboration on global security. There are examples in each case of collaborative learning ranging from the analysis of joint operations to the dissemination of best practices.

In all three cases, there is no discussion of incentives by the participating organizations that links performance in collaboration to professional rewards and promotion opportunities. It is impossible to know whether this is because systems do not exist or because reports were not focused on this aspect of the organizations. Research indicates that attention to reward systems is often a lagging factor in building collaborative capacity.[49] But as collaboration becomes an integral part of organizational expectations, rewards and incentives should be appropriately aligned.

The three cases of collaboration in the maritime domain demonstrate deliberate attention to the development of collaborative capacity. The ICC model provides a framework for systematic organizational design strategies that positively benefit collaboration. There are other collaborative initiatives under way to strengthen security in the domain including the Maritime Organization of West and Central Africa, the Contact Group on Piracy off the Coast of Somalia, and the EU policy on the integration of maritime surveillance.[50] Chapter 4 in this book offers another area of application for collaboration in the maritime domain—seabasing for the forward deployment of US forces.[51] This concept has particular appeal in areas such as the Asia-Pacific region, where land basing is a challenge.[52] Achieving the joint mission capability offered by seabasing requires interservice collaboration. An even more challenging argument has been made for security across all domains in the global commons. Although this chapter focuses on intradomain collaboration, there are proposals for interdomain collaborative planning to bring together stakeholders of maritime, air, space, and cyber domains.[53] Such efforts reflect growing attention to interorganizational factors in a global environment, and as such will benefit from systematic work on the organizational design factors that affect collaborative capacity.

NOTES

This chapter was written as part of the author's official duties at the Naval Postgraduate School and thus is in the public domain.

1. Scott Jasper and Paul S. Giarra, "Disruptions in the Commons," in *Securing Freedom in the Global Commons*, Scott Jasper, ed. (Stanford, CA: Stanford University Press, 2009), 2.
2. See "Introduction: A Comprehensive Approach," in this volume.
3. See chapter 3 in this volume, "Strategies of Deterrence," and also Roger G. Harrison, Collins G. Shackelford, and Deron R. Jackson, "Space Deterrence: The Delicate Balance of Risk," *Space and Defense* 3, no. 1 (2009): 1–30.
4. See also Schuyler Foerster, "Deterrence Strategies in and for the Global Commons: Cooperation and Conflict in the Global Commons," remarks presented at the 2010 Global Commons Conference, Virginia Beach, Virginia, June 29, 2010.
5. Jeffrey E. Kline, "Maritime Security," in *Securing Freedom in the Global Commons*, Scott Jasper, ed. (Stanford, CA: Stanford University Press, 2009), 75–76.
6. A definition used by James T. Conway, Gary Roughhead, and Thad W. Allen, in "A Cooperative Strategy for 21st Century Seapower" (Washington, DC: Department of Defense, October 2007), 1.
7. Peter Avis, "Best Practices for Canadian Maritime Security: A Comparison of Three National Approaches," *Canadian Military Journal* 7, no. 4 (2008), www.journal.forces .gc.ca/vo7/no4/notice-avis-eng.asp.
8. Susan Page Hocevar, Gail Fann Thomas, and Erik Jansen, "Building Collaborative Capacity: An Innovative Strategy for Homeland Security Preparedness," in *Advances in Interdisciplinary Studies of Work Teams: Innovation through Collaboration*, Michael M. Beyerlein, Susan T. Beyerlein, and Douglas A. Kennedy, eds. (Oxford: Elsevier JAI Press, 2006), 12: 255–74.
9. Examples include Hocevar, Thomas, and Jansen, "Building Collaborative Capacity"; "The Global Maritime Partnership Initiative of CNO Mullen," *Defense Daily*, October 25, 2006, www.navy.mil/navydata/cno/mullen/DEFENSE_DAILY_25OCT06_ Global_Maritime_Partnership_Gaining_Steam_At_Home_And_With_Interna tional_Navies.pdf. Reported outcomes based on data presented at the Secure Trade in

the APEC Region Conference, *APEC Newsletter*, March 2004, www.apec.org/apec/enewsletter/march_vol2/onlinenewsb.html.

10. US Government Accountability Office, "Interagency Collaboration: Key Issues for Congressional Oversight of National Security Strategies, Organizations, Workforce and Information Sharing" (Washington, DC: Government Accountability Office, September 2009), www.gao.gov/new.items/d09904sp.pdf.

11. Hocevar, Thomas, and Jansen, "Building Collaborative Capacity"; Erik Jansen, Susan Page Hocevar, Rene G. Rendon, and Gail Fann Thomas, "Interorganizational Collaborative Capacity: Development of a Database to Refine Instrumentation and Explore Patterns" (Monterey, CA: Naval Postgraduate School, NPS-AM-08-148, November 24, 2008).

12. Jansen et al., "Interorganizational Collaborative Capacity," 1.

13. Ibid.

14. Gaye Christoffersen, "Japan and the East Asian Maritime Security Order: Prospects for Trilateral and Multilateral Cooperation," *Asian Perspective* 33, no. 3 (2009): 107–49.

15. Adapted from J. Galbraith, *Designing Organizations: An Executive Guide to Strategy, Structure and Process* (San Francisco, CA: Jossey-Bass, 2002).

16. Susan Page Hocevar, "Inter-Organizational Collaborative Capacity: A Conceptual Model and Measurement Tool," remarks presented at the 4th Annual Homeland Defense and Security Education Summit, Georgetown University, Washington, DC, February, 24–25, 2010, www.chds.us/resources/uapi/summit10/Track2/Hocevar-Inter-Organizational-Collaborative-Capacity-02-031510-01.pdf.

17. Avis, "Best Practices," 3.

18. Ibid.

19. Ibid., 6.

20. Ibid.

21. See Joshua Ho and Jan Chan, "Case Study: Ensuring Safety and Security in the Straits of Malacca and Singapore," unpublished paper (Monterey, CA: Naval Postgraduate School, 2010).

22. Sam Bateman, Joshua Ho, and Jan Chan, *Good Order at Sea in Southeast Asia* (Singapore: Nanyang Technological University, April 2009).

23. Ibid.

24. "Agence France Presse—Key Malacca Strait Route Not a War Risk: Industry" (London: International Institute of Strategic Studies, December 29, 2005), www.iiss.org/whats-new/iiss-in-the-press/press-coverage-2005/december-2005/key-malacca-strait-route-not-a-war-risk/; Yann-huei Song, "Regional Maritime Security Initiative (RMSI) and Enhancing Security in the Strait of Malacca: Littoral States' and Regional Responses," in *Maritime Security in the South China Sea: Regional Implications and International Cooperation*, Shicun Wu and Keyuan Zou, eds. (London: Ashgate, 2009), 109–34.

25. Ho and Chan, "Case Study."

26. Republic of Singapore, Ministry of Defence, "Factsheet: Milestones of Malacca Strait Patrols" (March 28, 2008), www.mindef.gov.sg/content/imindef/news_and_events/nr/2008/mar/28mar08_nr/28mar08_fs.print.html?Status=1.

27. Ho and Chan, "Case Study," 4.

28. Graham Gerard Ong and Joshua Ho, "Maritime Air Patrols: The New Weapon against Piracy in the Malacca Strait," *Institute of Defense and Strategic Studies Commentaries* 70 (2005), www.rsis.edu.sg/publications/Perspective/IDSS702005.pdf.

29. Ho and Chan, "Case Study," 4–6.

30. Joshua Ho, "Maritime Security in Southeast Asia" (Singapore: Institute of Defense and Strategic Studies, 2007).

31. Joshua Ho, "Enhancing Safety, Security, and Environmental Protection of the Straits of Malacca and Singapore: The Cooperative Mechanism," *Ocean Development and International Law* 40 (2009): 233–47.

32. Yoshiaki Ito, remarks presented at the International Maritime Bureau Conference on Piracy and Maritime Security, Kuala Lumpur, Malaysia, June 11, 2007, www.recaap .org/news/pdf/news/april07.pdf.

33. Joshua Ho, "Combating Piracy and Armed Robbery in Asia," *Marine Policy* 33 (2009): 432–34, www.mofa.go.jp/mofaj/gaiko/kaiyo/pdfs/kyotei_s.pdf.

34. ReCAAP website, www.recaap.org/index_home.html; Ho, "Combating Piracy."

35. Ho, "Combating Piracy."

36. Ibid.

37. Daisy R. Khalifa, "SeaHawk Milestone: DHS, Coast Guard Prepare to Move Forward with Port Security Command Centers," *Seapower* 52 (June 2009): 36–38, http://local host:51966/seapower/200906-offline2/index.html.

38. Teresa Anderson, "Holding the Line," *Security Management*, September 1, 2006, www .securitymanagement.com/print/1587. See also Antony Pate, Bruce Taylor, and Bruce Kubu, *Protecting America's Ports: Promising Practices* (Washington, DC: Police Executive Research Forum, November 20, 2007), www.ncjrs.gov/pdffiles1/nij/grants/221075.pdf; Stephen Metruck, "San Diego Joint Harbor Operations Center (JHOC)," *NDIA Homeland Security Symposium*, May 24, 2004, www.dtic.mil/ndia/2004homeland/2004home land.html.

39. Pate, Taylor, and Kubu, *Protecting America's Ports*.

40. Ibid.

41. Robert B. Watts, "Maritime Critical Infrastructure Protection: Multi-Agency Command and Control in an Asymmetric Environment," *Homeland Security Affairs* 1 (Fall 2005), www.hsaj.org/?fullarticle=1.2.3.

42. Stephen Metruck, "Leveraging People and Technology to Optimize Interagency Interoperability," *USCG Proceedings* 66 (Spring 2009): 78, www.uscg.mil/proceedings.

43. Ibid.

44. Briefing for congressional staffers, US Coast Guard Headquarters, San Diego, California, August 19, 2010.

45. Vincent B. Atkins, testimony before the Subcommittee on Homeland Security of the House Committee on Appropriations, 111th Cong., 2nd Sess., April 19, 2010, www .dhs.gov/ynews/testimony/testimony_1271690315007.shtm.

46. Metruck, "Leveraging People."

47. Pate, Taylor, and Kubu, *Protecting America's Ports*, 48.

48. Hocevar, "Inter-Organizational Collaborative Capacity"; Jansen et al., "Interorganizational Collaborative Capacity."

49. Ibid.

50. On the Maritime Organization and Africa, see "MOWCA update 2/10: Sub-Regional Coast Guard Network," www.mowca.org/new%20design/coast-guard-update0210. html; James Kraska and Brian Wilson, "Diplomatic Efforts against the Gulf of Aden Pirates," *Harvard International Review*, February 19, 2009, http://hir.harvard.edu/index .php?page=article&id=1822&p=1; see United Kingdom, Foreign and Commonwealth Office, "The International Response to Piracy," www.fco.gov.uk/en/global-issues/con flict-prevention/piracy/international-response; United States Department of State, "International Response: Contact Group on Piracy Off the Coast of Somalia," www.state .gov/t/pm/ppa/piracy/contactgroup/index.htm; "EU Reaches Agreement on Maritime Security," *Defence IQ Press*, November 11, 2009, www.defenceiq.com/article.cfm ?externalID=1606.

51. See chapter 4 in this volume, "The Maritime Commons and Military Power."
52. Sam J. Tangredi, "Sea Basing: Concept, Issues and Recommendations," *Naval War College Review* 64, no. 4 (2011): 28–41.
53. Mark E. Redden and Michael P. Hughes, "Global Commons and Domain Interrelationships: Time for a New Conceptual Framework?" *Strategic Forum* 259 (Washington, DC: National Defense University Press, October 2010), www.ndu.edu/inss.

CHAPTER 8

Assuring Joint
Operational Access

✧

PAUL S. GIARRA

The doctrine of joint operational access—getting forward, staying forward, and operating along secured lines of communication—is as expensive as it is critical.[1] Since World War II joint operational access has generated profound strategic, operational, and tactical advantages for the United States and its allies. Given current strategic and resource constraints on defense planning going forward, reconsidering its virtues, requirements, and costs is one of the more fundamental issues confronting military strategic planners.

Perhaps joint operational access has come to be taken for granted. Operating far forward emerged from the victories of World War II and was annealed by the exigencies of the Cold War. To be ready, victorious, and dominant meant to operate forward from beginning to end, every day, regardless of cost. Forward operations were synonymous with deterrence, reassurance, and immediate operational and enduring strategic advantage. As a doctrinal and cultural precept, the wisdom of expeditionary operations has become second nature.[2]

The end of the Cold War basically altered the nature of expeditionary operations. Suddenly it was not necessary to overcome geography to confront an enemy or fight to maintain a forward posture. Together with the fall of the Berlin Wall, any resistance to operational access collapsed. Although this was not the end of history or conflict, no threat was going to challenge the ability of the United States and its allies to project and sustain power in forward positions. As a result, warfighting took on a fundamentally different nature, defined by hider-finder competitions rather than by maneuver warfare and offense-defense correlations. Enemies went to ground because they could not compete on those terms: they reinvented the conduct of warfare in order to impose serious limitations on the traditional Western advantages of firepower, maneuver, and sensing.

ASYMMETRICAL CHALLENGES

Three developments with major strategic import came to the fore after the demise of symmetric competition. First, a pervasive form of globalization emerged in which envisioning, preserving, and defending the structure of the global commons and the access to them became a paramount security concern.[3] Second, the unprecedented openness and permeability of the commons, based on the conceptual ideal of universal access, had the unintended effect of making the entire global enterprise fragile and vulnerable to various state and nonstate actors, down to perversely motivated individuals. The systems in each domain became potential weapons. This development was brought home by the exploitation of the air domain on September 11, 2001. Third, national competition was revived. The emergence of China, the truculence of Iran, the calamity of North Korea, and the proliferation of nuclear weapons are the syndromes of this renaissance of nation-state warfare, with significant attendant challenges to joint operational access.

Until recently there has been scant consideration of the requirements for forward defense, joint operational access, and their relationship to national security. But these changes in the strategic environment raise serious questions about the unencumbered joint operational access that has predominated during the past two decades, and implications for the profound innate advantages offered by joint operational access. In particular, near-peer competitors or nonstate actors perceive that they can interfere with the forward operations by US and allied forces directly or by destabilizing the global commons. China and Iran have gone so far as to reveal how they propose to do so, touting new anti-access and area denial capabilities at the operational, strategic, and tactical levels of war, in each domain of the global commons.[4]

Reconsidering joint operational access raises a number of questions:

- What will be the purpose of joint operational access in the future? What does going and staying forward really mean?
- What are the implications for joint operational access of the emergence of a new concept of the global commons as an entity in itself rather than a medium of military operations? And if the commons are the fabric of globalization, should not they be protected under their own mandate?
- How should the concept of the security, defense, and preservation of the global commons as a fundamental military requirement be construed within the context of joint operational access? What are the implications for joint operational access of the commons as a discrete entity rather than a dimension of military operations?
- Why should joint operational access in, through, and from the global commons be taken for granted? Is achieving joint operational access by moving

forward, staying forward, and operating forward—largely in the global commons—an end in itself or in part necessitated by having to defend the commons in the first instance?

- How does the rise of peer and near-peer competitors challenge the American way of war? Is the prevailing assumption correct, that joint operational access in, through, and from the global commons is something perennially secured?

IN, THROUGH, AND FROM THE COMMONS

The global commons represent the current and future trading space of international security and stability.[5] If the commons are secured, then each and every nation can be secure. This judgment captures the implications of securing the global commons for military operations in general, and of joint operational access as a means to that end in particular. Today the commons encompass outer space, international waters and airspace, and cyberspace.[6] They are not under the control of any nation or group of nations but nevertheless are critical in providing access around the world.[7] Together they "constitute the fabric or connective tissue of the international system."[8]

Because the global commons are new conceptually, it is worthwhile, even if incomplete, to consider them in terms of the traditional maritime domain. The great powers that once controlled the high seas assured their strategic mobility and regional and global access. The Etruscans and Greeks intervened when and where they desired, and prevented enemies from doing the same. Those powers were capable of operating militarily in and between regions and, over time, globally, and preventing their opponents from doing so. Having the resources and organizational wherewithal to do so, and especially in more than one domain, defined greatness. Ancient history is replete with examples of the interdependence of land and sea warfare, with the battle of Thermopylae being the event that decided the outcome of civilization in the trans-regional Persian invasion of Greece.

During the late eighteenth and early nineteenth centuries, Britain commanded the oceans and contained Napoleonic designs to become economically dominant. As Admiral of the Fleet John Jervis remarked in 1801: "I do not say the Frenchman will not come; I say only that he will not come by sea." Conversely, Britain surrendered to the American colonists as the Royal Navy temporarily lost control of the seas in 1781 off the Virginia Capes. During the twentieth century, command of the maritime domain enabled power projection and military operations on a global scale, with Anglo-American sea power trumping the domination of Eurasia by rising hegemons. Practical command of the high seas passing from the Royal Navy to the US Navy in 1942 did not change the doctrinal relevance for geopolitical power in the maritime domain.

The lessons of maritime history are simplistic and one-dimensional when compared with the complex realities of the global commons. Until the end of the Cold War the commons, with the exception of cyberspace that had yet to emerge, were seen largely in military terms as domains through, in, and from which the United States and its allies could wield power, and not yet the fabric or connective tissue of a new world order to be defended as well as exploited.

COMMAND OF THE COMMONS

Doctrine on the global commons and its implications for political, economic, and military power are complicated by several factors. The emergence of three additional domains to be mastered, integrated, and defended makes securing the high seas appear simple by comparison. For instance, efforts by Giullo Douhet, Billy Mitchell, Hugh Trenchard, Hap Arnold, and Curtis LeMay created airpower doctrine during the early decades of aviation, but not for the air domain as a military concept. Similarly, treaties and other international arrangements during the Cold War hampered the development of space doctrine in practical terms, despite its growing influence on communications, commerce, trade, and military operations. The cyber domain, so new and so immediately pervasive, has only just begun to emerge as a military concept, although it is notably immature with respect to doctrine.

Moreover, the intricacies and transcendence of connections and relationships among the four domains that constitute the global commons further complicate the concept of securing freedom for the global enterprise in them, not least because doing so must be accomplished simultaneously. These linkages are so numerous that so far it has been difficult enough to conceive of them, let alone describe and understand them in detail.

Nevertheless, it is clear that even temporary loss of control in the commons can have serious implications. The loss of local control by the Royal Navy of the Virginia Capes and the approaches to the Chesapeake in the American Revolution had major operational consequences. Similarly, the consequences of loss of air control by the Royal Air Force over Britain would have been equally disastrous in 1940.

Because of the nature of the commons, which are explicitly designed for maximum access by global populations, the entry costs for disruptive operations are drastically reduced. This is true because nations have a fundamental interest in making the global commons accessible, which underlies the reality of globalization, and competitors and enemies have decided to exploit this apparently irreversible trend. They have learned that threatening the integrity of the commons does not involve expensive or complex operations, which formerly were exclusive capabilities of large nations. As a practical matter this implies that nonstate actors with low profiles can operate effectively alongside near-peer competitors and powerful nations by taking advantage of systemic infrastructure and organizational vulnerabilities, particularly in electronic and cyber networks. These developments have unhinged conventional definitions and calculations of deterrence and military power in the commons on the strategic, operational, and tactical levels of war.

Civilian and military enterprises operate side-by-side in each domain, dependent on access to and stability in the commons while becoming increasingly interdependent. In part a function of the civilianization of military operations for both supplies and functions, with each sphere interdependent and thereby vulnerable to one another, this interdependence is not well understood. It puts civil-military relationships in a new, more tangible perspective, and is a significant new factor underscoring the issue of what must be defended, where, and by whom.

Essential civil-military relations introduce systemic vulnerabilities, which previously were only associated with weapons of mass destruction. This means that intimidating vulnerabilities, inflated risks, severe temptations, and the benefits of preemption will create escalatory threats in the future for the global commons. This fragility applies to conflicts instigated by both peer and near-peer competitors in the traditional nuclear warfighting environment; to regional intervention from offshore; and to events caused by nonstate actors, groups, and even individuals.

Given the high level of infrastructure integration throughout the commons, and the ease of access to and enhanced ability to exploit its vulnerabilities, fragile indefensibility imparts exceptionally high risk for nations and organizations. Especially for nations (but not limited to them), this new escalation dynamic is particularly unstable. Because vulnerability is so high, and will remain so until physical and cyber infrastructures and systems can be more reasonably protected, nations must live with much higher levels of risk. Andrew Marshall of the Office of Net Assessment at the Pentagon and others have concluded that the systemic and societal—perhaps even civilization—damage that can be done by even a single individual has increased dramatically.[9]

A NEW AGE OF NATIONAL SECURITY

In doctrinal terms, these observations suggest that we are at the theoretical and doctrinal outset of a new age of national security, defense planning, and military operations. This is distinct from debates over large wars/small wars, peer-competition, counterterrorism/counterinsurgency, and hybrid warfare. Similar to the wrenching discontinuities in the early years of the Cold War, this new reality of the pervasive, integrated, accessible, and simultaneous concept of global commons means that they must be defended, and not just exploited. The national security agenda must take into account the security and defense of the commons for their own sake, not simply as an enabler for domain warfare (although that, too), because they are key to the entire global enterprise.

Doing so will affect every aspect of defense: warfighting theory and doctrine; strategic formulation; defense policy development; defense research and development; capability development; defense organization and national security reform; defense industrial relations; acquisition; training and education; and recruitment. In its infancy, thinking through and implementing the synthesizing global commons effort potentially compares with the striving for effective jointness in military operations, but will be even more complex.

The initial step in conceptualizing the global commons is recognizing its emerging reality, and then clearly defining the nature of the task of securing it. This thought leadership, begun by Michèle Flournoy, Abraham Denmark, James Mulvenon, Scott Jasper, Dick Bedford, and others must be accomplished in terms sufficiently practical for a subsequent process of national security enterprise review and revision. Completing this initial conceptual effort will provide a basis for determining the significance of contemporary joint operational access, which requires mutual agreement on what must be defended, why, where, by whom, and with what means.

CHALLENGING THE AMERICAN WAY OF WAR

An understanding of joint operational access must define a problem that is perceived but not yet sufficiently articulated domestically: Security competitors, at differing levels of effort and capability, are intent on denying the United States and its allies the operational access to the global commons battlefield. Competitors sense that they are at the leading edge of warfare. They have studied the American way of war: its preference for forward operations, its leveraging of great strategic depth, its dependence upon strategic sanctuaries from which to mount operations. They said they will keep us out of distant but crucial theaters by challenging our ability to get forward, and have told us how they propose to do so. They have also announced the development of area denial attack capabilities that will make it difficult to stay forward. Measures are already being developed and proliferated that make it difficult to operate forward.

Basically competitors are challenging the contemporary American way of war. By contrast the characteristics of the traditional American way of war are rooted in geography, history, and military doctrine, which have deep-seated national associations that are reinforced by a century of international successes. These characteristics exhibit the following imperatives:

- Insisting upon open access (traditionally in the maritime domain) to markets overseas, which has been a national priority since before the United States enforced free trade and political access with its first six heavy *Constitution*-class frigates.[10]

- Intervening when national interests are threatened, ranging from small wars in Central America; to the World War I, World War II, and Cold War strategy of containment over the last century; to the interventions in Afghanistan and Iraq.

- Leveraging the profound strategic depth of the nation with its vast oceans to the east and west and friendly neighbors to the north and south. This strategic depth is not only a great geostrategic advantage, but the conceptual motivating basis for expeditionary operations that take the fight to the enemy.

- Controlling and exploiting external lines of communication. This is a reflection in particular of the naval heritage of the United States, and a profound advantage of great maritime powers able to exploit the seas.

- Building and preserving an overwhelming defense industrial base, and protecting the sources of raw materials that fuel it.

- Closing with enemies and defeating them through direct and close combat. This characteristic emerged from the Civil War, enabled by strategic, operational, and tactical maneuver.

- Fighting as close as possible to the enemy homeland. This is the conceptual core of operational access: getting to the point of decision, as close to the enemy base of operations as possible; being able to stay on the point of decision for as long as necessary, often in the face of savage resistance; and projecting maximum military power from the point of decision to defeat an enemy. Seizing and holding forward a base is key to the traditional American way of war, one reason that the marine corps and airborne troops loom so large in US doctrine on strategic maneuver.

- Incorporating sanctuaries that are out of reach of the enemy into strategic, operational, and tactical plans. The proximity of sanctuaries to the battle has changed over time but not their significance; sanctuaries remain a strategic priority for commanders, and current force structure and doctrine largely rely on their availability.

- Preferring short-range tactical firepower that assumes and is designed around the foregoing positions of strategic, operational, and tactical advantage.

- Imposing unacceptable attrition upon enemies, while preserving forces through the combination of astute battle commanders; overwhelming technological and material superiority; and the substitution of maneuver and firepower for manpower.

- Employing aerial bombardment and naval interdiction as key elements of the American way of war.

- Committing total national strength to winning total wars, including the concept and doctrine of escalation dominance.

THE TRADITIONAL AMERICAN WAY OF WAR

During the Cold War the elements of the traditional American way of war, re-inforced by the success of World War II, played significant roles in the containment and eventual collapse of the Soviet Union. Not all elements of US military doctrine remained in constant balance throughout those decades. When this imbalance occurred by internal miscues, lack of action, or Soviet strategy, the balance shifted to the detriment of the United States. But that situation was self-correcting because the Soviets were symmetric adversaries striving for a reciprocal balance.

When all elements of national security doctrine were accounted for and thereby in balance, the cumulative strategic effect on the Soviet Union was significant. This occurred in the 1980s when the US Navy maritime strategy was applied to maximum effect; when powerful land forces were closely integrated with air forces and fixed the Soviets in position in Central Europe; when the United States escalated horizontally; when strong alliances provided cascading benefits; and when technological surprise destabilized the Soviet military.

THE CONTEMPORARY AMERICAN WAY OF WAR

With the eclipse of the Soviet Union several influences diminished the doctrinal balance in the traditional American way of war. Because the United States no longer had a symmetric peer competitor, and in effect no rationale for the full panoply of major combat operations, it was no longer necessary to prepare for combat operations to fight in order to go forward or stay forward. Unfettered power projection became the *new* American way of war, and it was no longer self-correcting.

As a result, the US military de-emphasized en route and forward base combat operations. The doctrine and capabilities necessary for such warfighting tasks atrophied, and primary attention went to the application of power from secure forward positions. Strategic mobility became taken for granted, while enabling functions such as antisubmarine warfare atrophied. Among other things, this hyper-emphasis on power projection resulted in a focus on much shorter-range combat, from intrinsically secure positions, at the task force level. Consequently, the sort of command and control and doctrinal capabilities required for intertheater and strategic-depth warfare that were once familiar to practitioners of the traditional American way of war have eroded. This means that we cannot even *see* the need for large-scale combat operations such as countering anti-access and area denial warfare: except episodically, no commander has been assigned to take charge of that level of effort.

Potential adversaries, confronted by a seemingly unrestrained superpower, carefully studied the American way of war and came to understand its key doctrinal tenets of strategic depth: getting forward, staying forward, and fighting forward. They recognized the vulnerability, and in some cases the frailty, of US and allied lines of communication, which absent a perceived threat were no longer a priority. These competitors decided to challenge declining US naval power that would have been spread thin by global missions even if naval force levels had not declined, including asymmetric challenges such as Chinese shore-based antiship ballistic missiles (ASBMs) and Iranian swarm formations. They also recognized that land attack ballistic and cruise missiles could reduce US and allied forces and forward basing without developing first-rate, symmetric air combat assets. Moreover, the adversaries employed concealment and deception in urban and other terrain that precluded the advantages of command and control as well as intelligence, surveillance, and reconnaissance. They also adopted command and control techniques and distributed fires that used crude but effective improvised explosive devices to achieve maximum psychological effect.

Over the last two decades China has taken the lead in anti-access and area denial systems.[11] Beijing has been developing the doctrine and capabilities virtually in public to interrupt the flow of forces and reduce en route bases and forces along strategic lines of communication as well as defeat forward forces in detail.[12] Beijing has embarked on strategic competition with a theater campaign based on anti-access and area denial doctrine and capabilities. Tehran is pursuing a similar course by developing capabilities for asymmetric warfare intended to put US and allied forces at risk in the Arabian Gulf.

THE DEVELOPING OPERATIONAL ENVIRONMENT

Even more than the chaotic international political environment, this developing operational environment as redefined by adversaries is meant to give pause to allied commanders, and it is having that effect through its consciously public articulation in a persistent psychological operations campaign. Although many have been holding out hope for more cooperative and constructive outcomes, China is emerging as a strategic competitor instead of as a responsible stakeholder, essentially challenging current doctrine.[13] Beijing intends to exploit vulnerabilities apparent in the contemporary American way of war. Likewise, Tehran has fortified its maritime approaches, behind which it is building a nuclear arsenal, exemplifying and underscoring the dangers of continued nuclear proliferation. The net effect has been to underscore the imperatives for the United States of the traditionally balanced American way of war. These new realities will not improve with age: The doctrines, techniques, and capabilities being developed in China, Iran, North Korea, Iraq, and Russia have proliferated and will continue to do so, combining against US and allied troops wherever they deploy.

The recent *Quadrennial Defense Review Report* refers to the mounting threat posed by anti-access and area denial capabilities. Iran, North Korea, and even Hezbollah qualify in this regard. However, perhaps most alarming is the situation in China, which has been actively "developing and fielding large numbers of advanced medium-range ballistic and cruise missiles, new attack submarines equipped with advanced weapons, increasingly capable long-range air defense systems, electronic warfare and computer network attack capabilities, advanced fighter aircraft, and counter-space systems."[14] These advances constitute an impressive array of anti-access and area denial capabilities.

Nevertheless, the other primary sources of guidance for US planners—the *National Security Strategy, National Defense Strategy, National Military Strategy,* and *Capstone Concept for Joint Operations*—treat critical issues of getting forward, staying forward, and fighting forward only tangentially. They seem to presume that getting and staying forward are givens, and that fighting forward is an exercise in precision fires and coordinating land combat from secure enclaves.

THE STRATEGIC TRIANGLE

Today, military planners face a strategic triangle with the following points: first, what has been taken for granted; second, en route and forward-deployed infrastructure realities; and third, how other actors exploit the situation. While the salient details of these three consequential realities have not sufficiently impressed the authors of the planning documents highlighted above, there are many opportunities in the unclassified literature to examine the writing and thinking of Chinese and Iranians on these subjects, and a rich store of American analysis in response.

Assumptions that take for granted that access will be available—and that requirements for doctrinal, technological, and capability enhancements all concentrate on the forward edge of the battle area—are deeply rooted in current thinking. This assumes a shrinking of the battle space, even if the maneuver space remains virtually global. In fact, potential adversaries are enlarging the battle space by advancing into previously sacrosanct strategic and operational rear areas.

When not totally ignored, it is presumed that en route and forward deployed infrastructure is robust and defensible, even if it needs to be defended in the first place. If that is true, as US Transportation Command contends, that sometimes there are multiple routes forward, then maintaining that advantage requires each route to be sustainable, sustained, and defensible. Furthermore, this infrastructure has numerous nodes that, if they were not single points of failure, would disrupt or unhinge forward-deployed operations and deployments themselves if they were lost.[15] The reality is that numerous austere forward-operating bases and staging locations make sense only when an opponent has not ranged and targeted them.

Adversaries talk openly of making forward deployment and operations more difficult and more expensive. Their careful study of the traditional and contemporary American ways of war has highlighted the dependence of Western military organization on both operational sanctuary and freedom of maneuver. The same adversaries understand the consequences of not challenging military forward deployment and operations by US and allied forces. They aspire to strip away the inherent but presently unbalanced and fragile advantages of the American way of war.

MORE THAN DOCTRINE

The foregoing challenge to the American way of war means that the Pentagon can no longer plan for uninterrupted forward deployment and forward operations without significant intervention at all points on the strategic planning triangle. Thinking, active-minded, resourceful, and resource-rich opponents simply will not allow this luxury. The ability to get forward, stay forward, and operate forward is fundamental to assuring joint operational access, and that ability will become a major combat operation itself.

This is more than a doctrinal debate. Existing anti-access and area denial capabilities such as ballistic and cruise missiles, sophisticated air defense systems, swarm formations, and diesel submarines are proliferating. New anti-access and area denial Assassin's Mace capabilities are being developed, such as cyber warfare, electronic warfare, and antiship ballistic missiles. In fact, the single most notable aspect of the new joint operating environment will be the density of both anti-access and area denial defenses in a geostrategically enlarged battle space.

Fortunately there are various precedents from the last century that planners, commanders, and national leaders can review. A series of twentieth-century enemies attempted to deny strategic and operational military access to the United States and its allies. They were defeated or contained through a combination of strategic maneuver and defense in depth, fighting to preserve global strategic mobility, enabling alliances, industrial capacity, and technological superiority. Such advantages still largely exist. Artfully restored and combined, they can provide answers to anti-access and area denial threats. First, however, we have to see the problem and elevate operational access planning to a new strategic context.

DOCTRINAL AND CAPABILITY REQUIREMENTS

There are numerous challenges to the development of doctrine for joint operational access. First of all, the concept must not fall back on current strategic pronouncements. The last useful strategic planning relevant to joint operational access under modern conditions was conducted in the 1980s, in the context of the Cold War, thirty years on from foundational post–World War II planning. Before the 1950s, the period from the Washington Naval Conference until Pearl Harbor was rich in relevant and instructive strategic planning. The book *War Plan Orange* by Edward S. Miller has detailed the range (forty years) and the scale (total war) of planning during that period.[16] National-level guidance thus far has not achieved a strategic renaissance in the traditional American way of war or established the planning requirements for a balanced force and operational posture assured of winning in contested environments.

THE fielding of capabilities for implementation of a Joint Operational Access Concept requires making important choices.[17] Today, adversaries assert they are challenging the approach to military operations preferred by the United States and its allies, namely, the contemporary American way of war that assumes access to and the security of forward sanctuaries. In fact, they are provoking the reconsideration of traditional balanced forces that are sufficient to fight forward, stay forward, and operate forward while exploiting the profound geostrategic advantages of global mobility. Moreover, such forces assume new conceptual and operational responsibilities for assuring access to the global commons.

NOTES

This chapter benefited from conversations with colleagues at the Naval Postgraduate School, especially Scott Jasper and Scott Moreland, from my collaboration with Dick Bedford at Allied Command Transformation, and from an ongoing dialogue with partners involved in developing the Joint Operational Access Concept at the Joint Forces Command.

1. These lines include command and control, supply, and public and alliance relations.
2. North Atlantic Treaty Organization, "Strategic Concept for the Defense and Security of the Members of the North Atlantic Treaty Organization," November 20, 2010, www .nato.int.
3. See Scott Jasper, ed., *Securing Freedom in the Global Commons* (Stanford, CA: Stanford University Press, 2010). See also Mark A. Barrett, Dick Bedford, Elizabeth Skinner, and Eva Vergles, "Assured Access to the Global Commons" (Norfolk, VA: Allied Command Transformation, April 2011).
4. Andrew F. Krepinevich, "Why AirSea Battle?" (Washington, DC: Center for Strategic and Budgetary Assessments, 2010), 7–11.
5. See Dick Bedford and Paul S. Giarra, "Securing the Global Commons," *RUSI Journal* 155 (October–November 2010): 18–23.

6. United States Department of Defense, *The National Defense Strategy of the United States of America* (Washington, DC: Office of the Secretary of Defense, March 2005), 13.

7. Barry R. Posen, "Command of the Commons: The Military Foundation of US Hegemony," *International Security* 28 (Summer 2003): 5–46.

8. Michèle A. Flournoy and Shawn Brimley, "The Contested Commons," *Proceedings* 135 (July 2009): 17.

9. Roger C. Molander, Peter A. Wilson, and Robert H. Anderson, "US Strategic Vulnerabilities: Threats against Society," in *Strategic Appraisal: The Changing Role of Information in Warfare*, Zalmay Khalilzad and John P. White, eds. (Santa Monica, CA: Rand Corporation, 1999), 253–56.

10. On this issue, see James Bradford, "Defending US Maritime Commerce in Peacetime from 1794 to Today," *Footnotes* (Foreign Policy Research Institute) 15 (September 2010), www.fpri.org/footnotes/1506.201009.bradford.usmaritimecommerce.html.

11. See Jason E. Bruzdzinski, "Military Operations Research in the People's Republic of China: The Influences of Culture, 'Speculative Philosophy' and Quantitative Analysis on Chinese Military Assessments" (McLean, VA: Mitre Corporation, June 2007). For some time bloggers in China have been covering the development of ASBMs.

12. Robert F. Willard, testimony before the House Armed Services Committee, 111th Cong., 2nd Sess., March 23, 2010; Paul S. Giarra, "A Chinese Anti-Ship Ballistic Missile: Implications for the US Navy," in *Chinese Aerospace Power: Evolving Maritime Roles*, Andrew S. Erickson and Lyle J. Goldstein, eds. (Annapolis, MD: Naval Institute Press, 2011), 359–74; Mark A. Stokes and Ian Easton, "Evolving Aerospace Trends in the Asia-Pacific Region" (Arlington, VA: Project 2049 Institute, May 27, 2010), aerospace_trends_asia_pacific_region_stokes_easton.pdf; Mark A. Stokes, "China's Evolving Conventional Strategic Strike Capability: The Anti-Ship Ballistic Missile Challenge to US Maritime Operations in the Western Pacific and Beyond" (Arlington, VA: Project 2049 Institute, September 14, 2009); Wendell Minnick, "China Builds First Anti-Ship Ballistic Missile Base?" *Defense News*, August 5, 2010, www.defensenews.com/story.php?i=4735654.

13. "The Soviet Union never successfully 'Finlandized' Europe. But the threat has returned—from China, which is now trying to do the same in the Western Pacific. . . . China's goal is to stop the United States from protecting its longstanding interests in the region—and to draw Washington's democratic allies and partners (such as Japan, South Korea and Taiwan) into its orbit." Andrew F. Krepinevich, "China's 'Finlandization' Strategy in the Pacific," *Wall Street Journal*, September 11, 2010.

14. United States Department of Defense, *Quadrennial Defense Review Report* (Washington, DC: Office of the Secretary of Defense, February 2010), 31, www.defense.gov/qdr/QDR%20as%20of%2026JAN10%200700.pdf.

15. Michelle D. Johnson, testimony before the Subcommittee on Air and Land Forces, House Armed Services Committee, 111th Cong., 2nd Sess., April 28, 2010, www.airforce-magazine.com/SiteCollectionDocuments/Testimony/2010%20docs/042810.JohnsonM.pdf.

16. Edward S. Miller, *War Plan Orange: The US Strategy to Defeat Japan, 1897–1945* (Annapolis, MD: Naval Institute Press, 1991).

17. United States Department of Defense, *Joint Operational Access Concept (JOAC)* (Washington, DC: Office of the Chairman, Joint Chiefs of Staff, January 17, 2012), 33–36.

CHAPTER 9

Shaping the Outer Space and Cyberspace Environments

✧

MARC J. BERKOWITZ

> The space and cyberspace capabilities that power our daily lives
> and military operations are vulnerable to disruption and attack.
> —*National Security Strategy*

The international security environment is uncertain, dynamic, complex, and
dangerous. This is due in part to the emergence of outer space and cyberspace as new arenas of competition and conflict. In the twenty-first century the
United States and its allies must be able to deter and, if necessary, to fight and win
wars in multiple domains (land, sea, air, space, and cyber) and modalities (irregular, conventional, and nuclear).[1]

The bipolar structure that characterized international relations during most of
the last century was transformed by dramatic and disruptive changes in the aftermath of the Cold War. Today there is a diffusion of political, military, and economic power in the international system. This structural shift is altering power
relationships and the dynamics of international politics.

Although the changed security environment eased tension between the United
States and Russia, it unleashed latent forces of instability around the world. Absent
the restraints imposed by the superpowers and their associated blocs, cautious of
miscalculations that might ignite the powder trail to global thermonuclear war,
state and nonstate actors are more assertive in pursuing their interests. Political,
sociocultural, economic, and other antagonisms have reemerged to fuel crisis and
conflict.

Conflict remains a prominent feature of international relations. In addition to
traditional challenges, asymmetric threats now emanate from subnational groups

in failed states and ungoverned areas as well as regional powers exploiting modern technology. In an era of hybrid, multimodal warfare involving national and transnational actors, nations must be prepared to address the challenges to security in the space and cyber domains.[2]

This chapter examines how to shape the space and cyber environments. It discusses the terms of art, the interdependency between space and cyber, and threats to space and cyberspace as domains of the global commons. Finally, it proposes a comprehensive, whole-of-nations approach to protect and execute operations in the space and cyber domains.

LEXICON

Outer space and cyberspace are separate and distinct domains with unique characteristics. They are cross-cutting domains that utilize the electromagnetic spectrum. Space and cyberspace encompass the terrestrial mediums of land, sea, and air. They potentially flank any terrestrial battlefield.

Outer space exists in the void beyond the atmosphere of the earth and other celestial bodies. The space environment is defined as "the environment corresponding to the space domain, where electromagnetic radiation, charged particles, and electric and magnetic fields are the dominant physical influences, and that encompasses the earth's ionosphere and magnetosphere, interplanetary space, and the solar atmosphere."[3] It includes space systems that consist of spacecraft; mission packages; ground stations; data links among spacecraft, mission, or user terminals; launch systems; and directly related supporting infrastructure for space surveillance, battle management, and command and control.[4]

Cyberspace is described as the "global domain within the information environment consisting of the interdependent network of information technology infrastructures."[5] The information environment is composed of the "aggregate of individuals, organizations, and systems that collect, process, disseminate, or act on information."[6] It includes the Internet, telecommunication networks, computer systems, and embedded processors and controllers.[7]

As an operational medium, space is characterized by global perspective, reach, speed, and persistence. The cyber medium is characterized by global connectivity, ubiquity, and mobility. In contrast to outer space and other natural (land, sea, air) domains, cyberspace is a human-made domain. Although some orbits in near-earth space are crowded, the majority of the environment is devoid of activity. Cyberspace is a dense, constantly changing environment by comparison.

There are also significant differences in the cost of entry to access and operate in the space and cyber domains. Expensive launch vehicles and ranges, ground control systems, and satellites are required to deliver payloads into space and operate on-orbit. Anyone with an inexpensive computer and wireless connections can access the cyber domain. Despite their differences, space and cyberspace are interdependent domains unconstrained by political limits or geographic boundaries.[8]

SPACE AND CYBERSPACE INTERDEPENDENCY

Our economy, society, and way of life rely on access to and use of space and cyberspace. We rely and, in some cases, depend upon space and cyber capabilities to conduct diplomatic, law enforcement, emergency response, homeland security, intelligence, and defense activities. Consequently, unimpeded access to and freedom of operations in the space and cyber domains are vital national interests.

Space and cyberspace are used for commerce, trade, and other purposes to the benefit of humanity. Like the high seas or international airspace, they are a shared resource typically outside the sovereignty or jurisdiction of any nation. Collectively these areas known as the commons are part of the underlying foundation of the international system of commerce, communications, and governance.

Moreover, space and cyberspace are interconnected domains. The nexus is information. Space and cyberspace are important conduits for the free flow of information, finance, commerce, and trade around the world. Information and knowledge are now the engines of economic prosperity and military strength.

The global knowledge-based economy depends as much on information lines of communication through space and cyberspace as on the transportation lines across oceans and continents. In the past, national security interests focused on assuring the availability of natural resources to power an industrial economy. In the future, security interests will increasingly focus on accessing and assuring the free flow of information.

Space and cyberspace are integral to global, national, and defense information infrastructures. Space and cyber capabilities collect, generate, and relay information around the world as well as control physical assets in nearly every sector of critical infrastructure including energy, finance, transportation, and telecommunications. The space and cyber lines of communication are extensions of our homeland linked to our centers of gravity. Moreover, space and cyber assets enable all elements of national power.

Space and cyberspace are mediums—like land, sea, and air—within which military operations and intelligence activities are conducted to achieve national security objectives. Indeed, space and cyber capabilities provide a comparative security advantage. Command, control, communications, computers, intelligence, surveillance, and reconnaissance (C4ISR) assets operating in space and cyberspace support the execution of defense strategy and joint doctrine. They are advanced technology force multipliers that increase the operational effectiveness of our military forces.

The global access, speed, and precision delivered by space and cyber capabilities enable information and decision superiority. The ability to sense, comprehend, and act first provides the joint force with the ability to make informed decisions faster than an enemy. The ability to create such effects is a foundation of Western military operational style. Formations of smaller, dispersed forces can maneuver in nonlinear operations, synchronize actions, and mass coercive effects against the enemy in large part because of space and cyber capabilities.

SPACE AND CYBER THREATS

The space and cyberspace domains are increasingly congested, competitive, and contested. The number of actors capable of launching payloads into outer space and/or operating satellite systems as well as Internet protocol addresses in cyberspace has grown exponentially. Concurrently, the amount of spacecraft and debris on-orbit has created congestion around the earth that increases the risk of collisions. There are more than 21,000 objects in the space catalog maintained by US Strategic Command and over 1,100 active systems on-orbit.[9]

Although nations compete for prestige and power through space and cyber activities, commercial enterprises compete to generate wealth. There is also a growing competition over scarce space and cyber resources. This includes competition for positions in geosynchronous orbit and allocations of radio-frequency spectrum.

Moreover, foreign nations and subnational entities are pursuing counterspace and computer network attack capabilities to deceive, disrupt, deny, degrade, and destroy space and cyber systems. Such weapons are proliferating around the world through indigenous development, transfers of goods and services, and transnational collaboration.

Space and cyber assets are held at risk. They are targets of purposeful interference by both state and nonstate actors. Satellite communications as well as positioning, navigation, and timing have been jammed in peacetime and wartime. Computers and networks are constantly being probed, exploited, and infected with malicious software. Many incidents of interference in space and intrusion in cyberspace have been reported (see table 9.1).[10]

Threats to national security in space and cyberspace have become more obvious in recent years.[11] Interference with satellite operations is occurring with greater frequency. The information technology infrastructure has experienced intrusion, exploitation, and attack by criminals, terrorists, and nations.

Attacks on space and cyber assets can be accomplished remotely (for example, by botnets), inexpensively, and anonymously.[12] Anonymity, of course, makes attribution of the origin of the attack very difficult. Space and cyber attacks can be mounted instantaneously, prosecuted at the speed of light, with little or no

Table 9.1 Space and Cyberspace Incidents

Space	Cyber
1993 Indonesia jammed Tongasat over a dispute on geosynchronous orbital slot	2007 Russia distributed denial of service attack on Estonia
2002 Falun Gong hijacked Apstar television signals	2008 Russia emplaced malicious software in US Department of Defense networks via a thumb drive
2003 Iraq jammed global positioning systems during Operation Iraqi Freedom	2008 Russia denial of service attack on Georgia
2003 Iran jammed Telstar transmissions	2009 Russia denial of service attack on Kyrgyzstan
2005 Libya jammed Telstar transmissions	2009 Russia and China placed malware in the US electric power grid
2006 China lased US reconnaissance satellite	2010 China hacked Google after the company threatened to leave the country over censorship of its search results
2007 China tested direct-ascent antisatellite	2010 China rerouted both US and foreign Internet traffic through China for eighteen minutes
2010 Iran jammed Eutelsat transmissions	2010 US Department of Defense networks were probed 250,000 times per hour
2010 North Korea jammed global positioning system	2010 Stuxnet worm attacked Iranian nuclear program

warning. As US Deputy Secretary of Defense William Lynn has observed, "cyber is also attractive to our adversaries because it is hard to identify the origin of an attack. A keystroke travels twice around the world in 300 milliseconds. But the forensics necessary to identify an attacker may take months."[13]

Space and cyber attacks can have devastating effects that could impact an entire nation or region. Their effects can propagate rapidly with global implications. The speed and global reach of such attacks greatly compress decision cycles and stress laws, policies, and procedures designed for less demanding times.

In particular, cyber attacks pose a dangerous threat to space systems. Intrusion, exploitation, denial of service, corruption, and manipulation of data and information can counter the operational utility of a space system. An adversary will target the weakest node in the network such as the supply chain, supporting infrastructure, or telemetry, tracking, and commanding subsystem.

Hostile acts against space and cyber assets can influence perceptions; corrupt, disrupt, or usurp decision making; and create intended or unintended effects on a cascading, global scale. Such effects may occur at an exponentially faster pace than ever experienced, endure for very long periods of time, and inflict large-scale collateral damage on nonbelligerents. In an increasingly interconnected world, an attack on the space or cyber networks of one nation can be an attack on all nations.

Allied dependence on space and cyber capabilities creates asymmetry of value compared to potential adversaries that are less reliant on them for mission-critical purposes. Dependence on vulnerable space and cyber assets is provocative. It may lead to miscalculations about our political will and provide incentives for adversaries to threaten or attack such capabilities in crisis or conflict with adverse consequences for deterrence and escalation control.[14]

Counterspace and computer network attack capabilities pose serious threats to national interests in space and cyberspace. An adversary may attack space or cyber assets as part of an anti-access or area denial strategy involving either traditional or hybrid modes of warfare.[15] The objective of such aggression could be to undermine political will, societal cohesion, and morale; harm economic vitality; counter intelligence capabilities; and reduce combat effectiveness of military forces.

COMPREHENSIVE APPROACH

The nature of the space and cyber domains necessitates a holistic approach to address security challenges. This approach would utilize all elements— diplomatic, informational, military, and economic—of national power to create whole-of-government solutions to protect space and cyber systems, support infrastructure, and operations.[16]

Of course, military or hard power will be an essential tool to protect and defend the space and cyber domains. However, military power alone may be too blunt an instrument to deal with all of the threats to space and cyber security. The right mix of soft and hard power must be blended into smart power that can be tailored to solve problems endangering the space and cyber domains.

Leveraging and synchronizing all instruments of statecraft would improve the ability to shape the space and cyberspace environments and enhance deterrence, and if deterrence fails, to control escalation and terminate conflict on favorable terms. A whole-of-government approach would generate greater agility and versatility to deal with the complexity and speed of a crisis or conflict in the space and cyber domains. It would empower all of the pertinent elements of the government and private sector to ready resources, deter or withstand attack, and provide consequence management, reconstitution, and recovery. The commander of US Cyber Command remarked that defense relies "on the shared efforts of agencies, industry, allies, and mission partners who watch their own networks for problems that could affect all."[17]

The United States should work in concert with its allies, coalition partners, and friends in the international community when it can, or independently when it must, to advance and protect its interests in space and cyberspace. Consequently, the whole-of-government approach should be extended to a whole-of-nations approach. This would bring the resources and power of many nations and international partners to bear on the challenges of space and cyber security.

Such an approach will require cooperation and partnerships with allies and friends based on the tangible, mutual benefit of achieving shared objectives. Purposeful interference or hostile acts against space and cyber systems demand a coordinated response from governments, the private sector, and the international community. The United States should be positioned to ensure such a response by taking the lead in creating a mutual security framework for space and cyberspace.

DIPLOMACY, DETERRENCE, AND REASSURANCE

The practice and art of diplomacy are integral to developing a comprehensive approach. Skillful communications and management of relations among members of the international community are essential to protecting space and cyberspace. Both state and nonstate actors should be persuaded to align around a shared interest in acting responsibly to sustain the space and cyber environments for the benefit of humanity.

Developments in cyberspace have arrived at a point that is comparable to the advent of the space age. US leadership, reinforced by precedents of customary international law established by operational behavior in the medium, helped to shape the extant international legal regime for space. Similar leadership now is needed to increase the number of adherents to existing treaties and agreements, evolve the regime to address the growth of commercial and international space activities, and create an international cyber legal regime.

The United States is a party to multilateral treaties and international agreements that provide basic principles on governing the exploration and use of space that include the following:

- All states have the right to explore and use space.
- Space is not subject to appropriation by claim of sovereignty, use, or occupation.
- International law applies to space.

- Space is to be used only for peaceful purposes.
- States must settle disputes by peaceful means and not threaten or use force against the territorial integrity or political independence of another state.
- States have an inherent right to individual and collective self-defense.
- States retain jurisdiction and control over their space objects, are responsible for regulating their citizens' space activities, and are liable for damage caused to another state's space object.[18]

In addition, the United States is an adherent to bilateral and multilateral treaties and agreements that establish prohibitions and limitations on certain military space activities. These constraints include the following:

- Nuclear and other weapons of mass destruction may not be placed into orbit, installed on celestial bodies, or stationed in space.
- Detonations of nuclear weapons in space are prohibited.
- Testing any kind of weapons, establishing military bases, and conducting military maneuvers on celestial bodies are prohibited.
- Interference with national technical means of verifying compliance with strategic arms reduction treaties is prohibited.[19]

Several of the space principles clearly are worth considering as to whether they might be useful for cyberspace. Although it might be desirable to prohibit the deployment, testing, and use of weapons of mass effect in cyberspace, it is not clear that such constraints are feasible. The history of space arms control may be instructive in this regard.

Comprehensive and limited measures to ban or restrict the deployment, testing, and use of antisatellite (ASAT) weapons were examined by the United States and the Soviet Union in arms control negotiations during the Cold War. Neither the ASAT Talks nor the Defense and Space Talks produced an agreement. US administrations of both political parties rejected space arms control proposals on the basis that they were not verifiable, equitable, effective, or compatible with the security interests of the United States and its allies.[20]

Nonetheless, nations including Canada, France, Russia, and China have advocated new space arms control measures at the United Nations. For instance, in 2008 the Russians and Chinese proposed a draft Treaty on the Prevention of the Placement of Weapons in Outer Space, the Threat or Use of Force against Outer Space Objects.[21] However, such measures are flawed by problems of definition, commonality between civilian and military technologies, information disclosure, verification, and enforcement.

Consequently, collateral measures that build on the body of practical experience and laws regulating the orderly use of space and cyberspace offer a more pragmatic and effective diplomatic focus.[22] These measures might include transparency and confidence-building measures (TCBMs) that establish rules of the road, codes of conduct, or procedures for dealing with incidents that specify certain rules for space or cyber operations.[23] Such measures would aim to reduce the prospect of operational mishaps or misunderstandings arising from instances where apparently provocative or threatening actions are observed but not readily explained. They also could be constructed to enable verification and increase the effectiveness of unilateral space or cyber asset survivability measures.

The United States and its allies should reinforce existing, and establish new, international norms of acceptable space and cyberspace behavior. Such norms should encourage respect, safety, and order for the global, networked domains of space and cyberspace. Norms should facilitate information sharing and increase transparency to reduce misperceptions arising from provocative or ambiguous behaviors. In particular, attention should be focused on TCBMs for environmental preservation and enhanced operational safety given the growth of commercial and international activity. With respect to the space environment, for example, this includes collision avoidance, orbital debris mitigation, and noninterference by radio-frequency emissions and laser illuminations.

Reducing mishaps, misperceptions, and misunderstanding by regulating the orderly use of space and cyberspace will help draw clearer distinctions between acceptable, nonaggressive behaviors and unacceptable, aggressive behaviors in space and cyberspace. US and alliance red lines or zones, thresholds, and triggers for defensive actions will be geared to such aggressive behaviors that are considered hostile intentions or actions. Diplomacy thus will help establish the conditions necessary for effective deterrence.

Deterrence involves threatening the use of force to persuade an adversary not to behave or cease behaving in an undesirable way. For threats of deterrence (either punishment or denial) to be effective, they must be credible. Threats must be backed by political will and the military means to enforce the threatened consequence. Deterrence should work when an adversary believes the costs of aggression will outweigh the risks. Deterrence will not work, however, if the adversary misunderstands or is unconvinced of the threat's credibility.[24]

Deterrence is a state of mind that depends upon the stakes of the conflict and an adversary's risk calculus. Despite America's apparent successful reliance on the threat of nuclear retaliation to contain Soviet power and influence during the Cold War, deterrence is an inherently uncertain psychological proposition. History is replete with instances where deterrence failed or failed to apply.[25] A madman, religious zealot, or terrorist could be irrational and beyond deterrence.

Deterrence based on the threat of retaliation may be difficult to apply in the space and cyber domains because of the asymmetry of value and difficulty of attribution. In outer space, attributing the origin of an attack because it is a remote and harsh environment can be complicated by naturally occurring sources of interference, technical anomalies, mechanical failures, or inadvertent collisions of space objects. Similarly, it may take months of forensic work to identify the perpetrator of a cyber attack. Deterrence based on denial of benefit thus may be the more credible and effective approach.

Diplomacy is also an essential tool for reassuring America's allies and international partners of our will, resolve, and capability to support our foreign policy and defense commitments in peace, crisis, and war. Whereas deterrence involves the adversary, reassurance is focused on allies and friends. Such reassurance is required to reinforce the alliances and coalitions America relies upon to underpin our prosperity and security. Given the relationship between nuclear deterrence operations and C4ISR assets in space and cyberspace, reassurance is integral to the functioning of extended deterrence.

Even after the onset of hostilities, diplomacy and strategic communications must be employed and synchronized with other lines of operations to sustain the political cohesion of an alliance or coalition and win the battle for world opinion that is a precondition for overall success. In a space and cyber conflict where global effects can directly impact the lives of people around the world, public international diplomacy and strategic communications will be as important as information operations and other military capabilities.

One can hope that the prospect of despoiling space with thousands of pieces of debris that will remain in the earth's orbit for a millennium or unleashing self-replicating malicious code that infects cyberspace could provide restraints equivalent to the horrors of thermonuclear war. However, hope is not a strategy. Prudent defense and security planners should recognize that threats of diplomatic isolation, economic sanctions, military responses-in-kind, and even escalatory military actions within the space and cyber domains may not be sufficient to persuade an adversary against aggression. Consequently, the comprehensive approach must include hard-power instruments of statecraft for passive and active defense as well as vertical and horizontal cross-domain escalation.

DYNAMIC, MULTILAYERED, DEFENSE-IN-DEPTH STRATEGY

A dynamic, multilayered, defense-in-depth strategy is a key aspect of the comprehensive approach. Collective, mutual, or individual self-defense measures are necessary to ensure that hostile actions by nations, subnational entities, or individuals cannot prevent either access to or use of space or cyberspace. Self-defense measures should seek to deny an adversary the benefit of hostile acts and/or inflict punishment for aggression.

The strategy should be based on a theory of victory (and war termination) for conflict in the space and cyber domains. It should address the relationships among deterrence, dissuasion, passive and active defenses, and offensive measures. The strategy should link ends, ways, and means to protect the space and cyber assets the United States and its allies own, operate, or employ.

The strategy should recognize that, in the event of deterrence or dissuasion failure, we must be able to deal with a surprise attack and absorb an aggressor's first blow against our space or cyber assets. It must take into account the consequences of loss or disruption of space and cyber capabilities and services. This includes understanding their potential secondary and tertiary implications. We must be able to operate through an attack and the resulting degraded environment. As a senior allied officer recently concluded, "this demands we consider contingency requirements for resilience and redundancy, such as the need for hardened or protected systems, alternative means, procedures to deal with degradation, and operationally responsive arrangements."[26] Subsequently seizing the initiative and reasserting at least working control of the operating mediums will be essential to defending the freedom of the space and cyberspace domains.

The strategy should establish priorities and direct actions for mission assurance, resilience, protection, security, reconstitution, and recovery. This should encompass all space and cyber system segments and functions end to end. We should seek to channel adversary threats into costly and unproductive areas. Although avoiding the imposition of unaffordable costs, the strategy should ensure that space and cyber mission capabilities will be sufficiently ready, secure, resilient, and survivable to meet national and homeland security needs. Indeed, such resilience and survivability are directly tied to issues of self-deterrence and reassurance.

Establishing alliance or coalition arrangements to protect against threats to international security in space and cyberspace will be an important component of the strategy. This includes new public–private sector partnerships in recognition that many of the pertinent assets and infrastructure are privately owned and operated. Such arrangements will contribute to deterrence by sharing the defense burden and complicating a potential adversary's risk calculus. They will also contribute to escalation control and warfighting by increasing the resources and options for responding to aggression.

CENTRALIZED PLANNING, DECENTRALIZED EXECUTION

Preparations for crisis management, conflict prevention, and warfighting should recognize that policies, processes, and structures established for the Cold War might not be up to this century's threats to space and cyber security.[27] They may need to be altered or replaced. A comprehensive approach cannot be undertaken on an ad hoc, disjointed basis. It will require comprehensive strategic planning.

Implementing a comprehensive approach will require new policy and guidance, intra- and intergovernmental planning mechanisms and processes, and organizational constructs. A new paradigm and broader system are needed to accomplish the holistic planning necessary for a comprehensive, whole-of-nations approach. The National Security Council system provides a potential mechanism for comprehensive planning at the strategic level. Similarly, the Combined Joint Task Force, Joint Interagency Task Force, and Combined Operations Center constructs could provide a basis for orchestrating integrated planning and execution at the operational levels.

Deliberate, whole-of-nations, preplanning for plausible space and cyber contingencies is an essential basis for concerted action. Such centralized planning is necessary to coordinate, deconflict, synchronize, and, as appropriate, integrate decentralized execution of lines of operations. It should produce a rich menu of preplanned courses of action for all elements of power, ranging from flexible deterrent to major attack options. In addition, it should align conditions, postures, rules of engagement, and authorities to enable those alternative courses of action.

The options should encompass all phases of operations and involve all available instruments of statecraft. Military options should range from conditioning and signaling to preemptive and preventative actions. Response options may range from demarches, sanctions, and responses-in-kind to asymmetric (horizontal or vertical), cross-domain escalation.

Planning should clarify our red lines (or zones), thresholds, and triggers for responding to aggressive, hostile intentions and actions (for example, corrupting sensitive data or maneuvering in close proximity to spacecraft). We should recognize that unintended or unanticipated effects might contribute to inadvertent escalation. Consequently, our red lines or zones must be clearly articulated through communications of declaratory policy, conditioned by operational behavior, and understood by both allies and adversaries alike.

Although no plan can be expected to endure beyond contact with the enemy, the process of comprehensive, whole-of-nations planning will enrich strategy formulation and its operational execution. Given the dynamic and complex nature of the space and cyber mediums, the intellectual engagement of senior political authorities, diplomats, and operational commanders before the emergence of a deep crisis or outbreak of hostilities will pay dividends. Moreover, it will put us in a far better position for effective crisis action planning by establishing a foundation to meet the exigencies of specific crises.

Decision making must be prepared to address the speed of battle in the space and cyber domains. Command and control processes must be adapted to operate at network speeds to enable US, allied, or coalition forces to seize and maintain the initiative. Rapid decision making will require combined, cross-domain situational awareness and command and control structures. Alliance or coalition political authorities, diplomats, and commanders must have common understanding of different national policies, red lines, and rules of engagement. Alliance or coalition members must be clear about strategic intentions, war aims, political-military objectives, and the desired end state.

Of course, self-defense measures will include the use of force to respond to an infringement on our rights. Authorization for employment of force may be predelegated to commanders, in accordance with approved war plans or rules of engagement. Such predelegations will have to be justified in advance given that employment authority may be delegated, but responsibility still resides with elected and confirmed political officials. Predelegation of employment authority may be necessary to enable forces to be postured properly for speed-of-light warfare.

OUTER space and cyberspace are interdependent domains with unique operational characteristics unconstrained by boundaries. They are contested operating environments where assets are held at risk because of threats posed by counterspace and computer network attack weapons. The emergence of space and cyberspace as new dimensions of competition and potential conflict has made the international security environment more uncertain, dynamic, complex, and dangerous. Shaping the space and cyber environments prior to a crisis thus is essential to international peace and order.

The United States and its allies have vital national interests in ensuring unimpeded access to and use of the space and cyber domains. Our prosperity, well-being, and security are enabled by information and knowledge collected, generated, and transmitted through space and cyberspace. The global economy depends upon the information lines of communication through the space and cyber domains. The operational efficiency and effectiveness of our military forces also rely upon the information and decision superiority provided by space and cyber C4ISR capabilities. Consequently, we must be prepared to address the challenges to international security in space and cyberspace.

A comprehensive, whole-of-nations approach will enable the United States and its allies, coalition partners, and friends to take concerted actions to shape the space and cyber environments, deter aggression, and, in the event of a deterrence failure, control escalation and terminate conflict on favorable terms. Such an approach will enable decision makers to leverage all instruments of statecraft to tailor smart power solutions to space and or cyber security challenges. In particular, the approach will facilitate leveraging and synchronizing multiple, concurrent lines of nonlinear operations to mass effects at the speed and point of need.

Centralized planning and decentralized execution of the comprehensive approach will permit us to take the diplomatic and informational initiative to establish the conditions required for effective deterrence and reassurance. They will also enable us to implement a dynamic, multilayered, defense-in-depth strategy to ensure an adversary cannot achieve its political aims through the threat or use of force in space or cyberspace. Implementation of the comprehensive approach will require the national security community to adjust its policies, processes, and organizational constructs to enable the complex operations that will protect and advance our vital interests in today's security environment.

NOTES

The epigraph appeared in the *National Security Strategy* issued by the Executive Office of the President (Washington, DC: The White House, May 2010), 8.

1. See United States, Joint Forces Command, *Joint Operating Environment 2010* (Suffolk, VA: US Joint Forces Command, February 8, 2010); United Kingdom, Ministry of Defence, *Future Character of Conflict* (London: Development Concepts and Doctrine Center, February 2010).

2. On the advent of hybrid warfare, see William S. Lind, Keith Nightengale, John F. Schmitt, Joseph W. Sutton, and Gary I. Wilson, "The Changing Face of War: Into the Fourth Generation," *Marine Corps Gazette* 73 (October 1989): 22–26; Frank G. Hoffman and James N. Mattis, "Future Warfare: The Rise of Hybrid Wars," *Proceedings* 132 (November 2005): 18–19.

3. United States Joint Chiefs of Staff, *Department of Defense Dictionary of Military and Associated Terms*, Joint Publication 1-02, as amended December 31, 2010 (Washington, DC: Joint Chiefs of Staff, November 8, 2010), 336.

4. Ibid., 338.

5. Ibid., 92.

6. Ibid., 175.

7. See the above definition of *cyberspace*, ibid., 92.

8. United States Joint Chiefs of Staff, *Space Operations*, Joint Publication 3-14 (Washington, DC: Joint Chiefs of Staff, January 6, 2009); United States Department of the Air Force, *Cyberspace Operations*, Air Force Doctrine Document 3-12 (Washington, DC: Department of the Air Force, July 15, 2010).

9. See the summary of the 2009 *Space Posture Review Interim Report* in James N. Miller, testimony before the Subcommittee on Strategic Forces, House Committee on Armed Services, 111th Cong., 2nd Sess., March 16, 2010.

10. "Tonga Accuses Indonesia of Jamming Satellite Signals," *Satellite News*, March 3, 1997; "Chinese Satellite TV Hijacked by Falun Gong Cult" (Washington, DC: Embassy of the People's Republic of China, July 8, 2002); Jeremy Singer, "War in Iraq Boosts Case for More Jam Resistant GPS," *Space News*, April 8, 2003; "Libya 'Jammed' Media Satellites," *Middle East Times*, December 5, 2005; "Iran Jams TV Channels," *Courier Mail* (Brisbane), June 7, 2005; Vago Muridian, "China Tried to Blind US Sats with Laser," *Defense News*, December 5, 2005; Warren Ferster and Colin Clark, "NRO Confirms Chinese Laser Test Illuminated Spacecraft," *Defense News*, October 2, 2006; Edward Cody, "China Confirms Missile Test," *Washington Post*, January 27, 2007; Stephanie Nebehay, "UN Tells Iran to Stop Jamming Eutelsat," Reuters, March 26, 2010; "North Korea Appears Capable of Jamming GPS Receivers," Voice of America, October 7, 2010; Mark Lander and John Markoff, "Digital Fears Emerge after Data Siege in

Estonia," *New York Times*, May 29, 2007; William J. Lynn III, "Defending a New Domain: The Pentagon's Cyberstrategy," *Foreign Affairs* 89 (September–October 2010): 97–108; John Markoff, "Before the Gunfire Cyberattacks," *New York Times*, August 12, 2008; William Matthews, "Cyber Assault Cripples Web in Kyrgyzstan," *Defense News*, January 29, 2009; Siobahn Gorman, "Electricity Grid in US Penetrated by Spies," *Wall Street Journal*, April 8, 2009; Ariana Eunjung Cha and Ellen Nakashima, "Google China Cyberattack Part of Vast Espionage Campaign, Experts Say," *Washington Post*, January 14, 2010; *2010 Report to Congress* (Washington, DC: US-China Economic and Security Review Commission, November 2010); General Keith B. Alexander, USA, testimony before the House Committee on Armed Services, 111th Cong., 2nd Sess., September 23, 2010; Mark Clayton, "Ahmadinejad Admits Cyberweapon Hit Iran Nuclear Program," *Christian Science Monitor*, November 30, 2010.

11. Dennis C. Blair, "Annual Threat Assessment of the US Intelligence Community for the Senate Select Committee on Intelligence" (Washington, DC, February 2, 2010).

12. Botnets are collections of software agents that run automatically to compromise machines for malicious purposes. See *Emerging Cyber Threats Report 2011* (Atlanta: Georgia Tech Information Security Center, October 7, 2010), 3–5, http://gtiscsecuritysummit.com/.

13. William J. Lynn III, remarks presented at the Security Defense Alliance, Brussels, Belgium, September 15, 2010, www.defense.gov/speeches/speech.aspx?speechid=1503.

14. Marc J. Berkowitz, "The Strategic Value of Schriever V: Policy and Strategy Insights for the Quadrennial Defense Review," *High Frontier* 5 (August 2009): 32–36.

15. United States Department of Defense, *Quadrennial Defense Review Report* (Washington, DC: Office of the Secretary of Defense, February 2010).

16. Marc J. Berkowitz, "A Comprehensive Approach to Space and Cyberspace Operations," *High Frontier* 7 (November 2010): 44–47.

17. Alexander, testimony before the House, September 23, 2010.

18. United Nations, "Treaty on Principles Governing the Activities of States in the Exploration and Use of Outer Space" (1967), "Convention on International Liability for Damage Caused by Space Objects" (1972), and "Convention on Registration of Objects Launched into Space" (1976).

19. See United Nations, "Treaty Banning Nuclear Weapons Tests in the Atmosphere, in Outer Space, and Underwater" (1963) and "New Strategic Arms Reductions Treaty" (2010).

20. See, for example, United States Executive Office of the President, *The US Anti-Satellite (ASAT) Program: A Key Element in the National Strategy of Deterrence* (Washington, DC: The White House, May 1987).

21. United Nations, "Treaty on the Prevention of the Placement of Weapons in Outer Space, the Threat or Use of Force against Outer Space Objects" (Geneva, June 27, 2008).

22. Both the George H. W. Bush and William J. Clinton administrations asserted there was no need for space arms control measures because there was no arms race in outer space and existing laws were adequate. Although the George W. Bush administration supported tacit transparency and confidence-building measures, his administration opposed new legal regimes or other restrictions that prohibited or limited US access to space. Subsequently, President Barack Obama directed that "the United States will consider proposals and concepts for arms control measures if they are equitable, effectively verifiable, and enhance the national security of the United States and its allies." See United States Executive Office of the President, *National Space Policy of the United States of America* (Washington, DC: The White House, June 28, 2010), 7.

23. See, for example, the proposed "Code of Conduct for Outer Space Activities" (Brussels: Council of the European Union, December 17, 2008), www.consilium.europa.eu/show

Page.aspx?id=1570&lang=EN; Michael Krepon, "Model Code of Conduct for Space-Faring Nations" (Washington, DC: Stimson Center, October 24, 2007), www.stimson.org/images/uploads/research-pdfs/Model_Code_of_Conduct_for_Responsible_Space-Faring_Nations.pdf.

24. See, for example, Marc J. Berkowitz, "Protecting America's Freedom of Action in Space," *High Frontier* 3 (March 2007): 13–18; Roger G. Harrison, Deron R. Jackson, and Collins G. Shackleford, "Space Deterrence: The Delicate Balance of Risk," *Space and Defense* 3 (Summer 2009): 1–4; Kevin P. Chilton, opening remarks presented at the 2009 Deterrence Symposium, Omaha, Nebraska, July 29, 2009.

25. See, for example, Robert Jervis, Richard Ned Lebow, and Janice Gross Stein, *Psychology and Deterrence* (Baltimore, MD: Johns Hopkins University Press, 1985).

26. Andrew Dowse, "Schriever—An Australian Perspective," *High Frontier* 7 (November 2010): 19.

27. See Clark A. Murdoch, Pierre Chao, Anne A. Witkowsky, Michele A. Flournoy, and Christine E. Wormuth, *Beyond Goldwater-Nichols Phase III Report: US Government and Defense Reform for a New Strategic Era* (Washington, DC: Center for Strategic and International Studies, July 28, 2005); *Project on National Security Reform: Forging a New Shield* (Arlington, VA: Project on National Security Reform, November 2008); Steven J. Hadley and William J. Perry, *The QDR in Perspective: Meeting America's National Security Needs in the 21st Century* (Washington, DC: US Institute of Peace, 2010).

PART IV

INTERFACE MECHANISMS

CHAPTER 10

Maritime Security Consortiums

❖

GORDAN E. VAN HOOK

> For whosoever commands the sea commands the trade; whoso-
> ever commands the trade of the world commands the riches of
> the world, and consequently the world itself.
> —Sir Walter Raleigh, "A Discourse of the Invention of Ships"

The ocean covers 71 percent of the earth's surface.[1] The ability to traverse, exploit, and share this vast expanse is crucial to the security and prosperity of every nation around the world. The maritime domain is essential to global mobility and trade and is an abundant source of vital resources, from food to energy. Because of its indispensability, Alfred Mahan regarded the ocean as "the great common" of mankind.[2] In an existential sense, the maritime domain could be considered the "critical infrastructure" of global society, which must be preserved and protected for the benefit of all nations.[3]

The shared imperative and responsibility for maritime security necessarily transcend the capabilities of individual nations and navies. The realization of the potentialities of collective security through shared awareness demands new approaches to public-private partnerships in the maritime domain. These partnerships are known as maritime security consortiums and enlist multinational, federal, state, local, and private sector entities that, when combined, leverage their shared situational awareness to enhance international security. This chapter explores the ways in which maritime security consortiums could be an important future component of the maritime domain awareness necessary to achieve security in the maritime commons.

THE NECESSITY FOR COOPERATION

Preventing conflict and encouraging cooperation to secure the maritime domain start with the hard task of gaining and maintaining awareness of the environment. The maritime environment is especially challenging in this respect. Awareness can be difficult ashore even given total control of sovereign ground and air space. On the high seas that challenge is far more daunting. In the age of high-speed, high-endurance aircraft, commercial satellite imagery, long-range surveillance, and global digital communications, the ocean remains the "great unknown." It presents an often turbulent surface, marine life, complex weather systems, and attenuating atmospheric conditions that conspire to suboptimize the human senses and the most highly advanced of technological sensors. These conditions are combined with a plethora of small craft that ply the seas, especially their crowded littorals, and engage in trading, fishing, sports, recreation, and even smuggling as well as more traditional maritime crimes such as armed piracy.

This great unknown also carries upon it the massive maritime trade that is the linchpin of the global economic system, carrying 74 percent of the volume of goods on a complex network of liner, bulk, and tanker vessels that form a virtual set of conveyor belts to keep the global manufacturing engine whirring.[4] Raw materials are moved from their origin in bulk carriers to countries that form base materials. These are shipped to other countries in bulk to form subcomponents that are then moved via containers to other countries, where they are formed into subassemblies that are then forwarded for assembly of a final product. Between each of these steps are usually one or more transshipment nodes, or gathering points for the efficient grouping and forwarding of multiple shipments to common destinations. Although product labels may indicate the items were made in country x, it should read they were final assembled in country x. Although this virtual maritime conveyor belt is a modern marvel of globalization, it is simply a matter of time before it becomes vulnerable to those seeking to disrupt the global economic system.

Complete disruption of the maritime domain would be difficult because the global economic system has inherent redundancies and thousands of vessels. However, disruptions could have profound local and regional effects on smaller, fragile nations highly dependent on few or single ports, which support most of their trade and link them to the larger systems. The social impact of disruptions may be severe and lead to inevitable civil unrest. Many nations suffer from weak governance and brittle control of their populations, and disrupting their economies may have disastrous effects, tipping them toward failed states, which can breed terrorists with the threat of further disrupting the global system. Additional civil unrest and human suffering can result when humanitarian food aid is interdicted, as has happened in East Africa by Somali pirates.

Disruption of maritime trade also can affect the flow of certain critical commodities and production volumes, temporarily raising the cost of goods even for advanced nations. For example, insurance rates for passage through the Gulf of Aden rose from $500 to $20,000 per trip in one year.[5] Moreover, ransom payments charged by Somali pirates in 2010 amounted to an average of $5.4 million, with the largest at $9.5 million for the South Korean oil tanker *Samho Dream*.[6] Thus the results of such disruptions are felt by consumers. Action by maritime security forces to address regional disruptions and maritime disorder, such as the multinational counter-piracy efforts conducted off the Horn of Africa, incur additional costs that ultimately result in higher taxes in the participating countries or greater risks to national security interests.

Commercial shipping companies engaged in trading in the maritime domain are responsible for assessing risks to their vessels and cargoes and taking prudent actions to safeguard them. This process normally involves a vessel security plan, which is periodically updated based on the operational profile of each vessel.[7] In the case of piracy and maritime crime, there is much debate over the mitigating actions that should be taken by shipping companies and those that should be carried out by maritime security forces.[8] Most responsible commercial companies understand their obligations to follow the best management practices accepted by the industry.[9] They include both active and passive measures such as additional watches, laying out and activating fire hoses, stringing barbed and razor wire, locking exterior hatches, and others. The current distinction between the responsibilities of the private and public sectors is centered on whether shipping companies should be obligated to arm their crews or use armed force in regions where maritime disorder is prevalent.

Many nations as well as private operators consider armed security to be inappropriate on board commercial ships. They believe arming civilians for this purpose only increases risks of escalation and injury to the innocent and raises rules of engagement, liability, and sovereignty issues. This debate exists among commercial operators and internally between management and crewmembers. As more operators use private armed security companies to mitigate risks in dangerous waters, questions will arise on the extent of reasonable measures. For example, if commercial shippers deploy separate security vessels, what would be their functional relationship to coast guards and sovereign navies?

Given this debate over the effectiveness and appropriateness of active and passive measures by shipping companies, maritime security forces cannot neglect their inherent responsibility to prevent the disruption of trade. If national or regional security forces continue to play a role in protecting transportation in the maritime domain, they must leverage every possible source of awareness to include commercial maritime traffic. From their mutual self-interest to maintain peace in the maritime domain, the public and private sectors must collaborate.

A view of global electronic emissions from space displays an impressive array of electronic ribbons covering swaths of the open ocean, highlighting the major trade routes traveled by the tens of thousands of ships engaged in maritime trade. The world's commercial fleet is registered in more than 150 nations, and manned by over a million seafarers of virtually every nationality.[10] Yet despite their presence on the high seas, most commercial vessels operate in their own domes of awareness, sharing very little with each other and maritime security forces operating within the same region. Meanwhile, the security forces maintain their own surveillance pictures, and sharing information, even among their closest allies, presents unique operational and technical challenges. In the past five years, there has been extensive international dialogue among naval forces and coast guards regarding their shared responsibilities for maritime security in a globalized and interconnected world.

The concept of the Thousand-Ship Navy developed by the US Navy influenced global maritime partnerships, which have attracted widespread attention and comment.[11] The initiative has continued to evolve and recently was manifested in the cooperation reached among more than two dozen national navies combating piracy in the waters of the Gulf of Aden and the Somali Basin. However, many of the original thinkers who support global maritime cooperation like the chairman of the Joint Chiefs of Staff, Admiral Michael Mullen, envision it going beyond individual navies to a diverse array of multinational, federal, state, local, and private-sector capabilities.[12] If the private-sector entities are understood to include the commercial maritime industry and multinational conglomerates with interests that span well beyond national boundaries, the distinct opportunity exists to leverage collective awareness to enhance maritime security. Such awareness requires developing advanced concepts and a reconsideration of public-private cooperation efforts in the form of Maritime Security Consortiums.[13]

SCALE OF THE SURFACE PICTURE

In addition to recognizing the complexity of the maritime environment, any approach to gaining awareness of the maritime domain must recognize the inherent difficulty posed by its sheer immensity, which yields the relative freedom and danger of this domain. Awareness of the vast maritime domain requires a comprehensive approach that draws on all potential resources.

Although satellite communication and twenty-four-hour news cycle coverage provide a growing and unparalleled awareness of the universe, operators at sea often remain ignorant of anything over the visual horizon. Aerial reconnaissance and intelligence satellites can furnish naval forces with a wide range of data and electronic emissions that point to the pathways of global commerce. Although such assets can be focused on discrete areas that maritime security forces want to monitor and investigate, naval commanders understand all too well the difficulty in maintaining a coherent surface picture of assets under their charge, even with constant vigilance and dedicated surface and air surveillance assets.

While transiting busy chokepoints such as international straits, the problem of maintaining maritime situational awareness can become insurmountable. For example, a chokepoint such as the Babel Mandeb that separates Africa from Arabia registers more than 22,000 annual transits of commercial vessels. The difficulty intensifies on entering the Gulf of Aden, with thousands of small fishing and trading dhows and skiffs weaving over thousands of square miles.[14] As pirates began to expand their range from the Gulf of Aden to the vast expanses of the Somali Basin and Indian Ocean, in some cases commandeering large merchant ships as mother ships, the issue has become less of congestion and more of the enormity of an area larger than the state of Texas.[15] It is no wonder that piracy has flourished in this vast region, where by the end of 2011 suspected Somali pirates held eleven vessels for ransom with 193 crewmembers, despite the efforts of the United States, the North Atlantic Treaty Organization (NATO), the European Union, and a dozen nonaligned nations.[16]

MARITIME AWARENESS

Known as Maritime Domain Awareness (MDA) or Global Maritime Situation Awareness (GMSA), depending upon the government agency or country discussing the topic, the US government defines MDA as "the effective understanding of anything associated with the global maritime domain that could impact the security, safety, economy, and environment of the United States. MDA is a key component of an active, layered maritime defense in depth. It will be achieved by improving our ability to collect, fuse, analyze, display, and disseminate actionable information and intelligence."[17]

Understanding the traffic traversing the maritime domain is a vital safety and security concern. Yet although greater situational awareness may enhance global security and stability as well as economic progress, there are major barriers to increased awareness because of commercial and national competition and distrust in addition to the sheer challenge of millions of square miles of ocean and paucity of open ocean surveillance assets.

The International Maritime Organization requires the majority of commercial maritime traffic to carry collision-avoidance equipment such as radars, emergency beacons, satellite communications, and, for vessels displacing more than 300 gross tons, the Automatic Identification System (AIS). That last capability is a shipboard VHF radiobroadcast system that automatically transmits a ship's identification, position, course, and speed to surrounding vessels and shore stations within the ship's visual range or horizon. A relatively recent requirement, the AIS, has greatly enhanced the safety of ocean traffic, but it has not been fully leveraged to provide the awareness critical for regional stability and security.

The Volpe Center has become a leader in developing marine traffic management systems for specific geographic straits and waterways. Under the Research and Innovative Technology Administration of the US Department of Transportation, the Volpe Center has recognized the potential for the Automatic Identification System to meet the challenges posed by the *National Strategy for Maritime Security* and its attendant guidance in *A National Plan to Achieve Maritime Domain Awareness.*[18] The plan directs both the defense and homeland security communities to achieve maritime security through maritime domain awareness, for which the Volpe Center has provided the technological support.[19] In addition, the commander of US Naval Forces Europe has pioneered an effort to link NATO surveillance systems within the Mediterranean region to provide an unclassified common picture of the maritime environment.[20]

Recognizing the potential of the AIS to complete the surface picture, the US Navy embarked on a cooperative effort with Volpe to develop an unclassified network to collect and share AIS data. Known as the Maritime Safety and Security Information System (MSSIS), this effort proved useful not only in enhancing security and safety but also in enhancing international cooperation and trust in the region.[21] However, the system only functions among national governments and their armed forces and is not available to commercial operators. To realize the full potential of the system in a maritime security consortium, this system would have to be expanded to include commercial vessels.

The AIS offers a quantum leap in the consistency and quality of information made available to commercial and government mariners. Combined with the MSSIS, it provides an increased regional awareness to both national command center activities such as sector command centers operated by the US Coast Guard, which are evolving into interagency operational centers, and maritime security forces through the power of networks.[22] However, experienced mariners understand that the AIS has limitations. Because it is unencrypted, that system can easily be spoofed or altered, or it can simply malfunction to provide misleading or erroneous information.[23]

Professional mariners regard the AIS as only one fallible piece of data and constantly scan the horizon visually and electronically with installed radars to gather, correlate, and cross-check all surface contacts. Maritime security forces could leverage the regional and local awareness of professional mariners to enhance their awareness of the maritime environment if they could see the correlation and comparison of the AIS with its other shipboard sensors. Current technology may be paired with satellite communications and the MSSIS to provide this local awareness to both regional maritime commanders and their operational centers within their area of responsibility.

Starting in 2006, the largest US flag carrier for the US government, Maersk Line Limited, collaborated with Lockheed Martin in an effort to conduct their own feasibility demonstration of this concept. Maersk ships hosted a Lockheed Martin prototype AIS and radar correlation system known as Neptune. The system compared AIS data aboard ships to organic radar system contacts and beamed the information via Inmarsat satellite to a networked data services and analysis system, which could conceivably be used by a maritime operations center.[24] The results of this demonstration indicated the potential of the system to correlate thousands of discrete ship identifications made beyond the range of shore-based AIS collection systems as well as to detect various anomalies such as misidentified ships, ships changing their names in transit, ships not transmitting AIS, and visual identifications that did not match AIS data. Maersk continued this type of work with an experiment conducted in 2010 for US Southern Command in the Caribbean area known as the Ships AIS and Radar Correlator (SARC) system using technology developed by the Naval Research Laboratory. The SARC system was mounted in container ships transiting the region and automatically provided information from their surroundings with no input required by crewmembers, and the system imposed no costs on the commercial operators.

Correlated AIS data and radar contact information can greatly enhance regional maritime awareness and security for transiting commercial vessels as well as maritime security forces in the region. For example, correlated information could increase the fidelity and quality of surface surveillance for naval forces transiting heavily trafficked chokepoints and provide invaluable data on approaches to ports and harbors. However, it is critical that public-private correlation systems are properly developed with the right mind-set. The systems must evolve into totally free and open self-regulating networks, available to all mariners with minimal technical and financial investments. The MSSIS is available to government operators but could be expanded for commercial operators. Built to meet the standards sanctioned by the International Maritime Organization, the public-private correlation systems must not be regarded as either intelligence or surveillance systems but rather as awareness-enhancing systems to provide situational awareness much as international air traffic control systems function. Like air traffic control, the benefit of such a correlation system may include greater coordination of effort, safety, and reduced risk of collisions and near misses by identifying larger patterns in high-traffic areas and finding solutions.

CONSORTIUM COMPONENTS

The power of shared information networks, such as correlated AIS data and radar contacts, combined with new approaches to maritime security arrangements, enables cooperative public-private partnerships in the form of maritime security consortiums. Incorporating governmental and commercial maritime entities in consortiums may lead to assured maritime situational awareness at a time when the reliance on global maritime highways is expected to increase. In order to form public-private partnerships, the principles of cooperation and collaboration must be followed to achieve situational awareness while minimizing potential distrust and national competition. By allowing commercial participation in government information-sharing networks such as the MSSIS, installation of the AIS and radar correlators on ships can improve the quality of data on a mutually beneficial network. Standardizing correlation equipment through entities like the International Maritime Organization could also improve the quality of the network. Participation in the network would be strictly voluntary, but the attraction would be greater safety and security at sea.

Maritime security consortium activities could be coordinated through regional maritime security operational centers that monitor the maritime domain. An example is the way in which ships coordinate their movement through the pirate-infested waters of the Gulf of Aden by checking in with either the United Kingdom Maritime Transportation Operations Office in Dubai or the European Union Maritime Security Centre, Horn of Africa at Northwood.[25] Ships that check in and coordinate their movements with these operation centers greatly reduce their risk of successful hijacking in dangerous waters.

Such a scheme could become fully automated with voluntary participation in the MSSIS and the installation of AIS and radar correlators. With the enhanced situational awareness of commercial mariners, the regional operations center, and maritime security forces, all could benefit from greater safety and security. Joining a regional maritime security consortium network would only require the proper equipment and dedication to accurate self-reporting of contacts in the vicinity of a vessel within a given region, resulting in a voluntary maritime form of neighborhood watch.

In keeping with the principles of global maritime partnerships, participation in maritime security consortium network activities would be voluntary, self-regulating, and self-governing. The price of admission would be investment in additional equipment and communications, well worth the benefits of greater security and awareness. Maritime nations of the world could take the lead in investing in such equipment and encouraging commercial participation through regional maritime security operations centers. Ideal regions to start such consortiums would be the high-risk waters of the Red Sea and Gulf of Aden, North Arabian Sea, Strait of Malacca, South China Sea, and Gulf of Guinea. Regional operations centers already exist or are starting to form in some of these hot spots of the world, such as the Gulf of Guinea and Horn of Africa. These operations centers could be collectively manned by regional nations, and locations could be rotated to share costs and relative influence for all players.

The commercial maritime industry could be further encouraged and incentivized to equip their assets and participate in consortium networks through existing national subsidies, tax breaks, contractual preferences on government cargo, and other financial inducements. For example, sixty US-flagged ships are subsidized today under the Maritime Security Program to maintain sufficient strategic sealift capacity.[26] Installation of required network equipment and participation in a maritime security consortium might represent a reasonable prerequisite for companies that receive subsidies. Similar programs exist in many other maritime nations and could provide a significant start to a maritime security consortium initiative.

As interdependence continues to grow within an evermore globalized economic system, commensurate vulnerabilities also will expand. In addition, as transport systems become more optimized for efficiency in an interconnected world that depends on maritime highways of commerce, the oceans and maritime domain can no longer be considered the great unknown.

NOTES

The epigraph appeared in "A Discourse of the Invention of Ships, Anchors, Compass, &c," *The Works of Sir Walter Raleigh Kt*, vol. 8, reprinted 2010 (Oxford: The University Press, 1829), 325.

1. National Oceanic and Atmospheric Administration, "Ocean" (Washington, DC: Department of Commerce, n.d.), www.noaa.gov/ocean.html.
2. Alfred Thayer Mahan, "Influence of Sea Power upon History, 1660–1783," 12th ed. (Boston: Little, Brown, 1918), 25, www.gutenberg.org/files/13529/13529-h/13529-h.htm.
3. "United States–Japan Seapower Alliance for Stability and Prosperity on the Oceans" (Tokyo: Ocean Policy Research Foundation, April 17, 2009), 2, www.sof.or.jp/en/report/pdf/200906_seapower.pdf.
4. Randy Young, "Global Maritime Trade Overview," remarks presented to the Global Shipping Wargame at the Naval War College, Newport, Rhode Island, October 2010.
5. Alessandro Scheffler, "Piracy—Threat or Nuisance?" (Rome: NATO Defense College, February 2010), 1–10.
6. Anna Bowden, "The Economic Cost of Maritime Piracy," Oceans beyond Piracy Project, PowerPoint presentation (London: Chatham House, January 13, 2011), http://oceansbeyondpiracy.org/sites/default/files/documents_old/The_Economic_Cost_of_Piracy_Presentation.pdf.

7. US Code of Federal Regulations, 33 CFR 104.400 subpart d, "Format of the Vessel Security Plan (VSP), Navigation and Navigable Waters," 2008, http://edocket.access .gpo.gov/cfr_2008/julqtr/pdf/33cfr104.405.pdf.

8. Leslie Anne Warren, "Pieces of Eight: An Appraisal of US Counter-Piracy Options in the Horn of Africa," *Naval War College Review* 63 (Spring 2010): 68–69.

9. Allied Maritime Command, "Best Management Practices Version 3" (Northwood: NATO Shipping Centre, June 2010), www.marisec.org/BMP book_high.pdf.

10. Allied Maritime Command, "Shipping Facts: Information about the International Shipping Industry" (Northwood: NATO Shipping Centre, n.d.), www.marisec.org /shippingfacts/home/.

11. Michael G. Mullen, remarks presented at the 17th International Seapower Symposium on "A Global Network of Nations for a Free and Secure Maritime Commons," Naval War College, Newport, Rhode Island, September 21, 2005; John G. Morgan and Charles W. Martoglio, "The Thousand Ship Navy: Global Maritime Network," *Proceedings* 132 (November 2005): 14.

12. Michael G. Mullen and Michael W. Hagee, "Naval Operations Concept" (Washington, DC: Department of the Navy, 2006).

13. The term *maritime consortiums* was coined by the Chief of Naval Operation Strategic Studies Group 24 in July 2005.

14. Skuld, "Sustainable Growth: Skuld Annual Review 2009" (Oslo: Assuranceforeningen Skuld, 2009), www.skuld.com/templates/Page.aspx?id=2888.

15. Lauren Gelfand, "Somali Pirates Venture Further Out to Sea," *Jane's Defence Weekly*, December 22, 2010, 16; Cheryl Pellerin, "Piracy Challenges Maritime Security off Somalia," American Forces Press Service, January 26, 2011; Hannah McNeish, "Madagascar Captures Somali Pirate 'Mother Ship,'" *Christian Science Monitor*, March 1, 2011.

16. International Maritime Bureau, "Piracy and Armed Robbery against Ships," Annual Report: January 1–December 31, 2011 (London: International Chamber of Commerce, January 2012), 20.

17. United States Executive Office of the President, *National Plan for Achieving Maritime Domain Awareness* (Washington, DC: The White House, October 2005), www.dhs .gov/xlibrary/assets/HSPD_MDAPlan.pdf.

18. United States Executive Office of the President, *The National Strategy for Maritime Security* (Washington, DC: The White House, September 2005), www.dhs.gov/xlibrary /assets/HSPD13_MaritimeSecurityStrategy.pdf; United States Department of Homeland Security, "A National Plan to Achieve Maritime Domain Awareness" (Washington, DC: US Department of Homeland Security, May 26, 2008), www.dhs.gov/xlibrary /assets/HSPD_MDAPlan.pdf.

19. See *Volpe Center Highlights*, May–June 2006, www.volpe.dot.gov/infosrc/highlts/06 /mayjune/focus.html.

20. Henry G. Ulrich, remarks presented to the Chief of Naval Operations Strategic Studies Group, May 2006.

21. Alan L. Boyer, "Maritime Security Cooperation," *Newport Papers* 22 (July 2010): 50–51.

22. An explanation of this concept can be found at www.uscg.mil/acquisition/ioc.

23. Abbas Harati-Mokhtari, Alan Wall, Philip Brooks, and Jin Wang, "Automatic Identification System (AIS): Data Reliability and Human Error Implications," *Journal of Navigation* 60 (2007): 373–89, doi:10.1017/S0373463307004298.

24. John M. Doyle, "US May Monitor Pirates from Space," *Aviation Week and Space Technology*, April 29, 2009, www.aviationweek.com/aw/generic/story_channel.jsp ?channel=defense&id=news/SATS042909.xml.

25. The UK Maritime Trade Operations Office in Dubai is the point of contact for merchant ships with security forces in the region. It also administers the Voluntary Reporting Scheme whereby ships report their position, course, speed, and expected arrival time in the next port. Moreover, it tracks vessels and passes positional information to Coalition Maritime Forces; see the Maritime Security Centre, www.mschoa.org/Pages/default.aspx.

26. The Maritime Security Act of 1996 established the Maritime Security Program. Subsequently, the National Defense Authorization Act for 2004 reauthorized the program through 2015. See www.marad.dot.gov/ships_shipping_landing_page/national_security /maritime_security_program/maritime_security_program.htm.

CHAPTER 11

Cyber Security
Social Contract

❖

LARRY CLINTON

In the 20th century, developing, testing, and possessing nuclear
weapons conferred special power on a select group of nations. . . .
In the 21st century, this same power will be held by those who
control the network.

—David N. Senty, Internet Security Alliance Meeting

The strategic importance of cyberspace networks and the absence of the preparedness measures to deal with cyber threats against them are recognized
by both civil and military constituencies.[1] The unfettered use of the other
domains—air, sea, and space—largely depends on cyber systems for their management and control. As a result the challenge of developing practical and sustainable systems to administer and secure the cyberspace domain is critical to
effectively operating in the global commons. In the words of the president of the
United States, "this cyber threat is one of the most serious economic and national
security challenges we face as a nation. . . . We're not as prepared as we should
be, as a government or as a country."[2]

Although the global commons often are defined as vast expanses of unoccu-
pied space, the privately held network known as the Internet customarily delin-
eates cyberspace. Yet unlike other domains, cyberspace is organized by man around
a complex system of standards, practices, and technologies. Perhaps more importantly from a security perspective is the fact that although the commons have been
understood traditionally as the purview of nations, this is not necessarily true of
cyberspace. The Internet is unique as a broad-based infrastructure with different
owners and systems of governance and issues. It is deliberately manipulated at the

micro and macro levels for widely divergent purposes. As a result, it remains problematic at best for one nation or group of nations to attempt to govern cyberspace.

The unique characteristics of the Internet raise fundamental questions about long-held national security assumptions. For instance, the oceans that traditionally protected the United States have become essentially irrelevant in cyber warfare. In addition, the strategy of the North Atlantic Treaty Organization during the Cold War that depended on the US nuclear umbrella to deter attacks on members of the alliance no longer is relevant. Indeed, the roles and functions of military organizations and combatant forces may need to be fundamentally rethought within the cyber context.

Two recent cyber attacks targeted Estonia and Georgia. Although both attacks presumably served the interests of nations, the best evidence indicates they were conducted by civilians against civilian targets and probably without direct military assistance.[3] What is the military role in countering cyber attacks in these cases? Are traditional defense organizations capable of combating such attacks? Most practitioners agree that effective cyber defense cannot be developed without a creative partnership between the public and private sectors, possibly necessitating new roles and responsibilities for both. Few think that such a partnership exists today in a sustainable and effective form.

THE ECONOMICS OF CYBER SECURITY

In constructing the sort of sustainable partnership required to meet the modern threat, it is important to understand aligned though not necessarily identical perspectives that public and private entities have with respect to security. The nature of the cyber threat has evolved and is likely to continue to evolve, which means doing more than identifying discrete solutions to various forms of technological attacks. Controlling or protecting the cyber domain requires integrating advanced technology with economics and public policy that create a sustainable system to secure this domain. As a former director of national intelligence characterized this indispensable partnership to Congress, "the national security of the United States, our economic prosperity, and the daily functioning of our government are dependent on a dynamic public and private information infrastructure."[4]

The majority of work in the field of cyber security, especially that done by governments, has been focused almost exclusively on technology. Nevertheless, analyzing technological vulnerabilities and exploits only can provide better understanding of how cyber attacks occur. In order to develop a sustainable system for securing the cyber domain, it is also necessary to understand why the cyber attacks have occurred and why they have not been adequately addressed.

The primary reason that cyber attacks are launched against the private sector is economic. Moreover, the main reason adequate defenses are not deployed against them also is economic.[5] According to one study, because "distributed systems are assembled from machines belonging to principals with divergent interests, we find that incentives [become] as important as technical design. . . . Security failure is caused at least as often by bad incentives as by bad design."[6]

In the early days of cyber security most attacks were benign with many expressly designed to show off expertise. That is not the case with recent attacks such as Stuxnet, which is intended to debilitate systems. Modern cyber attacks such as advanced persistent threats are designed to be stealthy. Such threats can be directed at business and political targets over a prolonged duration of operations.[7] In most instances, these new attacks are not designed to take down the Internet but rather to use the Internet to steal information for strategic or financial gain.

Virtually all the economic incentives with respect to cyber security favor the attackers. Cyber attacks have become easy as well as cheap and can be outsourced inexpensively through the Internet. In addition, attacks are extremely profitable, with the estimates of annual theft ranging in the billions of dollars, and the chances of being caught are slim; estimates indicate that fewer than 2 percent of cyber criminals are successfully prosecuted.[8]

By contrast, cyber defense has numerous economic disincentives, with the defenders usually lagging a generation behind the attackers. The perimeter to be defended is virtually limitless. Return on investment, a critical calculus in the private sector where firms are obligated to be profitable, is difficult to demonstrate. It is complicated by mandated compliance regimes that are counterproductive because they can drain resources without improving security. Even with a return on investment, success requires preventing something from happening, which is almost impossible to measure.

As long as the economic equation for cyber security remains unbalanced, it will not matter whether the technological solutions are good in remedying the problem. The incentives to attack will virtually guarantee continued successful attacks by continually more sophisticated attackers. Another concern resulting from the modus operandi of cyber criminals is that their activities generate an ever-expanding pool of cyber mercenaries available to either unfriendly nations or terrorist organizations. Indeed, there is evidence that Russian organized crime might well have been responsible for the attacks on both Estonia and Georgia— and perhaps Chinese criminals in the 2010 Google attacks as well.[9]

Economics is not only the driving force behind cyber attacks; it is also the principal reason cyber defenses are insufficient. One consistently demonstrated although least-known fact is that tools are available to stop or substantially mitigate most attacks but they are not used because of cost. The Central Intelligence Agency and the National Security Agency have indicated that between 80 and 90 percent of attacks could be prevented easily by consistently applying existing standards, practices, and technologies.[10] Research conducted by PricewaterhouseCoopers, Verizon, and the US Secret Service reported similar findings. In 2010, Verizon and the Secret Service found that well-known and largely inexpensive measures could have prevented 94 percent of successful attacks.[11] Governmental and private sector research confirmed the major reason for not fielding such measures is cost. One recent study found that cost remains "the biggest obstacle to ensuring the security of critical networks."[12]

Using an entirely different methodology, the White House performed a comprehensive assessment of the roles of both the public and private sectors in cyber security, which reported that "many technical and network management solutions that would greatly enhance security already exist in the marketplace but are not always used because of cost or complexity."[13]

One complication in the economics of the cyber domain is that existing policies have created misalignments that must be redressed. In the cyber security world, negligent or culpable entities are not necessarily penalized for their actions. A review of the literature on information security similarly discovered that jurists "have long known that liability should be assigned to the part that can best manage the risk. Yet everywhere we look we see online risk allocated poorly.... People who connect insecure machines to the Internet do not bear the full consequences of their actions ... [and] developers are not compensated for costly efforts to strengthen their code."[14]

One obvious example is personal liability associated with lost credit cards. If one engages in risky behavior that results in credit card theft and thousands of dollars being charged against the accounts, what is the personal liability? In the United States it is a minimal amount of fifty dollars. Banks, on the other hand, which are not culpable for such losses, bear most of the cost, and they pass that cost on to their customers in transaction fees and interest rates.

A similar complication arises in the theft of corporate intellectual property. The problem of interdependent risk occurs when corporate information technology infrastructure is connected to other entities in such a way that it leads to failures elsewhere.[15] This risk will lead firms to underinvest in security technology and cyber insurance. For example, assume that a rogue state or criminals attempt to steal intellectual property from a high-value target. Accessing the target may be difficult because of substantial investments made to prevent unauthorized entry to its system. The same information may be found, however, on less protected networks belonging to a partner or contractor. Thus the attack could be mounted against a weaker element in the system.

In such instances, which may include attacks on the defense industrial base, the edge entity on the point of attack may not suffer any economic impact and has little incentive to prevent similar attacks. On the other hand, the ultimate target not only would suffer potentially severe impacts, it also reveals that investments are being undermined by an entity on the edge of the attack. Research has confirmed the security downside of such interdependency: "Further externalities can be found when we analyze security investment, as protection often depends on the efforts of many principals. Budgets generally depend on the manner in which individuals' investments translate into outcomes, but the impact of security investment often depends not only on the investor's own decisions but also the decisions of others. . . . Systems are particularly prone to failure when the person guarding them is not the person who suffers when they fail."[16]

One other complication arises from competitive economic pressures that lead enterprises to employ dubious security measures. It is argued that deploying unified communications (UC) platforms such as the Voiceover Internet protocol yields substantial cost savings but "while unified communications offer a compelling business case, the strength of the UC solutions in leveraging the Internet is also vulnerability. Not only are these solutions exposed to security vulnerabilities and risk that the Internet presents but the availability and relative youth of UC solutions encouraged malicious actors to develop and launch new types of attacks."[17]

A similar example of this phenomenon involves cloud computing. Just like the Voiceover Internet protocol and other unified communications, platform cloud computing has emerged as one of the hottest developments in information technology, which is largely driven by perceived economic benefits from cost savings.[18] Moreover, like the Voiceover Internet protocol and unified communications, deployment security has fallen aside because of competitive pressures driving cost reductions. A survey of 49 percent of enterprises by a professional services company reported that they had deployed a cloud solution, although 62 percent of them acknowledged having little or no faith in the security of the data in the cloud.[19]

CYBER SECURITY RESPONSIBILITIES

As well as understanding relationships between business economics and cyber security, policymakers must be mindful that the responsibilities of public and private entities are not the same. The role of the federal government enshrined in the US Constitution is providing "for the common defense" although the role of industry, which is supported by nearly 100 years of case law, involves maximizing shareholder value. These traditional roles produce significantly different approaches to making critical decisions on issues such as investments in cyber security.

Although no one wants to be the victim of attacks, for example, industry traditionally may have a higher tolerance for lax security than a government entity. Indeed, it is commonplace for retailers to accept that a certain amount of their inventory walks out the back door every month. However, some businesses tolerate this situation because the expense of hiring guards, installing cameras, and other measures may exceed the value of the merchandise being stolen and the lack of security is written off as a cost of doing business. Anecdotal evidence suggests that this attitude may have influenced the prevailing view of many business firms toward emerging cyber attacks.

Because governments are charged with defending their citizens and not concerned with profit margins, they may have a lower level of tolerance for poor security. It has been widely acknowledged in the security community that in the age of advanced persistent threats defensive measures and investments must be risk-based, but which standard of risk should be used in calculating a public-private partnership?

Perhaps national security may demand governmental standards to assess a particular risk. One cannot assume, however, that private enterprise will fund risks over the long term beyond their business plans to accommodate risk tolerance determined by the government. Also, given the world economy, the traditional ability of government to mandate private investment for the public good is eroding as corporations move to less regulated environments offshore.

The public sector, especially the federal government, can generate funds to pay for services through higher taxes and deficit spending without the constraints faced by the private sector. For example, the US government responded to the financial crises in 2008 with increased spending. Although the private sector remained cautious about investments, the Department of Homeland Security nearly tripled the size of its National Cyber Security Division. In fact, studies indicate that notwithstanding the tremendous increase in cyber vulnerabilities and attacks, spending on cyber security was deferred or reduced in half by two-thirds of US corporations.[20] Spending by the private sector is not expected to return to the pre-2008 level until as late as 2013.[21]

Developing a sustainable model to secure the cyber domain will require doing more than funding awareness programs and research on new technologies. It must recognize the realities of cyber economics and provide incentives for private sector investments in security at levels higher than those found in business plans and perhaps even assume uneconomic responsibilities. The National Infrastructure Protection Plan acknowledged this need, noting that the success of its partnership "depends on articulating the benefits to government and the private sector partners. Although articulating the value proposition to the government typically is easier to achieve, it is often more difficult to articulate the direct benefits of participation for the private sector. In assessing the value proposition for the private sector, there is a clear national interest in ensuring the collective protection and resiliency of the Nation's [critical infrastructure and key resources]."[22]

The "Cyberspace Policy Review" articulated a requirement for market incentives to promote cyber security in the private sector for the public interest: "The government should identify procurement strategies that will incentivize the market to make more secure products and services available to the public. Additional incentive mechanisms that the government should explore include adjustments to liability considerations, indemnification, tax incentives, and new regulatory requirements and compliance mechanisms."[23] Unfortunately, little has been achieved within the government to implement needed policy enhancements in cyber security.

SOCIAL CONTRACT MODELS

Early in the twentieth century, electrical power and telephones were transformative technologies that initially proved to be uneconomical in addressing broader social needs. Nevertheless, policymakers blended the public interest with pragmatic business sense to establish a social contract that guaranteed investment in the technology, which remained privately owned, in return for their widespread public application. This was the beginning of rate of return regulation.

A similar though not identical social contract can be created with respect to cyber security. Government needs the private sector to provide enhanced cyber security beyond what is justified by business needs of most enterprises. Government should deploy a range of market incentives sufficient to overcome the cyber security gap that now exists and is rapidly growing. The actual expenditure needed to close this gap is not as substantial as one might assume. For example, the Verizon–Secret Service study concluded that 94 percent of security breaches could have been prevented by deploying simple and cheap practices and technologies.[24] In return for these incentives, industry will harden and maintain national and global cyber security systems.

A MARKET INCENTIVE SYSTEM

The three main issues in designing a system to create sufficient incentives to make investments in cyber security, which are not justified by business plans, include developing a mechanism to determine the sort of behaviors that merit incentives, incentives powerful enough to change the behavior of specific businesses that can be made available to those entities that adopt desired behaviors, and mechanisms to assure that incentives are not fraudulently assessed.

The US Food and Drug Administration (FDA) uses a model that could be adapted for this purpose. The agency does not create drugs, but rather evaluates them to determine their efficacy. Multiple drugs are routinely deemed acceptable for various levels of effectiveness, and they are often categorized depending on their strength and effectiveness. For example, there are pain remedies available over the counter, a higher category of drugs for pain available by prescription, and others administered only with medical supervision.

There are many sets of standards and best practices designed for security purposes by the National Institute of Standards and Technology, International Organization for Standardization, American National Standards Institute, and other smaller and discrete bodies. One reason for myriad standards and practices can be attributed to different systems that serve various purposes in diverse cultures. No one size of standards or practices fits every situation.

Governmental concerns by agencies such as the FDA should not be raised on who creates standards and best practices but on how well they work. A cyber FDA would be tasked with evaluating standards and practices to determine their effectiveness. Private entities would voluntarily adopt these standards and practices and then would apply for incentives based on increasingly higher-level practices, with the greater incentives for more stringent processes (for example, a system of perhaps a 2 percent tax credit for adopting effective class-A practices and a 5 percent credit for adopting a higher-level set of practices).

The government already uses various incentives to promote pro-social action in areas like the environment, agriculture, and transport that promote cyber security. Among these measures are streamlined regulatory requirements, liability benefits, insurance, government procurement, marketing benefits (Safety Act), small business association loans, stimulus grants, tax incentives, and others. Incentives do not necessarily impose great costs on the government. Insurance, for example, can be furnished by the private sector. Some incentives such as streamlined regulations could generate less cost for both government and industry, while others like loans and procurement already are borne by the government.

The last major aspect is developing a mechanism to assess compliance with the provisions that warrant market incentives. For regulated sectors such as chemicals, energy, utilities, and telecommunications, the existing regulatory structure could be adapted to evaluate compliance. Broader mechanisms to assess compliance with effective cyber security would call for a more vibrant insurance industry. Cyber insurance not only endorses good practices but also provides privately funded mechanisms for assessing compliance. When insurance companies put their money on the line, they have an enormous incentive to assure that the insured practices are being followed with a concomitant social advantage of further assuring better cyber security.

ADDRESSING CYBER SECURITY

Although the adoption of effective security practices by the private sector could mitigate 80 to 90 percent of cyber attacks, there still are problems requiring more sophisticated analysis and intervention. Among the outstanding critical issues in cyber security that must be resolved are supply chain management, information sharing, and enterprise risk management.[25]

Supply Chain Management

A compelling difference between the economics of the public sector and that of the private sector in developing cyber security policies is supply chain management. Both sectors have vulnerabilities with respect to compromising the information technology supply chain. From a military perspective, threats to the hardware supply chain are particularly serious. By compromising the hardware in weapons, adversaries could debilitate entire systems or turn them against their operators when launched. Hardware that has been compromised is virtually undetectable. A simple, unthinking reaction would be to manufacture every weapon within the security of US facilities, but that is economically impractical and limits access to higher-quality and unique components.

From a risk management perspective the private sector has greater interest in combating attacks on the software supply chain than those targeting hardware. This is true because almost every attack on the hardware supply chain can be achieved more easily as well as less expensively by attacking the software supply chain. In addition, attacks against the hardware supply chain may undermine confidence in the supply chain, which in turn undermines the long-range plans of organized crime. Therefore hardware attacks are less of a threat to the private sector.

Nations might have interest in installing sleeper, one-use attack tools in hardware because one of their responsibilities is preparing defensive tools for extreme circumstances like conflicts. They will accept extended preparation times to acquire enduring capabilities and target hard-to-access systems such as highly protected military, intelligence, and infrastructure facilities.

Although malicious hardware creates a problem for the government, its effect is limited in the case of the private sector relative to attacks on the software supply chain. Because of varying levels of threat the private sector might assign a low priority to preventing hardware attacks and committing appropriate budget resources to do a risk management assessment. As a result, from the perspective of the government the degree of involvement by the private sector is liable to be less than optimum for sound, risk-based reasons. The answer is resolving the problem of malicious hardware in a manner that produces security benefits of interest to the private sector. In that way the other benefits can justify required expenditures on hardware security.[26]

Even if businesses do not experience major losses from malicious hardware, they do suffer the theft of intellectual property, interruptions in the supply chain resulting in production delays and increasing costs, and poor quality control. In addition, they face the problem of counterfeit products that threaten lost sales and damage to their brand names when proven defective. The key to solving the problem of malicious hardware is making the entire global supply chain more secure in order to cope with all of these threats. This requires that measures to protect against malicious hardware must form part of a comprehensive program that prioritizes the economic concerns of the business community in conjunction with national security priorities.

Unfortunately, improved security has not featured in supply chain management programs. Typical efforts have been focused primarily and sometimes exclusively on technical standards and procedures with business economics being considered only afterward, if at all. In 2006 the Internet Security Alliance in conjunction with Carnegie Mellon University and the US Cyber Consequences Unit, which is a private, nonprofit organization, initiated a program to address supply chain management. A framework based on this approach was contained in the Obama administration's cyberspace review and subsequent reports on management procedures.

Information Sharing

An inescapable truth of the cyber security environment is that determined intruders cannot be prevented from getting into a network as long as e-mail and web surfing exist, yet no business can survive without those two bedrocks of the information age.[27] The gaping hole in cyber information sharing is that most governmental and commercial small- and medium-sized organizations do not participate in the Information Systems Audit and Controls Association or other information-sharing groups and lack the resources to take advantage of information. Unfortunately, for many in critical infrastructure sectors, those organizations represent a major portion of the supply chain and thereby pose a significant risk to the cyber ecosystem.

The best way to address the reality of cyber security is to recognize that although networks may be invaded, the attackers are successful only when they escape with stolen information. Therefore, if we can alter our strategy away from the traditional perimeter defense, which attempts to keep attackers out, and instead reformulate our defensive actions to detect, disrupt, and deny attackers' command and control communications back out to the network, we may have a better chance to mitigate the modern attacks.

This strategy acknowledges the fact that there are fewer and relatively noisier ways to get out of a network than to get into it. Such an approach is focused on identifying the websites and addresses used by attackers to communicate with a malicious code infiltrated in computers and reducing the amount of dwell time attackers have in the system, which effectively locks the bank robbers in the vault, where they can do little damage. This dwell time can be reduced either by making a considerable investment in traffic analysis and analytical methods to detect malicious outbound traffic in a network or through collaboration with other operational entities.

Currently, many firms perceive command and control in relatively narrow terms. Collectively, however, they see a wide swath of the threat environment. By establishing a central clearinghouse, which includes well-funded organizations that detect and share information on unauthorized outbound traffic, the process might be simplified. This step will make it practical to provide a large portion of the community that is left out of the existing complex model with simple, actionable information. This basically adopts the successful antivirus model that enables receipt of security information as a passive activity for the vast majority of the population who will simply block the malicious command and control centers that are identified by the trusted and certified providers.

The model also eliminates the biggest obstacles to robust information sharing, namely, the fact that the private sector and the government do not trust one another. The private sector is reluctant to share data because it does not believe the latter can protect the confidentiality of a company that has been attacked, which may devalue stocks or compromise proprietary information to the advantage of competitors; the government is reluctant to share information for fear of revealing sources and methods and alerting targets of investigations. Both concerns are obviated, however, by only disclosing unauthorized outbound traffic, and if compromised, the government does not have to disclose sources and methods, just the suspected websites and URLs.

This information-sharing model has five built-in incentives for all participating parties. First, large commercial entities will receive significant branding and marketing benefits from becoming certified trusted reporters. Second, the government benefits from information created by a near–real time common operating picture that truly reflects the current threat environment. Third, vendors of firewall devices will attract new customers looking for high-payoff defensive measures. Fourth, both small- and medium-sized organizations will be able to take advantage of investigative work by the best organizations in the nation. Fifth, once this model is up and running, it could be readily extended to provide cyberspace security internationally.

Enterprise Risk Management

Because the cyber domain is predominantly owned and operated by the private sector, security management must seek to address economic issues associated with enterprise risk management. Although cost represents the single biggest variable with respect to adequate security in 95 percent of US firms, chief financial officers are not directly involved in managing security risks. In fact 65 percent of firms lack a process to assess cyber risk or a person in charge of a process, which amounts to no plan at all.[28] As a Carnegie Mellon study has found, "only seventeen percent of corporations had a cross-organizational privacy/security team. Less than half of the respondents had a formal enterprise risk management plan. In the one third of the forty-seven percent that did have a risk management plan, IT [was] not included."[29]

Modern corporations are integrated by technology. Yet corporate structures and decision-making processes have retained an antiquated model of independent departments and silos that do not facilitate interdependency today. In addressing this problem corporations should develop management systems under their chief financial officers or equivalent-level executives that bring all relevant parties to the table to address cyber security across the enterprise. This process would involve security and technology personnel, although they would not be placed in charge of cyber risk management. At a minimum such a corporate structure would include representatives of the financial, legal, operations, human resource, communications, public affairs, investor relations, compliance, and risk management offices as well as members of the upper echelons of the firm. In order to meet this new challenge the Internet Security Alliance and the American National Standards Institute have developed a practical methodology that corporations may employ in addressing the potential financial losses created by cyber risk interdependencies.[30]

THE cyber domain is critical for the defense of the global commons. This vital system of systems cannot be defended unless a reasonable government-industry partnership is established. Such a relationship must take account of changes in technology, economics, and public policy. A social contract model can be established that describes the roles and responsibilities of the public and private sectors. Such a model is capable of generating incentives to provide measures that have been empirically demonstrated to be successful in improving cyber security.

NOTES

The epigraph was contained in remarks presented by Major General David N. Senty, USAF, at the Internet Security Alliance board of directors meeting held in Arlington, Virginia, on November 18, 2010.

1. The author would like to thank Jeff Brown, vice president, Infrastructure Services and CISO Information Technology, Raytheon; Gary McAlum, senior vice president and chief security officer, USAA; Paul Davis, senior vice president and chief technology officer, NJVC; and Scott Borg, director, US Cyber Consequences Unit, for their valuable help with this chapter.
2. United States Executive Office of the President, "President Obama's Remarks on Securing US Cyber Infrastructure" (Washington, DC: The White House, May 29, 2009), www.america.gov/st/texttrans-english/2009/May/20090529161700eaifas0.1335871 .html.

3. John Bumgarner, "Overview by the US-CCU of the Cyber Campaign against Georgia in August of 2008" (Washington, DC: US Cyber Consequences Unit, August 2009), 2–4, 8.
4. Adm. Dennis C. Blair, USN (Ret.), testimony before the Senate Select Committee on Intelligence, 111th Cong., 1st Sess., February 2, 2010.
5. See, for example, Stewart Baker, Shaun Waterman, and George Ivanov, "In the Crossfire: Critical Infrastructure in the Age of Cyber War" (Santa Clara, CA: McAfee, 2009), 35.
6. Ross Anderson and Tyler Moore, "The Economics of Information Security: A Survey and Open Questions," *Science* 314 (October 27, 2006): 1.
7. "Advanced Persistent Threats (APT)" (Atlanta, GA: Damballa, 2010), www.damballa .com/knowledge/advanced-persistent-threats.php.
8. Robert M. Regoli and John D. Hewitt, *Exploring Criminal Justice: The Essentials* (Sudbury, MA: Jones and Bartlett Publishers, 2010), 378.
9. Iftach Ian Amit, "Cyber[Crime|War]: Linking State Governed Cyber Warfare with Online Criminal Groups," *Security & Innovation* (2010), 3–6, www.defcon.org/images /defcon-18/dc-18-presentations/Amit/DEFCON-18-Amit-Cyber-Crime-WP.pdf.
10. Quoted in Robert Bigman and Richard Shaffer, "Implementing the Obama Cyber Security Strategy via the ISA Social Contract Model" (Arlington, VA: Internet Security Alliance, 2009), 5, www.thecrimereport.org/wp-content/uploads/2009/12/Implement ing_the_Obama_Cyber_Security_Strategy-31.pdf.
11. Wade Baker, Mark Goudie, Alexander Hutton, C. David Hylender, Jelle Niemantsverdriet, Christopher Novak, David Ostertag, Christopher Porter, Mike Rosen, Bryan Sartin, Peter Tippett, and the men and women of the US Secret Service, "2010 Data Breach Investigations Report" (Verizon Business, 2010), www.verizonbusiness.com /resources/reports/rp_2010-data-breach-report_en_xg.pdf.
12. Baker, Waterman, and Ivanov, "In the Crossfire," 14.
13. United States Executive Office of the President, "Cyberspace Policy Review: Assuring a Trusted and Resilient Information and Communications Infrastructure" (Washington, DC: The White House, May 2009), 31.
14. Anderson and Moore, "Information Security," 2–3.
15. See Larry Clinton, "The Internet Security Alliance Answer to the Department of Commerce Notice of Inquiry: Cybersecurity, Innovation and the Internet Economy" (Arlington, VA: Internet Security Alliance, September 20, 2010), 9.
16. Anderson and Moore, "Information Security," 1, 4.
17. "Navigating Compliance and Security for Unified Communication" (Arlington, VA: Internet Security Alliance, 2009), 21.
18. Christopher S. Yoo, "Cloud Computing: Architectural and Policy Implications" (Washington, DC: Technology Policy Institute, January 2011), 6.
19. "PwC 2011 Global State of Information Security Survey" (PricewaterhouseCoopers, 2010), pwc.com/giss2011.2010.
20. See "Trial by Fire" (PricewaterhouseCoopers, October 2009), 5; see also Baker, Waterman, and Ivanov, "In the Crossfire."
21. Jon Brodkin, "Gartner: Enterprise IT Spending to Hit $2.5 Trillion Next Year," *Network World*, October 18, 2010, www.networkworld.com/news/2010/101810-enterprise -it-spending.html.
22. United States Department of Homeland Security, *National Infrastructure Protection Plan* (Washington, DC: Department of Homeland Security, 2009), 10, www.dhs.gov /xlibrary/assets/NIPP_Plan.pdf.
23. Executive Office of the President, "Cyberspace Policy Review," v.

24. Baker et al., "2010 Data," 56.
25. For more details, see "The Cyber Security Social Contract: 2.0" (Arlington, VA: Internet Security Alliance, December 2009).
26. Scott Borg, "A Framework for Securing the Global 'IT' Supply Chain," in "The Cyber Security Social Contract: 2.0."
27. Jeff Brown, "Disrupting Attacker Command and Control Channels: A New Model for Information Sharing," in "The Cyber Security Social Contract: 2.0."
28. Jody R. Westby, *Governance of Enterprise Security: CyLab 2010 Report* (Pittsburg, PA: Carnegie Mellon College of Engineering CyLab, December 2008).
29. Ibid.
30. "The Financial Impact of Cyber Risk: 50 Questions Every CFO Should Ask" (Washington, DC: American National Standards Institute and Internet Security Alliance, 2008), www.isalliance.org.

PART V

BEHAVIORAL NORMS

CHAPTER 12

Setting Norms for
Activities in Space

MICHAEL KREPON

Space is a very demanding domain in which to operate, even when nations choose not to impose barriers to each other's success. Space can easily become a chaotic domain as more countries, national enterprises, international consortiums, and nongovernmental entities with contesting agendas seek gains or seek to deny gains to others. Some barriers to successful space operations are growing markedly, such as space debris that can have indiscriminate and lethal effects. Other potential barriers in the form of multipurpose technologies such as lasers that could be used to interrupt, harm, or destroy spacecraft or their operations are not hard to acquire. Any space-faring nation that has the capability to launch and maintain satellites in orbit also has the capability to create havoc in space. Space is a domain where the prisoner's dilemma could fill many jail cells.

Without rules, there are no rule breakers. Norms establish standards, set expectations, and clarify irresponsible behavior. They can help nations that act responsibly to isolate and to facilitate appropriate actions against rule breakers. Norms can evolve from customary practices reflecting the self-interest of individual states. These norms can be clarified by the passage of national laws or regulations, and if enough countries agree to the same customary practices, they can become codes of conduct with international standing. Some codes are deemed important enough—such as the nonproliferation of nuclear weapons or a ban on the possession and use of chemical and biological weapons—as to warrant codification in treaty form. Even in the absence of formal codification, norm setting can help order potentially chaotic domains.

The magna carta that established norms for national operations in space is the Treaty on Principles Governing the Activities of States in the Exploration and Use of Outer Space, including the Moon and Other Celestial Bodies, also known as the Outer Space Treaty (OST).[1] This treaty was negotiated in 1967 during the Johnson administration. The nature and challenges of space operations have changed significantly in subsequent decades. Many more countries now use space for military, commercial, and other purposes.[2] National enterprises and multinational consortiums have become active in space, which was not the case at the outset of the space age. Geosynchronous orbit has become crowded and space debris has grown exponentially in recent years.[3] The principles and norms of responsible behavior established by the OST require updating. A rare opportunity exists to do so by crafting a code of conduct that responsible space-faring nations can adhere to, but many challenges lie ahead.

NORM SETTING FOR SPACE

In the 1960s there were concerns that a US–Soviet space race could spark a superpower conflict in which weapons would constantly be circling overhead. Instead, space became a domain of uncommon strategic restraint, even as Washington and Moscow produced and deployed many thousands of nuclear weapons. Why did the superpower arms race not extend into space? One reason was that strategic competition was dangerous enough on earth and both superpowers understood that it would become far more dangerous if elevated into space. The fragility of mankind's initial forays into the heavens and the promise of future steps were sufficiently understood that both the United States and the Soviet Union refrained from actions in space that could have had negative, spiraling consequences. The vehicles that the superpowers used to begin setting norms for responsible activities in space were two UN resolutions, Stationing Weapons of Mass Destruction in Outer Space of October 1963 and the Declaration of Legal Principles Governing the Activities of States in the Exploration and Use of Outer Space of December 1963. These resolutions were the precursors to the OST.[4]

Among the norms established by the OST are that the exploration and use of outer space are to be carried out for the benefit and in the interests of all countries, in accordance with international law, including the Charter of the United Nations; the deployment of nuclear weapons or any other kinds of weapons of mass destruction (WMD) is prohibited; the establishment of military bases, installations and fortifications, the testing of any type of weapons, and the conduct of military maneuvers on celestial bodies are prohibited; states bear international responsibility for activities carried out by governmental agencies and nongovernmental entities within their national jurisdiction; states are liable for damages resulting from their space launches; states retain jurisdiction and control over objects launched into space; states are to avoid the harmful contamination of outer space; states are to avoid activities that could cause potentially harmful interference with the activities of other states; and states are to undertake appropriate international consultations for activities that would cause potentially harmful interference in the peaceful exploration and use of outer space.[5]

The importance of the norms is best appreciated by considering the likelihood of increased friction between major space-faring nations in their absence. For example, today no one laments the OST prohibitions on nuclear weapons orbiting in outer space, but this was a distinct concern in the formative stages of superpower competition. Another way to consider the value of OST norms is to focus on their limits. The OST was silent on conventional weapons in orbit as well as destructive tests against satellites, which are both areas of concern. Anti-satellite (ASAT) tests are rare occurrences, so when any nation demonstrates this capability, it warrants great attention, especially when such testing results in debris fields that endanger space operations. The Chinese ASAT rocket test that used a kinetic kill vehicle to destroy an obsolete weather satellite in January 2007 and the US Navy shoot-down of a nonfunctioning reconnaissance satellite by a modified Standard Missile-3 in February 2008 raised international concerns about the weaponization of outer space.[6] Military demonstrations of ASAT capability also presumably prompted the more serious pursuit by major space-faring nations of offensive counterspace capabilities, countermeasures, and military planning in the event of space warfare. The absence of norms with respect to weapons in space employing conventional effects stands in stark contrast to the OST prohibitions on weapons of mass destruction in orbit.

One norm relating to space was codified in treaty form for three decades but is no longer in effect. In 1972, the Nixon administration negotiated the Anti-Ballistic Missile (ABM) Treaty with the Soviet Union. One provision of the treaty banned both space-based ABM systems and components. Soon after the Senate consented to the ABM Treaty with just two negative votes, its constraints became controversial in the United States. The Reagan administration sought to reinterpret, and considerably relax, these obligations, only to be rebuffed by the Senate. In 2001, the George W. Bush administration withdrew from this pact. The flight testing, development, and deployment of national missile defenses, especially space-based missile defenses and their components, remain politically controversial and have sparked diplomatic countermoves by Russia and China. The friction between major powers on the subject of missile defenses has not extended to other space-related activities in domains where norms have been established by the OST.

Subsequent to the OST, diplomatic accords that establish norms for responsible space-faring nations have been few and far between, and of limited scope:

• The Agreement on the Rescue of Astronauts, the Return of Astronauts and the Return of Objects Launched into Outer Space (the "Rescue Agreement"), adopted by the General Assembly in its resolution 2345 (XXII), opened for signature in April 1968, entered into force in December 1968. This agreement's central objective and purpose are, "States shall take all possible steps to rescue and assist astronauts in distress and promptly return them to the launching State, and States shall, upon request, provide assistance to launching States in recovering space objects that return to Earth outside the territory of the Launching State."

- The Convention on International Liability for Damage Caused by Space Objects (the "Liability Convention"), adopted by the General Assembly in its resolution 2777 (XXVI), opened for signature in March 1972, entered into force in September 1972. This convention's central objective and purpose are that "a launching State shall be absolutely liable to pay compensation for damage caused by its space objects on the surface of the Earth or to aircraft, and liable for damage due to its faults in space."
- The Convention on Registration of Objects Launched into Outer Space (the "Registration Convention"), adopted by the General Assembly in its resolution 3235 (XXIX), opened for signature in January 1975, entered into force in September 1976. This convention's central objective and purpose are, "Member States conducting space launches should provide the United Nations with the following information: registration number and general function of space object, and the date, territory and basic orbital parameters of launching."
- The Agreement Governing the Activities of States on the Moon and Other Celestial Bodies (the "Moon Agreement"), adopted by the General Assembly in its resolution 34/68, opened for signature in December 1979, entered into force in July 1984. This agreement's central objective and purpose are, "The Moon and other celestial bodies are a natural resource and the common heritage of mankind and should be used exclusively for peaceful purposes, [and] their environments should not be disrupted."[7]

Several treaties besides the now-defunct ABM Treaty, including treaties governing strategic arms reduction, affirm the norm first codified in the 1972 Strategic Arms Limitation accords obligating the parties "not to interfere" with each other's "national technical means" of monitoring compliance. This norm provides an explicit pledge of protection for certain satellites that have become important instruments of strategic stability.[8]

The OST and subsequent agreements leave much work to be done to strengthen norms of responsible behavior in space, particularly in three areas:

- debris mitigation, especially generated by ASAT tests
- purposeful, harmful interference against objects in space
- space traffic management, especially to avoid collisions

LIMITS OF NORM BUILDING

There are many reasons why American presidents do not focus on norm setting for space and why their record of accomplishments in space diplomacy is quite modest. They focus first and foremost on negotiations to reduce nuclear dangers, and thus space-related issues usually go to the rear of the queue. Nuclear weapons and launchers have distinct, circumscribed purposes, making it somewhat less difficult to negotiate constraints on their deployment and number. By contrast, space weapons can be fashioned from many technologies and can be used for other essential military and nonmilitary purposes. For example, lasers can be used for legitimate peaceful purposes such as range finding, station keeping, and verification but can also be used for dazzling and damaging satellites.[9] As a consequence, negotiations could produce results of broad scope that impair essential purposes and military capabilities or fail to effectively constrain space weapon capabilities by being too narrow in scope. In addition, space diplomacy has been moribund because the forum in which the talks are supposed to occur—the sixty-five-nation Conference on Disarmament in Geneva—operates by consensus under the chair of a rotating presidency and has been dysfunctional for more than a decade.[10]

Another reason why space diplomacy has been a backwater, marked by long periods of disinterest and only brief spurts of meaningful diplomacy, is that on those rare occasions when Washington has tried to negotiate seriously, Moscow has overreached badly. For example, when President Carter was interested in placing restraints on ASAT weapons, Soviet negotiators argued that the space shuttle with its Canadian-built arm for retrieving and deploying satellites was an ASAT. Nothing came of the space talks during the Carter administration.[11]

The administration of George W. Bush rejected diplomatic initiatives that might constrain freedom of action in space by the US military. The *National Space Policy* issued in August 2006 stated that "the United States will oppose the development of new legal regimes or other restrictions that seek to prohibit or limit US access to or use of space. Proposed arms control agreements or restrictions must not impair the rights of the United States to conduct research, development, testing, and operations or other activities in space for US national interests."[12] In support of this policy, Under Secretary of State for Arms Control and International Security Robert Joseph asserted "there is no arms race in space and we see no signs of one emerging."[13]

Skeptics of the need for a code of conduct during the George W. Bush administration might have viewed any initiative as a slippery slope toward the eventual reimposition of the ban on space-based missile defenses under the ABM Treaty. Others might have viewed a code of conduct as an impediment to their desire for dominant US military capabilities in, from, and through space. For whatever reason, the Bush administration was unwavering in its stance—even after the People's Liberation Army (PLA) carried out a kinetic energy ASAT test in January 2007 against a one-ton satellite that created the largest and longest-lasting man-made debris field in the history of the space age, generating roughly 2,500 pieces of debris larger than ten centimeters (big enough to destroy a satellite outright) that will remain in orbit at an altitude of 850 kilometers (a densely populated part of space) for many decades.[14]

The debris-generating ASAT test by the PLA was followed, in sharp succession, by three other wake-up calls attesting to the need for additional norms of responsible behavior in space. In February 2007, the upper stage of a Russian Proton rocket exploded over Australia, littering space with more than 1,000 pieces of junk in an elliptical orbit.[15] In February 2008, the US intercepted an errant spy satellite laded with toxic fuel and about to reenter the earth's atmosphere, as a possible danger to people in the reentry impact area, demonstrating a very agile ASAT missile capability without creating a lingering debris field.[16] Then, in February 2009, at an altitude of 790 kilometers above northern Siberia, a nonoperational Russian Cosmos 2251 satellite collided with a functioning American commercial Iridium communications satellite, causing another potentially lethal spike of more than 1,000 objects.[17]

Space developments during the last two years of the Bush administration badly undermined arguments against norm-setting measures and clarified that, even in the absence of an arms race in space, this domain could become far less hospitable and far more dangerous for space operations essential for US national and economic security. Although not reaching the threshold of an arms race in space, even limited ASAT testing could greatly complicate and potentially negate US military plans, programs, and policies. Developments in space during the end of the Bush administration clearly highlighted the absence of norms in the OST in the three crucial areas of debris mitigation (whether from ASAT tests or other means); purposeful, harmful interference against space objects; and space traffic management, especially to avoid collisions.

Recognizing the growing problem of space debris, the Bush administration continued to pursue long-standing, bottom-up efforts to draft voluntary debris mitigation guidelines at the Interagency Space Debris Coordination Committee. This forum, consisting of ten space agencies, drafted guidelines after almost twenty years of effort in 2002.[18] The United Nations approved the voluntary guidelines without dissent in December 2007.[19] The Bush administration steered clear of other space diplomacy initiatives that might in any way limit the action of the military in space. The net effect of this rejectionist stance was less US freedom of action in space because of the impetus given to ASAT testing and the exponential growth in space debris during the last two years of the Bush administration.

A CODE OF CONDUCT VERSUS A TREATY

Diplomatic options to enhance space security range from a code of conduct clarifying rules of the road and best practices for space-faring nations to an ambitious treaty banning space weapons and their threatened use. Some might object to a code of conduct as being too marginal, while others could object to a treaty of broad scope as being too ambitious.

In the four decades since the OST was agreed upon, no multilateral negotiations of comparable or greater scope have ever been undertaken. Negotiating a treaty to ban space weapons of all kinds is a very daunting undertaking, since many technologies or techniques used for peaceful purposes in outer space could also be employed to disable or destroy satellites. For example, the Chinese sets of maneuvers to coax their SJ-12 satellite into position beside the smaller SJ-06F satellite in August 2010 might have been to develop and practice rendezvous techniques for innocent close-up inspection or on-orbit servicing, but the activity could have been an antisatellite test.[20] Banning all multipurpose technologies or techniques is impractical, and banning technical applications dedicated to attacks against satellites does not provide reassurance, given unconstrained latent or residual capabilities.

Without launch payload inspections, verification of treaty limits or bans would also be problematic, as in the case of space mines that might be piggybacked on other payloads.[21] Payload inspections, first proposed in the Eisenhower administration, remain highly sensitive and unlikely. Another roadblock to negotiations on an ambitious space treaty comparable to the OST is that the negotiating forum established for this purpose, the Conference on Disarmament in Geneva, could not begin or complete work on any of its agenda items in the absence of a consensus. Since the advent of the Obama administration, talks on space security have been stalled at the Conference on Disarmament because Pakistan objects to negotiations on a fissile material cutoff pact.[22] Moreover, at the national level, the Senate reflects bitter political divides, making it very difficult for a president with modest, let alone ambitious, negotiating agendas to secure the necessary two-thirds vote for ratification.

Notwithstanding these daunting challenges, Russia and China filled the void in space diplomacy created by the Bush administration's withdrawal from the ABM Treaty by proposing an ambitious treaty to take its place. In June 2002, they submitted a paper at the Conference on Disarmament on "possible elements for a future international legal agreement on the prevention of the deployment of weapons in outer space, the threat or use of force against outer space objects."[23] Moscow and Beijing subsequently dipped into the old Soviet playbook to table a draft Treaty on the Prevention of the Deployment of Weapons in Outer Space (PPWT) in February 2008.[24] This draft treaty is of greater scope than the defunct ABM Treaty. It defines space weapons as "any device placed in outer space, based on any physical principle, which has been specially produced or converted to destroy, damage, or disrupt the normal functioning of objects in outer space, either on the Earth or in the Earth's atmosphere." The draft of the Russian and Chinese treaty states that "a weapon shall be considered to have been 'placed' in outer space if it orbits the Earth at least once, or follows a section of such an orbit before leaving this orbit, or is permanently located somewhere in outer space."[25]

The draft Russian and Chinese treaty raises problems of scope while avoiding problems of verification. It recognizes that technologies and equipment used for other purposes could be employed as space weapons, and hence defines the term *space weapon* as specially produced or converted for this purpose. Unless there are common understandings on whether a multipurpose device or technology has been "specially produced or converted" so as to qualify as a space weapon, the ban proposed by Moscow and Beijing has no practical effect. Ground-, sea-, or air-based capabilities could be used to attack objects in space, but have other military applications. For example, ground-based interceptor missiles could be tested and used for ballistic missile defense as well as ASAT purposes. It is unclear whether externally observable differences could help distinguish satisfactorily between these uses or whether such differences would have any credible meaning. An inclusive definition of space weapons would foreclose essential military capabilities, while a limiting definition would allow many kinds of latent ASAT systems to remain unconstrained.

The draft treaty's focus on banning Cold War–era "space strike weapons"—weapons based in space designed to attack targets on earth—is also problematic, as it tackles a problem that is not likely to materialize and yet which generates strong supportive feelings on Capitol Hill. The Russian and Chinese draft is also silent with respect to norm setting for space debris, the most pressing threat to satellites and space flight. Nor does this draft treaty address in a direct way kinetic energy ASAT tests or use by means of ground-based interceptors, actions that could make low earth orbit unusable for space operations, as was evident from the Chinese ASAT test in January 2007. In other words, the draft treaty focuses on weapons that are least likely to be deployed, while being silent on ASATs that have already been tested that have extremely destructive, indiscriminate, and long-lasting effects. ASAT weapons using nondestructive effects, such as cyber and jamming attacks, are far more likely to be employed in crises or warfare yet less likely to be included in a definition of space weapons in a prospective treaty.[26]

For these and other reasons, a code of conduct in the form of an executive agreement is a far more practical way than an ambitious treaty to set and strengthen norms of responsible behavior in space. Analogs for a code of conduct for space exist for US and Russian navies, armies, and air forces operating in close proximity. The 1972 Incidents at Sea Agreement negotiated by the United States and the Soviet Union during the Nixon administration establishes norms of responsible behavior for navies and aircraft operating in close proximity.[27] This model executive agreement has been adopted by other navies. The 1989 Dangerous Military Practices Agreement, signed by President George H. W. Bush and Soviet General-Secretary Mikhail Gorbachev, establishes comparable understandings for armies and air forces operating in close proximity.[28] These accords have demonstrated their utility and have not generated controversy. The domain of space, unlike the ground, the sea, and the air, is notable for its absence of rules of the road defining responsible military practices.

As a presidential candidate, Barack Obama endorsed the concept of a code of conduct for responsible space-faring nations, but once he was elected, the familiar obstacles stood in his way.[29] Faced with a deadline for the expiration of monitoring provisions of its strategic arms reduction accords with Russia, the Obama administration put completion of New START at the top of the agenda and undertook a series of time-consuming posture reviews on both space and nuclear issues. The resulting *National Space Policy*, unlike that of the previous administration, endorsed space initiatives that were equitable, verifiable, and consistent with national security interests.[30] The pursuit of initiatives that met these criteria took a back seat to gaining the required votes in the Senate for ratification of New START, which did not occur until December 2010.

The Stimson Center developed two model codes of conduct with the assistance of US experts and partnering nongovernmental organizations from other space-faring countries.[31] The multilateral initiative championed by the Stimson Center framed its code of conduct in terms of the following rights and responsibilities of space-faring nations.

Rights of Space-Faring Nations:
- The right of access to space for peaceful exploration and uses and safe operations, including military support functions.
- The right of self-defense as enumerated in the Charter of the United Nations.
- The right to be informed on matters pertaining to the objectives and purposes of this code of conduct.
- The right of consultation on matters of concern and the proper implementation of this code of conduct.

Responsibilities of Space-Faring Nations:
- The responsibility to respect the rights of other space-faring nations and legitimate stakeholders.

- The responsibility to regulate legitimate stakeholders that operate within their territory or that use their space launch services to conform to the objectives and purposes of this code of conduct.
- The responsibility to develop and abide by rules of safe space operation and traffic management.
- The responsibility to share information related to safe space operations and traffic management and to enhance cooperation on space situational awareness.
- The responsibility to mitigate and minimize space debris in accordance with the Inter-Agency Debris Coordination Committee guidelines or possible future international standards.
- The responsibility to refrain from harmful interference against space objects.
- The responsibility to consult with other space-faring nations regarding activities of concern in space and to enhance cooperation to advance the objectives and purposes of this code of conduct.[32]

The European Union also found utility in a code of conduct and engaged in a multiyear effort that resulted in the public release of a draft in December 2008.[33] The European Union's draft code of conduct covers the three most important missing bases of the OST: debris mitigation, harmful interference, and space traffic management. It places particular emphasis on "the responsibility of States to take all the appropriate measures and cooperate in good faith to prevent harmful interference in outer space activities." One of its "general measures" is for subscribing states to "establish and implement national policies and procedures to minimize the possibility of accidents in space, collisions between space objects or any form of harmful interference with other States right to the peaceful exploration and use of outer space." Another is "to promote the development of guidelines for space operations within the appropriate fora for the purpose of protecting the safety of space operations and long-term sustainability of outer space activities." The draft EU code addresses the issue of kinetic energy ASAT tests in the context of debris mitigation, calling on subscribing states to "refrain from intentional destruction of any on-orbit space object or other harmful activities which may generate long-lived space debris."[34]

AN INDIRECT APPROACH

Sir Basil Liddell Hart suggested there are times in military campaigns when it is wisest to adopt an indirect approach.[35] The same holds true in diplomacy. There are clear and compelling reasons to update norms of responsible behavior in space. Although it is true that treaties codify norms more definitively than codes of conduct, it is also true that a code of conduct for activities in space is a far more realizable objective than a treaty of ambitious yet vague scope. How nations act in space matters far more than how they define space weapons in long, arduous treaty negotiations. A code of conduct in the form of an executive agreement signed by major powers can help enumerate best practices and decrease worst practices in space. Executive agreements signed by US leaders have legal standing and are not subject to the consent of sixty-seven senators. On rare occasions, they are voted upon and passed, by simple majorities, by both houses of Congress.[36]

A code of conduct for space would establish standards of responsible behavior during peacetime. To be sure, practices in wartime differ from those in peacetime, but even warfare has norms (that are sometimes broken). Establishing a code of conduct for peacetime increases the likelihood that at least some rules of responsible behavior in space can be carried over during severe crises and warfare. Paradoxically, the protection of satellites rests, in part, on their vulnerability to attack, and on the retaliation that would occur if they were attacked. Satellites provide substantial benefits to all major powers, and once satellites are either interfered with or attacked, uncontrolled escalation could follow. This scenario benefits none of the combatants, especially because satellites are intricately connected to nuclear forces. This circumstance may help explain why, at least to date, satellites have not been interfered with at times of increased friction between the major powers. The likelihood of warfare between powers has been greatly diminished since World War II, but remains enough of a possibility for some nations to develop capabilities to interfere with satellites should this be deemed necessary. Deterrence in space as on earth relies on denying the potential benefits of an attack by reducing the chances of success and increasing potential costs through retaliation.[37] Acts of interference are more likely when nations with limited military capabilities face contests or crises with major powers.

WILL a code of conduct for responsible space-faring nations be negotiated? Many long-standing impediments remain in place. The Conference on Disarmament may no longer be able to negotiate significant agreements. Russia and China continue to promote overly ambitious accords. For these reasons, success may well remain elusive. Yet the European Union has stepped up to the challenge of drafting a code of conduct for others to accept or revise.

On January 17, 2012, Secretary of State Clinton did announce "the United States has decided to join with the European Union and other nations to develop an International Code of Conduct for Outer Space Activities," but with a caveat that "we will not enter into a code of conduct that in any way constrains our national security-related activities in space or our ability to protect the United States and our allies."[38] Nonetheless, key spacefaring nations have both the creativity and agility to mount a new diplomatic initiative to draft a code of conduct.

Some factors suggest a rare opportunity for a diplomatic success. International concerns over space debris, ASAT tests, and other counteroffensive space capabilities have been heightened. Moscow and Beijing, noting the volatile nature of US politics, may see the wisdom of accepting what they would term "interim measures" to their proposed treaty, including a code of conduct. And the Obama administration, or its successor, may demonstrate the necessary commitment to working together in achieving a historic success in space diplomacy.

NOTES

1. The agreement on the Outer Space Treaty was reached by the UN General Assembly in 1966. It was adopted under Resolution 2222 (XXI), opened for signature in January 1967, and entered into force in October 1967. The term *Outer Space Treaty* has become part of modern parlance. See Francis Lyall and Paul B. Larsen, *Space Law: A Treatise* (Surrey: Ashgate, 2009), 53–54.
2. See Friedrich Wilhelm Ploeger, "NATO Space Operations Assessment" (Kalkar: NATO Joint Air Power Competence Centre, January 30, 2009), especially tables 5 and 6, www .japcc.org.
3. Samuel Black and Yousaf Butt, "The Growing Threat of Space Debris," *Bulletin of the Atomic Scientists*, March–April 2010, 1–5, http://bos.sagepub.com/content/66/2/1.full.
4. See Raymond L. Garthoff, "Banning the Bomb in Outer Space," *International Security* 5 (Winter 1980–81): 25–40. For the text of the resolution of December 1963, see www .unoosa.org/oosa/en/SpaceLaw/gares/html/gares_18_1962.html.
5. United Nations Office for Outer Space Affairs, *Outer Space Treaty*, www.oosa.unvienna .org/oosa/SpaceLaw/outerspt.html.
6. Caitlin Harrington, "Chinese ASAT Test Rekindles Weapons Debate," *Jane's Defence Weekly*, January 24, 2007, 4; Nathan Hodge, "Shootdown of US Satellite Raises ASAT Concerns," *Jane's Defence Weekly*, February 27, 2008, 4.
7. For the texts of these agreements, see the United Nations Office of Outer Space Affairs, www.oosa.unvienna.org/oosa/en/SpaceLaw/treaties.html.
8. The Strategic Arms Reduction Treaty (START I) and the Treaty on Measures for the Further Reduction and Limitation of Strategic Offensive Arms (New START) are found on the website of the US Department of State, www.dod.gov/acq/acic/treaties /start1/text.htm#article9 and www.state.gov/documents/organization/140035.pdf.
9. Joan Johnson-Freese, *Heavenly Ambitions: America's Quest to Dominate Space* (Philadelphia: University of Pennsylvania Press, 2009), 11.
10. See Cesar Jaramillo, "Space Security 2010: Trend 3.2 COPUOS and the CD Continue to Be Key Multi-Lateral Forums for Outer Space Governance," August 2010, 70–74, Space Security Index, www.spacesecurity.org.
11. See James Clay Moltz, *The Politics of Space Security* (Stanford, CA: Stanford University Press, 2008), 185–87.
12. United States Executive Office of the President, *National Space Policy of the United States of America* (Washington, DC: The White House, August 31, 2006).
13. Robert G. Joseph, remarks presented at the Marshall Institute, Washington, DC, December 13, 2006, www.marshall.org/pdf/materials/481.pdf.
14. David Wright, "Space Debris from Anti-Satellite Weapons" (Cambridge, MA: Union of Concerned Scientists, April 2008), www.ucsusa.org/assets/documents/nwgs/debris -in-brief-factsheet.pdf.

15. Kelly Young, "Rocket Explosion Creates Dangerous Space Junk," *New Scientist*, February 22, 2007, www.newscientist.com/article/dn11239-rocket-explosion-creates-dangerous-space-junk.html.

16. Marc Kaufman and Josh White, "Spy Satellite's Downing Shows a New US Weapon Capability," *Washington Post*, February 22, 2008, www.washingtonpost.com/wp-dyn/content/article/2008/02/21/AR2008022100641.html.

17. Bill Harwood, "US and Russian Satellites Collide," CBS News.com, February 11, 2009, www.cbsnews.com/stories/2009/02/11/tech/main4792976.shtml; David Wright, "Colliding Satellites: Consequences and Implications" (Cambridge, MA: Union of Concerned Scientists, February 26, 2009), www.ucsusa.org/assets/documents/nwgs/SatelliteCollision-2-12-09.pdf.

18. Inter-Agency Space Debris Coordination Committee, "IADC Space Debris Mitigation Guidelines," action item 22.4 (IADC-02-01), revision 1 (September 2007), www.spacelaw.olemiss.edu/library/space/IntOrg/IADC/IADC-%2002-01%20-%20IADC%20Space%20Debris%20Mitigation%20Guidelines.pdf.

19. See the resolution on International Cooperation in the Peaceful Uses of Outer Space (A/RES/62/217) adopted on December 22, 2007 by the UN General Assembly, www.un.org/depts/dhl/resguide/r62.shtml.

20. William Matthews, "Chinese Puzzle: Beijing Offers No Explanation for Complex Satellite Maneuver," *Defense News*, September 6, 2010, 24.

21. According to Regina Hagen and Jurgen Scheffran, "immediately after its release from the launching vehicle a space mine could attempt to approach and attach itself to the target satellite unobserved—only to detonate when the destruction mechanism is triggered." See "Is a Space Weapons Ban Feasible? Thoughts on Technology and Verification of Arms Control in Space," *Disarmament Forum*, vol. 1 (Geneva: UN Institute for Disarmament Research, 2003), 44–45.

22. "Pakistan Objects to Conference on Disarmament Agenda," Global Security Newswire, January 19, 2010, www.globalsecuritynewswire.org/gsn/nw_20100119_9019.php.

23. Conference on Disarmament, "Possible Elements for a Future International Legal Agreement on the Prevention of the Deployment of Weapons in Outer Space, the Threat or Use of Force Against Outer Space Objects" (Geneva: United Nations, June 28, 2002), www.geneva.mid.ru/disarm/doc/CD1679-ENGLISH.pdf.

24. Conference on Disarmament, "Papers from the CD 2008," *Reaching Critical Will*, www.reachingcriticalwill.org/political/cd/papers08/.

25. Ibid.

26. See Debra Werner, "Satellite Security: Hacking Cases Draw Attention to Satcom Vulnerabilities," *C4ISR Journal* (January/February 2012): 16–17, and see Voice of America, "North Korea Appears Capable of Jamming GPS Receivers," *DefenceTalk*, October 11, 2010, www.defencetalk.com/north-korea-appears-capable-of-jamming-gps-receivers-29335/.

27. For the text of the agreement see the website of the Federation of American Scientists, www.fas.org/nuke/control/sea/text/sea1.htm. See also David F. Winkler, *Cold War at Sea: High-Seas Confrontation between the United States and the Soviet Union* (Annapolis, MD: Naval Institute Press, 2000); Sean M. Lynn-Jones, "A Quiet Success for Arms Control: Preventing Incidents at Sea," *International Security* 9 (Spring 1985): 154–84.

28. American Society for International Law, *International Legal Materials* 28 (July 1989): 877–95. See also United States Department of State, www.state.gov/documents/organization/139393.pdf; Kurt M. Campbell, "The US–Soviet Agreement on the Prevention of Dangerous Military Activities," *Security Studies* 1 (March 1991): 109–31.

29. Barack Obama, "A 21st Century Military for America on Defense Issue," www.barack obama.com/pdf/Defense_Fact_Sheet_FINAL.pdf.

30. United States Executive Office of the President, *National Space Policy of the United States of America* (Washington, DC: The White House, June 28, 2010).

31. On the proposal by the Stimson Center, see Michael Krepon, ed., *A Code of Conduct for Responsible Space-Faring Nations* (Washington, DC: Stimson Center, 2010), www.stim son.org/research-pages/model-code-of-conduct/.

32. Ibid.

33. European Union, "Council Conclusions and Draft Code of Conduct for Outer Space Activities" (Brussels: Council of Europe, December 17, 2008), http://register.consilium .europa.eu/pdf/en/08/st17/st17175.en08.pdf.

34. Ibid.

35. B. H. Liddell Hart, *Strategy* (London: Faber and Faber, 1954).

36. The SALT I interim agreement was approved by Congress in this unusual fashion because it constrained nuclear capabilities and a follow-on treaty was anticipated. The Incidents at Sea and the Dangerous Military Practices agreements were not subject to congressional approval.

37. See Forrest E. Morgan, "Deterrence and First-Strike Stability in Space" (Santa Monica, CA: Rand Corporation, 2010), 6.

38. Hillary Clinton, "International Code of Conduct for Outer Space Activities," press statement, January 17, 2012, www.state.gov/secretary/rm/2012/01/180969.htm.

CHAPTER 13

Establishing Rules for Cyber Security

❖

ENEKEN TIKK

The comparison of cyberspace to the high seas, civil aviation, and viral diseases has generated a debate on the applicability of their regulation to the cyber domain. A group of nations led by Russia and China is calling for a new regulatory approach to the cyber domain.[1] This debate has advanced efforts to explicate the definition, management, and regulation of information-driven society and the corresponding threats. However, before deciding on new regulatory steps, it is useful to look to existing legal concepts that have been designed with the cyber domain in mind or reflect upon accepted principles that can be applied to cyberspace. Considering the international legal and policy framework applicable to cyber security, many concepts useful in remedying cyber security exist but are scattered in various fields of law and often in need of interpretation in the context of current threats. Several of those concepts have proven useful in managing international cyber incidents by creating innovative legal practices. Those practices, if skillfully combined, could reduce the gray area that allows perpetrators of cyber crimes to get away with disruptive and other hostile acts that threaten international security.

CYBER SECURITY LAW

It is difficult to reach a consensus on an exact definition of cyber security. As one analyst opined, the mandate of computer security has grown in complexity and seriousness as information technology has saturated social life and sophisticated threats have multiplied. In order to understand laws applicable to cyber conflict, cyber security must be understood in conceptual terms.[2]

Cyber security originated with computer security, which is based on the scientific and technical field of the same name. In recent decades cyber security has

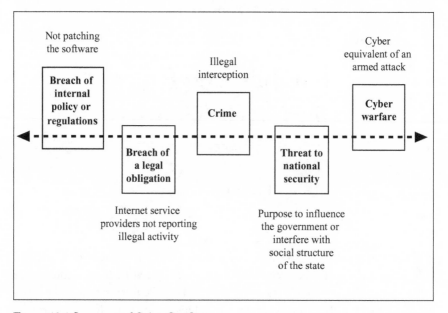

Figure 13.1 Spectrum of Cyber Conflict

Source: Eneken Tikk, "Frameworks for International Cyber Security" (NATO Cooperative Cyber Defence Centre of Excellence).

become complex and sophisticated and grown into network security, information systems security, and information assurance, which all describe measures for protecting computers, networks, and information from failures and breaches. Today the term *cyber security* links computer security to national security and engages the leaders of government, corporations, and nongovernmental organizations at varying levels of interest and involvement as Larry Clinton notes in chapter 11 to this volume. From an international legal perspective, cyber security has become more sophisticated as cyber crimes and other malicious acts in cyberspace become more organized and dangerous. Such acts threaten national security, can reach the threshold of an armed attack and require remediation from the perspective of computer security and information society.

The term *cyber security* appears frequently in US legislation whereas the North Atlantic Treaty Organization (NATO) has adopted *cyber defense*. In its polyglot style, the European Union in its numerous instruments refers to information and communication technology security, network and information security, information technology security, information security, network security, and cyber security. For the purpose of the following discussion, cyber security ranges from organization-centric computer and network security to global out-

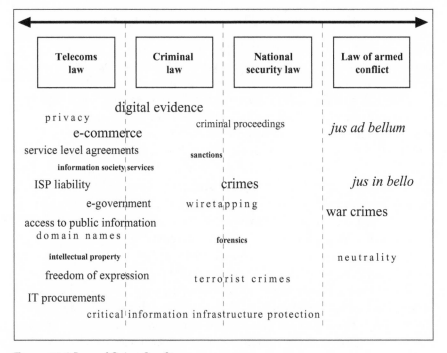

Figure 13.2 Law of Cyber Conflict

Source: Eneken Tikk, "Frameworks for International Cyber Security" (NATO Cooperative Cyber Defence Centre of Excellence).

reach to prevent or mitigate cyber warfare. Cyber conflict together with cyber security comprises different phases and invokes different legal remedies and responses (see figure 13.1).

Accordingly, cyber security begins with designing secure and resilient information systems in peacetime and ends with choosing and applying appropriate means of cyber warfare. Although the operational skills for cyber security are technologically similar throughout the spectrum, legal regimes and solutions can vary significantly. Thus it is crucial to understand and apply concepts from different legal fields to cyber security in a systematic manner, which is easier said than done (see figure 13.2). It is difficult to find experts skilled in every relevant legal field, while many groups are interested in the effect of cyber security on users, businesses, and the information society. With cyber security reaching across various fields of law, it has recently been seen as an interdisciplinary problem. Such approaches are not exceptional, but they rarely cover distinct fields of law with equal intensity.

EXISTING REGULATORY FRAMEWORK

In the massive body of material and case studies on cyber security that has appeared in recent years, a number of suggestions for improving legal clarity for cyberspace management recur within different contexts and with variations in wording. Some on the use of force and self-defense in cyberspace, for example, cover legal or technical issues that otherwise get lost in translation between academics and operators. Others reflect controversies or the divide between legal and nonlegal thinking about cyber security such as data protection and network monitoring. And there are observations from a policy perspective, developed over time and from experience like the need for cooperation, the extension of national sovereign rights to cyberspace, and responsibility for state-sponsored or state-tolerated cyber incidents. Finally, certain conclusions are drawn from cyber incident management. For instance, without the recent examples of Estonia and Georgia, it would not be possible to predict the legal futility of finger pointing at nations denying cooperation or involvement in the incident itself.

Before looking for a new consensus and enacting legislation on cyber security issues at the international level, it would be useful to exhaust the solutions, leads, and remedies existing under current legal frameworks and derived from legal practice. Also, customs of the Internet can answer legal questions given the lack of supranationally binding Internet law.[3]

Some authors use international law theory to explain how customary behavior of the Internet society could form the basis of a supranational legal framework for the commercial sphere of cyberspace or the Internet *lex mercatoria*. Internet customary practices are created unconsciously by user communities and enforced by software, which mechanically imposes norms. These practices can develop in years, months, or even hours in cases of widespread subscription to automatic online update facilities. The idea of custom has advantages. It is flexible and reflects changes in practices as soon as they occur. From the legal perspective, custom plays an important role in the interpretation and process of filling gaps between legal areas and instruments.

Major incidents demonstrate how nations handled national security-related cyber crime. These events have proven useful in discovering that cyber law in practice often differs from theory and serve as a basis for reviewing relevant legal concepts and approaches in other nations. Also, proposals for wholly new legal regimes have been made. Some have proposed a regime of International Law for Cyber Operations.[4] Others have come up with proposals on analogies such as the law of the sea and airspace.[5] On the international level, however, opposition has grown to creating new legal instruments. Overall, there is no consensus on whether added regulations are needed to better secure cyber domain.

The following argument builds on the concept of the ten rules for cyber security and introduces a set of rules derived from or inspired by existing international legal instruments and practices.[6] Some of these rules such as data exchange and cooperation of Internet service providers are mainly subject to regulation under telecommunications law, some issues relating to criminal law and process (criminalization, self-defense, criminal cooperation) and other issues (state responsibility, self-defense against armed attack) primarily belong to the regulatory field of international law and law of armed conflict. A few concepts (duty of care, mandate) are broad enough to embrace several fields of jurisprudence.

The idea behind introducing these rules is interpreting laws on the quality of existing legal frameworks and facilitating discussion of current regulatory approaches. These rules do not offer new regulatory measures, but are intended to invoke discussion among legal experts with different areas of expertise about the applicability of commonly accepted norms and practices for cyber security. Each rule is presented against a defined legal background and has exceptions and counterarguments. The concepts under question include territoriality, responsibility, cooperation, self-defense, data exchange, early warning, access to information, duty of care, criminality, and mandate. This rule set is derived from information technology or cyber, criminal, and international laws including the law of armed conflict. Some rules are long settled, while others require further discussion. Each of the rules is applicable in at least two of three perspectives: legal, policy, and technological. Where applicable, core issues related to practice and interpretation are provided.

1. Territoriality

The information infrastructure within national territory is subject to the territorial sovereignty of that nation. No one central body can govern the Internet by enacting and enforcing laws.[7] This is not to say that the Internet cannot or should not be governed on both the national and international levels. Although challenges in territorial regulatory approaches exist, obstacles to enforcement create even more incentive for nations to harmonize and synchronize their legal approaches to cyberspace.

A debate has evolved since the early days of the Internet over the ability to regulate the cyber environment under a territoriality-based legal order. Internet freedom was advocated in the legendary Declaration of the Independence of Cyberspace: "Governments . . . have no sovereignty [in cyberspace]. . . . Cyberspace does not lie within your borders. Do not think that you can build it. . . . It is an act of nature."[8] The unrestricted nature of the Internet has been characterized as free, not in the sense of free beer, but unrestricted like free speech, markets, trade,

enterprise, will, and elections.[9] Others argue that the whole conception of the
Internet as a place free from regulation is repealed and the Internet could be a
symbol of control just as it has been a symbol of liberty.[10] That inherent liberty
was used as a postulate until it was demonstrated that what the Internet could
provide depends on the laws of technology just as non-electronic action depends
on the laws of nature.[11] It also has been argued that the Internet cannot be regulated much in the same way that any other form of written or spoken word cannot be controlled.[12]

One popular argument for describing regulatory challenges is the cross-border
nature of the Internet, which contends computer network attacks differ from
other means of warfare in that geography ceases to be relevant to the security of
globally networked systems.[13] Similar observations come from the law of armed
conflict that concluded "unless the international community is willing to adopt a
de novo scheme for assessing the use of inter-state coercion, any justification, or
condemnation of [computer network attacks] must be cast in terms of the use of
force paradigm," which is inadequate to defend community values from attack.[14]
At the same time, the concept of territoriality encourages governments to use
regulatory tools at hand to improve public-private partnerships, support generally accepted security measures, and incentivize parties under their jurisdiction
to contribute to national and global cyber security.

The territorial imperative of public international law derives from the Declaration on Principles of International Law Concerning Friendly Relations and
Cooperation among States that affirms nothing "in its terms shall be construed
as authorizing or encouraging any action which would dismember or impair,
totally or in part, the territorial integrity or political unity of sovereign and independent States conducting themselves in compliance with the principle of equal
rights and self-determination of peoples."[15]

Despite general agreement that cyberspace as a whole cannot be subjected to
territorial jurisdiction, nations can work to exercise effective control over the information technology infrastructure within its territory, such as providing sustainable
policy support for investments in information architecture and telecommunications markets, developing an understanding of threats within its jurisdiction, and
balancing the development of the information society with national security
interests.

Control over information assets in sovereign territory provides national authorities with situational awareness of incidents as well as the actions required to
investigate and cooperate outside their jurisdiction. Moreover, those authorities
should not knowingly permit critical infrastructure to be used to launch attacks
on other nations.[16] In case domestic remedies are not exhausted, requests for information or cooperation from other nations would be hard to justify.

2. Responsibility

The fact that a cyber attack has been launched from an information system located in a State's territory invokes the responsibility of that State for the attack. It has been argued that an attack originating from an information and communication system in national territory is prima facie evidence of attribution to that state. Applying cyber attack attribution beyond the law of armed conflict, state and nonstate actors should be considered responsible for cyber attacks launched from within their infrastructure.[17]

In practical terms, the approach that holds the country where attacks originate accountable has been validated a number of times. Estonian authorities accused Russia of the cyber attacks launched in 2007 against its governmental and private infrastructure networks.[18] Although the parties responsible for the attacks were never identified, Russia was linked to the incident as well as the attacks in 2008 against Georgia and Lithuania.[19] China also was accused of conducting cyber espionage against the United States. The People's Liberation Army reportedly hacked into computer networks in 2007 in the most successful attack on the US Department of Defense.[20] Allegedly, it took three weeks and four million dollars for the Pentagon to rectify the situation after theft of an extensive amount of sensitive defense information.[21]

The United States is not the only nation that faces cyber issues vis-á-vis China. Similar allegations by Germany, Belgium, and India indicate that hackers trying to ferret information that could benefit the Chinese have targeted computer networks within their borders.[22] France, Australia, and New Zealand have raised additional concerns.[23] Moreover, the British Secret Service (MI5) alert in 2007 on Chinese spy threats resulted in government-level accusations that Beijing was carrying out state-sponsored espionage against the British economy.[24] At the same time, several NATO members have announced plans for defensive cyber capabilities.

The original wording of the responsibility rule only partly deals with the existing concept of state responsibility under international law. It also touches on accepted criteria of compensating for damages and engaging in damage control. The key issue with attribution appears to be that it is seen by many as mission impossible. From the standpoint of jurisprudence, attribution is not so much a legal concern as a technical aspect of cyberspace architecture. Apart from technical difficulties of identifying the computer operator, attribution relies upon country assistance to determine the source of an attack and information about the perpetrators, methods, and tools and to search, seize, and investigate the incident. From a legal perspective, different standards in attribution exist:

- To restrict access to communications in case of a malicious activity, there is no need to identify the actor—it is sufficient to point out the device.

- To request cooperation from or to impose economic sanctions against a country that lets its cyber infrastructure to be used for routing cyber attacks, there is no need to attribute the attacks to any specific person—it is necessary to define the networks or operators involved and the jurisdictions they belong to.
- To engage in collective self-defense against a nation-state, the decisive factor is the level of hostilities.

Therefore, any 100 percent attribution requirement largely applies to law enforcement or prosecution. Thus attribution often becomes a technical rather than a legal issue; law enforcement usually has the authority to gather and process evidence on the identity of the actor. When this approach is not feasible, it is presumed that lacking identification, hostile acts cannot be attributed to a person.

Under international law several threshold markers exist when it comes to responsibility of a nation for malicious cyber activity. According to one expert group, "if a cyber operation has been launched or otherwise originated from governmental cyber infrastructure there is a rebuttable presumption that the state in question is associated with the operation."[25] Courts also have looked into the question of attribution. For example, in the Nicaragua case concerning US support of Contra paramilitary activities the International Court of Justice determined effective control of financing, organizing, training, supplying, and equipping as well as target selection and planning was not sufficient to meet the attribution threshold.[26] In another case, overall control, beyond the mere financing and equipping of such forces and participating in the planning and supervision of military operations, was established as the threshold.[27]

Although no clear responsibility threshold exists for the attribution of a cyber attack launched from a nationally based information system, nations whose information infrastructure are vulnerable to abuse must expect to be accused of launching strikes from within their borders.

3. Cooperation

The fact that a cyber operation has been conducted via the cyber infrastructure located in a State creates a duty to cooperate with the Victim State. Both the essence and structure of critical information infrastructure depend on public-private collaboration, making it almost impossible to effectively protect infrastructure without cooperation from the private sector. With a considerable part of global information infrastructure in private hands, remedies to safeguard the cyber domain must be based on public-private partnerships. Under the contemporary cyber conflict paradigm, the private sector can fall under attack because of the actions undertaken by or against the government.

Although it is virtually impossible to establish governmental and military networks and information systems without contributions from the private sector, this relationship requires heightened standards of protection. On the other hand, private firms are generally responsible for securing their systems, which affects the different types of cyber attack that threaten them.[28] The Estonian confrontation with Russia in 2007 resulted in distributed denial-of-service attacks against communication service providers, online media, and banks. On the regulatory level, some private information services and equipment now have become part of the national critical infrastructure.

Under the Cyber Crime Convention, parties are requested to cooperate in criminal matters, arrangements agreed on the basis of uniform or reciprocal legislation, and domestic laws, to the widest extent possible for purposes of criminal investigations related to computer systems and data or the collection of evidence in electronic form of a criminal offense.[29] Another example is found in article 4 of the North Atlantic Treaty whereby the parties will consult together whenever they believe that their territorial integrity, political independence, and security are being threatened.[30] The existing provisions offer a broad legal framework for cooperation among interested parties for the purposes of enhancing cyber security.

De facto cooperation has also occurred without clearly defined legal bases. For instance, the activities of national-level computer emergency response teams involve constant consultation and information exchange as well as sharing expertise and practices to pattern, detect, analyze, and mitigate malicious activities that target national and critical private information systems and services. One practical example of ad hoc cooperation was third-party hosting of Georgian governmental websites during cyber attacks launched in 2008. Recently, several botnets including Mariposa, Bredolab, and Waledac have been taken down as a result of successful cross-border cooperation between law enforcement and Internet service providers (ISPs).

The cooperation rule is recognized as a legal concept and a practical behavioral pattern based on the cyber conflict paradigm and interconnectedness of the information infrastructure. Defense against cyber attacks is only possible with cooperation from nations whose infrastructure is used for routing attacks or those authorities with effective visibility of such acts. Even local crimes may have international ramifications, and assistance may be required from all nations through which the attacks are routed. One example is the case of Mafiaboy, whose distributed denial-of-service attacks conducted in 2000 revealed the gravity of the threat and vulnerability of e-commerce.[31]

Effective coordination of national capabilities also could exploit benefits of collective technical, legal, and policy solutions for the whole spectrum of cyber security. For example, the implementation of the directives on both personal data protection and data retention in a coordinated manner would result in availability of traffic data to all potentially interested security authorities as well as a more holistic approach to data protection.[32]

Interdisciplinary cooperation also is necessary among experts on legal, policy, military, technical, and other fields of expertise to combine various methods and solutions to create an effective cyber shield. Consulting, information exchanges, reallocated resources, and support services can be regarded as ways to implement this rule. The international legal framework for cooperation must be supported by national provisions on Internet service provider assistance, data exchanges, and partnerships as well as formal international coalition agreements.

4. Self-Defense

Everyone has the right to self-defense when facing a clear and imminent danger. The basis of this rule is the right to defend against interventions into one's legally protected goods and values. Known in both criminal and international law, the concept illustrates that in principle, everyone has the right to self-defense, with limitations deriving from the proportionality and necessity of such an action.

From a criminal law perspective, acting in self-defense excludes liability for an otherwise wrongful act. In other words, criminal law allows for the use of defense anytime the victim reasonably believes that unlawful action is or is about to be used against him. This is not to claim that every hack-back can be justified, because the concept of self-defense is usually seen as a last resort.

On the international level, criteria for individual and collective self-defense stem from customary law as well as the UN Charter and international case law. Article 51 of the UN Charter declares that nothing shall impair the inherent right to individual or collective self-defense if an armed attack occurs against members of the United Nations. Consequently, a cyber attack only invokes individual and collective self-defense if it rises to the threshold of an armed attack.

As noted more than a decade ago, "Unless the international community adopts a de novo scheme for assessing the use of interstate coercion, any justification or condemnation of computer network attacks must be cast in terms of the use of force."[33] The criteria defining the rights of a nation to respond in self-defense include severity—an armed attack threatens physical injury or destruction of property to a greater extent than other forms of coercion; immediacy—the negative consequences of armed coercion or threat of those consequences usually occurs with great immediacy, while those of other forms of coercion develop more slowly; directness—the consequences of armed coercion are more directly tied to the *actus reus* than in other forms of coercion, which often depend on numerous contributory factors to operate; invasiveness—the act causing the harm in armed coercion usually crosses the border into the target state, whereas in the use of economic warfare, the acts generally occur beyond the target's borders; measurability—whereas the consequences of armed coercion are usually easy to ascertain, such as a certain level of destruction, the actual negative consequences of other forms of coercion are harder to measure; and presumptive legitimacy—in most cases, whether under domestic or international law, the application of violence is deemed illegitimate absent some specific exemption such as self-defense.[34]

For a computer network attack to rise to the level of armed force, it must directly result in loss of life, human injury, or physical damage to tangible property in the same way as kinetic warfare. Thus far no cyber incident has triggered an act of self defense, but it appears that a certain degree of natural deterrence is present in the application of the law of armed conflict to cyber incidents of sufficient intensity. Although a decision on what constitutes a cyber-armed attack must undergo technical, legal, and policy debate, the practical aspect of self-defense requires the further understanding of the available remedies when this threshold is crossed.

5. Data Exchange

Information infrastructure monitoring involves processing personal data. Since the cross-border nature of cyber incidents and the architecture of the Internet do not allow centralized control of online activities, information exchanges on threat patterns, anomalies in network traffic, and ongoing incidents are critical to instituting appropriate security measures. The balance between network monitoring and information exchanges must be carefully struck with respect for an individual's right to privacy. From a legal perspective, data protection regulation is well established, particularly within the European Union. Currently, a considerable divide exists between the legal and technical approaches to managing data and cyber security.

Regulating data protection is controversial because information technology experts have varied legal and technical opinions on network monitoring directives. One interpretation of the Data Protection Directive issued by the European Union leads to the conclusion that collecting and exchanging Internet protocol (IP) addresses are subject to the terms and conditions in the directive. Another interpretation excludes IP addresses from the immediate scope of the applicability of the directive except when they identify those behind an attack.

Information related to identified and identifiable natural persons is considered personal data. EU authorities regard IP addresses and other network monitoring and incident handling data to be personal subject to restrictions under the directive including consent by the subject for processing data, prohibition to transfer data to third countries, and potential inadmissibility, which includes any evidence of data that has been obtained in an unlawful manner.[35] There are arguments against considering IP addresses as personal data, although it is noteworthy that this approach to the regulation of data protection can be mitigated only on the national level.[36]

6. Early Warning and 7. Access to Information

The public has the right to be informed about threats to their life, security, and property. The early warning principle, whereby an irrevocable threat needs to be reported to potential victims, has been regarded as technical rather than legal common sense. It is also based on the concept of access to information as well as being established as best practice among operational cyber security entities such as the computer emergency response teams. Legally, the right of the public and potential victims or affected parties to be informed about a threat is supported by the obligations of communication service providers.

A general right exists to receive and impart information under article 10 of the European Convention of Human Rights.[37] On the national level the right to access information has led to a more specific right to be informed on threats and risks. For example, the Estonian Public Information Act requires public authorities to disclose information promptly on dangers that threaten the life, health, and property of individual persons or the environment.[38]

The concept of early warning has been supported by cyber-incident handling practices. In 2008 three hundred Lithuanian websites were defaced in response to the Parliament's decision to ban the use of Soviet symbols. According to the Lithuanian computer emergency response team, most of those sites were hosted on a single web server. The fact that the Lithuanian government was warned of an impending web attack raises the issue of the standard of service level agreements (SLAs) for government information infrastructure, as well as considerations for defining a nondiscrimination duty to ensure Internet service providers and web hosts are warned about known threats.[39] Because governments use online services provided under SLAs with private sector ISPs, they should consider additional guarantees for their services and infrastructure in terms of the sustainability of electronic services, availability priorities, and reaction time.[40]

While early warning practices, if supported by legal constructs, provide transparency about threats and attacks, considerable counterarguments exist regarding disclosure of information about targets and remedies. The private sector is increasingly becoming a target of the politically motivated attacks and therefore subject to the overall threat picture. It may not be in the interest of companies, banks, and telecommunication service providers to publicly disclose information on their vulnerabilities and damage, but there is a growing trend in exchanging such information within trusted communities to enhance awareness of threats, attacks, and remedies.

8. Duty of Care

Each individual, company, and State has the responsibility to implement a reasonable level of security in their information and communication assets and activities. The concept of duty of care is well known in many areas of law. In the law of obligations, for example, this concept requires parties to exercise proper attention, skill, and stewardship when engaging in contractual relationships. In data protection law it requires those processing personal data to exercise a level of security corresponding to the risks related to confidentiality, integrity, and availability of the data in question. It is also known in the law of telecommunications, which requires service providers to ensure the general security of their networks. Further, the concept applies to legal issues involving consumer protection and information society services.

An obligation to patch software is not necessarily established directly in law. Imposing clear and ultimate obligations on service providers is not common practice in most nations. Although principles exist that require service providers to implement adequate measures to secure their networks, the exact standard of cyber security is often disputable from a legal perspective.

Under the EU Data Protection Directive, appropriate technical and organizational measures must be implemented to protect personal data against accidental or unlawful destruction or accidental loss, alteration, or unauthorized disclosure or access, in particular where the processing involves the transmission of data over a network, and all other unlawful forms of processing.[41] With regard to the state of the art and cost of their implementation, such measures shall ensure a level of security appropriate to the risks of processing and the nature of the data. The Directive on Privacy and Electronic Communications imposes similar safeguards whereby service providers are expected to take suitable technical and organizational measures to safeguard their respective services under article (4) 1.[42]

The duty of care concept can be used to develop and impose security standards for critical information infrastructure and governmental or military information services. Individual entities must assess risks not only from a business perspective but also in respect to national critical infrastructure lists and applicable threat assessments. Both defensive and mitigation measures must be developed in cooperation with respective supervisory authorities. In his chapter, Clinton explores mechanisms for promoting understanding and cooperation between government and industry through social contracts.

The emergency measures adopted by Estonia after the cyber attacks in 2007 illustrate this cooperation. They require the providers of life-critical services to implement the necessary level of security in information systems and information assets to support essential services. Although the providers are given the freedom to choose the means of providing an adequate level of security, they are responsible for the end result.

9. Criminalization

Every nation has the obligation to render possible the prosecution of cyber criminals. It is practically impossible to impose state coercion on any individual engaged in a cyber attack unless the specific activity, consequence, or both have been listed as a crime under national law. The need for reliable and efficient mechanisms for international cooperation in law enforcement matters is urgent. Given the cross-border nature of information architecture, a coordinated effort is needed to deal with international cyber crime. In the framework of relevant instruments and coordination, issues of both substantive and procedural law as well as matters that are closely connected with the use of information technology should be addressed in addition to matters of international cooperation.

The first round of criminalization was passed a decade ago when the Council of Europe adopted the Convention on Cybercrime in Budapest.[43] It aimed to deter actions directed against the confidentiality, integrity, and availability of computers, networks, and data by criminalizing illegal access and interception, interference with data and systems, misuse of devices, computer-related fraud and forgery, and offenses related to child pornography and copyright and other rights. The convention establishes a threshold and a template for harmonizing national penal laws with a view toward malicious acts that target computers or networks. This instrument lists the most common offenses and offers a framework for international cooperation for purposes of investigation, prosecution, and extradition of cyber criminals.

However, the Convention remains unevenly implemented on the national level. For instance, as regards illegal access and interception of data, some nations have decided to extend protection by criminalizing data espionage while others only criminalize such acts when secret information is obtained. Yet other nations have adopted a broader approach and criminalized the act of obtaining stored computer data even if those data do not contain economic secrets.

In principle, the Cyber Crime Convention in concert with national procedural laws address all investigatory techniques and measures required to fight cyber crime.[44] But criminal policies must be fine-tuned on the national level to address new issues like organized cyber crime and appropriately respond to specific cyber criminality issues in a given nation or region.

10. Mandate

An organization's capacity to act (and regulate) derives from its mandate. International bodies can play a major role in coordinating across-border cyber security. Their respective authority and action is covered by the general requirement to operate on a defined and transparent basis. To justify investments in cyber capabilities, international organizations should make use of and enhance efforts by other entities. Where it is possible and practicable, overlaps and gaps in mandates of different authorities must be avoided. Logically, every entity and organization has a unique niche in global cyber security while also being responsible for the security of its networks and services as well as involved in the activities of others. For example, although the primary NATO focus in the field may be related to collective self-defense, the organization still must handle cyber incidents below the threshold of a cyber armed attack targeted against it and individual allied nations. Before a decision is reached on which defensive measures to put in place, the existing framework should be understood to avoid conflicting practices and gaps in coordination. As one report emphasized, "NATO is by no means the sole answer to every problem affecting international security. NATO is a regional, not a global organization; its authority and resources are limited and it has no desire to take on missions that other institutions and countries can handle successfully."[45] The same principle applies to the European Union, which has played a major role in synchronizing data protection, e-commerce, and electronic communications law in about thirty countries. The International Telecommunication Union has provided technical standardization and the Council of Europe has contributed the Cyber Crime Convention and relevant infrastructure.

Currently, the mandates of international organizations are not sufficiently defined when it comes to cyber security. For example, cyber crime is tackled by several organizations, which can be categorized as professional, regional, multinational, or global.[46] The better the mandates of such organizations are aligned vertically and horizontally, the more efficient the investments into global cyber security by governments will become. States party to a number of international organizations must ultimately incorporate each organizational agreement into their national cyber security framework.

IT is difficult in legal terms to consider the cyber domain as a distinct aspect of the commons because cyber infrastructure and actors already operate in the other established domains. The satellites, undersea communication cables, and everyone operating from a location on earth are bound to some existing legal regulation. Cyber activities are directly or indirectly subject to legal instruments that must be reinforced with a contemporary cyber threat picture. If various legal constructs are interpreted and implemented with recent incidents and practices in mind, they could foster and support global and national efforts to counter cyber threats.

Even if not a global commons *strictu sensu*, the cyber domain should be regarded as common concern. The end goal is a shared understanding of the importance of cyber security issues and the need to face these threats in a coordinated and cooperative manner. The more nations are willing to recognize cyber as a component of the commons, the more incentive there will be for cooperation.

Potential upgrades and updates to already existing legal instruments are the focal point of international cyber affairs. In order to indicate gray areas and the need for additional regulation, international attention should be focused on how to use the existing regulatory framework to more efficiently combat cyber threats. Only after an interdisciplinary debate on the quality of the existing legal framework can conclusions be reached on which regulatory constructs are insufficient or lacking and therefore need to be addressed on an international or national regulatory level.

NOTES

1. David A. Gross and Ethan Lucarelli, "The 2012 World Conference on International Telecommunications: Another Brewing Storm over Potential UN Regulation of the Internet," *Who'sWhoLegal*, November 2011: http://whoswholegal.com/news/features /article/29378/the-2012-world-conference-international-telecommunications-brewing -storm-potential-un-regulation-internet.
2. Helen Nissenbaum, "Where Computer Security Meets National Security," *Ethics and Information Technology* 7 (2005): 61–73.
3. Przemyslaw Paul Polanski, Customary Law of the Internet: In Search for a Supranational Cyberspace Law (The Hague: T. M. C. Asser Press, 2007), 2.
4. Duncan B. Hollis, "Why States Need an International Law for Cyber Operations," 11 *Lewis & Clark Law Review* 1023 (2007), http://legacy.lclark.edu/org/lclr/objects/LCB _11_4_Art7_Hollis.pdf.
5. Julie J. C. H. Ryan, Daniel J. Ryan, and Eneken Tikk, "Cyber Security Regulation: Using Analogies to Develop Frameworks for Regulation," in *International Cyber Security Legal and Policy Proceedings*, Eneken Tikk and Anna-Maria Talihärm, eds. (Tallinn: NATO Cooperative Cyber Defence Centre of Excellence, 2010), 76–99.
6. The concept was developed by the author in collaboration with Julie J. C. H. Ryan of George Washington University, Daniel J. Ryan of the National Defence University, and Maeve Dion of Stockholm University. The main concept is introduced by Eneken Tikk in "Ten Rules for Cyber Security," in *Survival: Global Politics and Strategy* 53 (2011): 119–32.
7. Robert Kahn and Vinton Cerf proposed the Transmission Control protocol/Internet protocol in 1974. Kahn proposed four rules, the fourth of which proclaimed that "there would be no global control at the operations level."
8. John Perry Barlow, "A Declaration of the Independence in Cyberspace" (1996), http:// homes.eff.org/~barlow/Declaration-Final.html.
9. Lawrence Lessig, *Code and Other Laws of Cyberspace*, 1st ed. (New York: Basic Books, 1999), xiv.
10. Thomas Schultz, "Carving up the Internet: Jurisdiction, Legal Orders, and the Private/ Public International Law Interface," *European Journal of International Law* 19, no. 4 (2008): 802.
11. Ibid.
12. Melissa DeZwart, "The Future of the Internet: Content Regulation and Its Potential Impact on the Shape of Cyberspace," *Entertainment Law Review* 9 (February 1998): 92.
13. See Phillip A. Johnson, "Is It Time for a Treaty on Information Warfare?" in *International Law Studies* 76, Michael N. Schmitt and Brian T. O'Donnell, eds. (Newport, RI: Naval War College, 2002): 439–55.

14. Michael N. Schmitt, "Computer Network Attack and the Use of Force in International Law: Thoughts on a Normative Framework," *Columbia Journal of Transnational Law* 37 (1998–99): 886n38, 913.
15. UN General Assembly, resolution 2625, 25th Sess., Supp. 28 (New York: United Nations, October 24, 1970), 121, 124.
16. Wolff Heintschel von Heinegg, Europa-Universität Viadrina, who initiated the colloquy leading to this article with his presentation "Cyberwarfare: Necessity for New Rules," Conference on Cyber Conflict (Tallinn: NATO Cooperative Cyber Defence Centre of Excellence, June 16, 2010).
17. Ibid.
18. See Eneken Tikk, Kadri Kaska, and Liis Vihul, "International Cyber Incidents: Legal Considerations" (Tallinn: NATO Cooperative Cyber Defence Centre of Excellence, 2009).
19. See Eneken Tikk and Kadri Kaska, "Legal Cooperation to Investigate Cyber Incidents: Estonian Case Study and Lessons," proceedings of the 19th European Conference on Information Warfare and Security, University of Macedonia, Thessaloniki, July 1–2, 2010.
20. Demetri Sevastopulo and Richard McGregor, "Chinese Military Hacked into Pentagon," *Financial Times*, September 3, 2007.
21. Dan Goodin, "Pentagon Attackers Stole 'Amazing Amount' of Sensitive Data," *The Register*, March 6, 2008, www.theregister.co.uk/2008/03/06/pentagon_breach_assessment.
22. Dan Goodin, "India and Belgium Decry Chinese Cyber Attacks," *The Register* (London), May 8, 2008, www.theregister.co.uk/2008/05/08/belgium_india_china_warnings.
23. John Leyden, "France Blames China for Hack Attacks," *The Register* (London), September 12, 2007, www.theregister.co.uk/2007/09/12/french_cyberattacks.
24. Rhys Blakely, Jonathan Richards, James Rossiter, and Richard Beeston, "MI5 Alert on China's Cyberspace Spy Threat," *Times* (London), December 1, 2007, www.lexisnexis.com.
25. Discussions at a conference on cyber conflict sponsored by the NATO Cooperative Cyber Defence Centre of Excellence in Tallinn on June 16, 2010.
26. "Military and Paramilitary Activities in and against Nicaragua (*Nicaragua v. United States of America*)" (The Hague: International Court of Justice, June 27, 1986).
27. Tadic Case (International Criminal Tribunal for the former Yugoslavia, case IT-94–1).
28. See "Unsecured Economies: Protecting Vital Information," McAfee, January 21, 2009, www.mcafee.com/us/about/press/corporate/2009/20090129_063500_j.html.
29. Convention on Cybercrime of the Council of Europe, November 23, 2001.
30. See article 4, "The North Atlantic Treaty" (Washington, DC: North Atlantic Treaty Organization, April 4, 1949).
31. Roderic Broadhurst, "Developments in the Global Law Enforcement of Cyber Crime," *Policing: An International Journal of Police Strategies and Management* 29 (2006): 418.
32. European Union, Directive 95/46/EC of the European Parliament and the Council on the protection of individuals with regard to the processing and free movement of personal data, October 24, 1995; European Parliament, Directive 2006/24/EC of the European Parliament and the Council on the retention of data generated or processed in connection with the provision of publicly available electronic communications services or the public communications networks and amending, March 15, 2006.
33. Schmitt, "Computer Network Attack," 886.
34. Ibid.

35. Under article 7 of the Data Protection Directive, personal data may be processed only if their subject has given unambiguous consent, and under article 26 (1) the transfer to a third country of personal data being processed or intended for processing after their transfer may occur only if the third country in question ensures their adequate protection.
36. See Eneken Tikk, "IP Addresses Subject to Personal Data Regulation," in *International Cyber Security Legal and Policy Proceedings*, Eneken Tikk and Anna-Maria Talihärm, eds. (Tallinn: NATO Cooperative Cyber Defence Centre of Excellence, 2010), 24–40; see also Eneken Tikk, "Defining Critical Information Infrastructure in the Context of Cyber Threats: The Privacy Perspective," in *Modelling Cyber Security: Approaches, Methodology, Strategies*, U. Gori, ed., NATO Science for Peace and Security 59—E: Human and Societal Dynamics (Amsterdam: IOS Press, November 2009), 189–98.
37. "The European Convention on Human Rights" (Rome: Council of Europe, November 4, 1950).
38. Public Information Act, November 15, 2000, §30 (1), www.legaltext.ee/et/andmebaas/tekst.asp?loc=text&dok=X40095K4&keel=en&pg=1&ptyyp=RT&tyyp=X&query=avaliku+teabe.
39. Rytis Rainys, e-mail to the NATO Cooperative Cyber Defence Centre of Excellence Legal Team, December 10, 2008.
40. European Union, Directive 95/46/EC, n47.
41. Ibid., n64; ibid., article 17, n64.
42. European Union, Directive 2006/24/EC, n79.
43. Council of Europe Convention on Cybercrime, Budapest, November 23, 2001.
44. Stein Schjolberg and Solange Ghernaouti-Hélie, *A Global Treaty on Cybersecurity and Cybercrime*, 2nd ed. (Rome: Global Centre for Information and Communication Technologies in Parliament, February 2011).
45. Ibid., 9–10, n67.
46. Xingan Li, "International Actions against Cybercrime: Networking Legal Systems in the Networked Crime Scene," www.webology.ir/2007/v4n3/a45.html.

Conclusion
Avoiding Conflict and Facilitating Cooperation

SCOTT JASPER and SCOTT MORELAND

> The United States will continue to lead global efforts with capable allies and partners to assure access to and use of the global commons, both by strengthening international norms of responsible behavior and by maintaining relevant and interoperable military capabilities.
>
> —*Sustaining US Global Leadership: Priorities for 21st Century Defense*

This volume brings together both security precedents and best practices to guide strategies and partnerships for responsible and sustainable use of the global commons. Despite the imperative to respond to nefarious threats to security and prosperity, considerable debate persists regarding the most effective mechanisms for encouraging cooperative behavior. All the contributors have underscored the need for promoting international norms via voluntary adherence to established standards of conduct and universally recognized ethical behaviors; however, they refrain from prescribing international legal regimes as the preferred normative model. Inclusivity and incentives, rather than legal coercion, form the basis of the suggested codes of conduct.

The most generally accepted definitions of the commons are "an area not under the sovereign control of any one nation" or "shared areas, which exist outside exclusive national jurisdictions."[1] The cyber domain epitomizes how the distributed nature of transnational incidents underscores overlapping jurisdictions that pose complex control concerns in the commons. Although individual nations exercise jurisdiction over the servers, switches, and routers as well as intellectual property, they lack true control because of the seamless boundaries across which information moves globally.

As espoused by Ian Adam in chapter 2, recent incidents and developments reiterate that all four of the domains in the commons, not just cyberspace, are congested, contested, and competitive. However the complexity of malware seen in highly visible attacks in cyberspace outside sovereign authority reflects the pressing need to find innovative ways to facilitate cooperation to avoid persistent conflict in the commons.

PERSISTENT CONFLICT IMPLICATIONS

The major dispute over maritime territorial claims in the South China Sea, as described by Sam Tangredi in chapter 4, continues to be a potential source of conflict.[2] Tensions rose in May 2011 after Chinese ships tried to damage or cut seismic cables being towed by PetroVietnam survey vessels within the Vietnamese exclusive economic zone.[3] Vietnam responded by negotiating with Russia to purchase additional Baston-P mobile coastal defense systems armed with P-800 Yakhont ramjet-powered sea-skimming cruise missiles in addition to six Kilo class diesel-electric submarines to secure marine resources.[4] Although China and Vietnam agreed to establish a defense hotline to reduce tensions, China's insistence on bilateral talks contrasts with Vietnam's desire to negotiate multilaterally and base any settlement on the UN Convention on the Law of the Sea (UNCLOS).[5]

Chinese ability to coerce negotiations is expanded in the sea trials of the first PLA Navy aircraft carrier.[6] In addition to the PLA Air Force buildup of short- and medium-range ballistic missiles as illustrated by Mark Stokes and Ian Easton in chapter 5, China has added a new road-mobile brigade whose solid-fueled Dong Feng 31A missiles can reach any location in the continental United States.[7] This development could evolve into a slow-motion arms race as the need for ballistic missile defense is apparent because air strikes would be dubious against the road-mobile and not silo-based systems. Meanwhile, production and proliferation of fifth-generation aircraft, like the Sukhoi T-50 PAK-FA, complicate the US and allied air superiority calculus for operating deep inland.[8]

Rapidly accumulating man-made debris in low-earth orbit presents a daunting and urgent international challenge. The National Academy of Sciences asserts that the "current orbital debris environment has already reached a tipping point," wherein existing low-orbit detritus could continue to collide with itself and spawn more space debris, even without any future orbital launches.[9] Although capabilities exist in both the public and private sectors for removal of space junk, Michael Krepon warns in chapter 12 that extant space treaties do not adequately address the full implications of commercial technologies as ASAT weapons.[10] He notes that the United States and China have demonstrated military antisatellite capabilities while commercial firms are collaborating on an infrastructure servicing satellite to be launched in 2015. The latter system could refuel and repair satellites, although skeptics fear it could serve as an antisatellite weapon. As the efforts of the European Union and the United States to produce a space code of conduct languish, China and Russia appear to be pursuing an obstructionist approach to space by inserting opaque language on space weapons in a draft UN space treaty.[11]

Sophisticated intrusions into the security networks of Lockheed Martin and several other US defense contractors in May 2011, through use of duplicate SecurID electronic keys made with information extracted from RSA, the security division of EMC Corporation, highlighted the continued extent to which cyberspace is exploited by hackers, criminals, terrorists, and foreign powers.[12] In August 2011, McAfee uncovered an international hacking campaign dubbed Operation Shady RAT, conducted by one specific actor against the networks of seventy-one governments and corporations.[13] Although China denied involvement in Shady RAT, other state actors like Iran are actively contemplating cyber warfare against America and its allies.[14] A spate of targeted intrusions against US Energy Labs in April and June 2011 highlight existing vulnerabilities in various segments of critical infrastructure and key resources.[15] Given the integrated nature of cyberspace, computer-induced failures of power grids, transportation networks, or financial systems could cause massive physical damage and economic disruption.[16] Military operations, both at home and abroad, are dependent on this infrastructure.[17]

The malware seen in the above incidents are known as Advanced Persistent Threats. This class is commonly characterized as being

- targeted—where individuals with high-level access are approached through spear-phishing by spoofed e-mails with malicious links or attachments, frequently in a work context or through social media
- zero-day—where reconnaissance is conducted to understand target systems, applications, and networks to exploit unpatched or unknown computer vulnerabilities
- stealthy—where installed malware hijacks systems, creates back doors, and establishes connections to command and control servers to steal information or alter performance of critical infrastructure or manipulate operations

The severity and complexity of Advanced Persistent Threats and their effects necessitate cooperation among all stakeholders in industry, government, and defense spheres for prevention and mitigation.[18] The method to facilitate this cooperation is the comprehensive approach that can draw upon historical precedents and established tenets in the commons.

COMPREHENSIVE APPROACH SOLUTIONS

Admiral James Stavridis, supreme commander, Europe, articulates how the comprehensive approach is being applied in Afghanistan to secure the terrain and population from the Taliban while creating sufficient governance and security capacity. Admiral Stavridis considers the comprehensive approach to be the most recent manifestation of the idea of mobilizing the resources of an entire society to succeed in modern counterinsurgency missions.[19] The pool of potential assistance for a challenged state is vast and includes whole-of-government as well as individual capabilities and resources from contributing nations (political specialists, private medical bodies, and academe), international organizations (the United Nations, World Bank, and International Committee of the Red Cross), and nongovernmental organizations (Doctors Without Borders and Reporters Without Borders). The Afghan model aligns with the North Atlantic Treaty Organization (NATO) term for bringing together all elements of effort: political, economic, cultural, military, and others.

NATO media releases proclaim that "the need to promote a Comprehensive Approach applies not only to operations, but more broadly to many NATO efforts to deal with 21st century security challenges, such as fighting terrorism, improving energy security . . . protecting against cyber attacks and confronting the threat of piracy."[20] Although the NATO experiences of Afghanistan offer a starting point to design a comprehensive approach for the commons or a particular domain of interest, the methodology must be modified and translated for different operational environments, structural characteristics, and prominent partners, to include commercial actors. For example, a comprehensive approach for cyberspace security could be described as *the employment of unified principles and actions that integrate the capabilities of national governments, global industries, and international agencies to prevent, contain, or resolve conflict in cyberspace.* The objectives of this comprehensive approach would be twofold:

- Embrace security precedents and norms to enable responsible use of the domain.
- Identify best practices and compelling incentives to encourage cooperation.

And the tasks to implement this approach would include the following:

- Create public and private sector partnership forums to enhance shared awareness of threats and vulnerabilities and coordinate incident management efforts.
- Utilize a flexible deterrence strategy that considers the best way to alleviate complications in retaliation, preemption, and escalation.

- Build integrated, resilient, and responsive security systems through joint operating concepts and international collaborative mechanisms.

Consistent with the Afghanistan model, a comprehensive approach for cyberspace security would seek to achieve the highest possible degree of coordination, cooperation, and unity of effort from the different actors involved in achieving objectives and implementing tasks.

SECURITY PRECEDENTS

The oceans and airspace above them, as the first internationally recognized global commons, have established tenets, like the UNCLOS and International Civil Aviation Organization (ICAO), that can serve as the model for addressing security concerns. Space offers precedence for cooperative behavior in the 1967 Outer Space Treaty, even though it inadequately addresses mounting issues of space debris, orbital crowding, and commercial space flight.[21] For cyberspace, the Council of Europe's Convention on Cybercrime is a common framework for nation-states to pursue consistent sovereign criminal policy "on the basis of uniform or reciprocal legislation, and domestic laws."[22]

The Convention on Cybercrime was opened to signature by nonmember nations as an expression of good faith in adherence to cyber best practices. Signatory nations implicitly benefit from compliance as safe bets for corporate investment and preferred trade partners for Council of Europe nations that wish to conduct safe, legal, and transparent cyber transactions. They also signal clear and united enforcement intent to discourage would-be rogue actors in search of cyber sanctuaries. The Convention on Cybercrime is an important initial step, but it does not sufficiently address the inherently transnational nature of cybercrime or offer succinct legal terms of reference or implementation mechanisms for compliance with its provisions. The next critical phase for international cyber security is to establish clear and universally acceptable definitions and norms for nations to meet their traditional international obligations and responsibilities.

The language found in the UNCLOS could provide a useful template for identification of terms, rights, and duties that promote international cooperation while discouraging excessive sovereign government intervention and coercion in cyberspace. The UNCLOS preamble promotes an international order with "peace, justice, and progress for all peoples of the world." These principles should also resonate in a cyber environment that increasingly permeates and shapes our collective social interactions, entertainment, and professions.

UNCLOS provisions that limit state disruption of shared spaces are directly applicable to protecting unfettered cyber network access. For example, the article

125 "freedom of transit" provisions that empower land-locked states with the right of access to and from the sea are just as essential to securing freedom of access to cyber gateways and connectors. Both article 42 and 44 prohibitions against states bordering straits "denying, hampering, or impairing the right of transit passage" through sea lanes through coercive action or failure to communicate hazards are, with some modification, relevant to assigning custodial duties and state responsibilities for access to essential cyber nodes and connections that reside in or pass through sovereign spaces.[23]

The EU draft Code of Conduct for Outer Space Activities provides a clear set of norms and behaviors that could also be applied to cyberspace. The code of conduct centers on a set of best practices designed to enhance security, safety, and sustainability in space. Like the UNCLOS, this code counts the freedom to "access, explore, and use" space for peaceful purposes as its guiding principle. Space, like cyberspace, is a rapidly evolving domain whose utility is dependent upon technological innovation. Since capabilities, systems, and platforms are constantly changing, the code employs broad measures that prohibit "any form of harmful interference with other states" or "any action which intends to bring about, directly or indirectly, damage or destruction of outer space objects."[24]

Given cyberspace shares many of the same principles as other domains, every effort should be made to incorporate conventions or codes that guide behavior throughout the commons. In order to enforce criminal laws and prosecute actors for attacks in cyberspace generated from sovereign territory, nations need transnational investigative cooperation. Even when cooperative efforts are initiated they can be complicated by deliberately circuitous routing of attack traffic and exfiltrated information through compromised servers in third-party countries. In chapter 3, Schuyler Foerster admonishes that deterrence by punishment relies as much on shaping perceptions as it does on developing capabilities. Prosecuting enraged citizens, dedicated activists, and criminal elements for cyber attacks, many of which reside outside the targeted nation, as seen in the online assault by the "hacktivist" collective Anonymous on the Vatican in August 2011, might not be effective given attribution challenges and negative domestic and international reactions to a coercive state cyber posture.[25] Extraditing transnational perpetrators is not a viable option, especially when countries where servers reside will not cooperate. Internationally acceptable rules could help to deter bad actors in cyberspace by promoting appropriate cyber behaviors and entangling nations in a shared commitment for protection from crime and right of self-defense.[26]

The strength of the ten rules for cyber security that Enekin Tikk offers in chapter 13 is that they attempt to incorporate existing legal frameworks and relate them to cyber security best practices. The rules are based on a comprehensive approach that considers relevant legal, policy, technological, and cultural perspectives to identify effective and appropriate mechanisms for compliance, enforcement, and punishment in the cyber domain. By design, those rules can be effectively implemented only via interstate, interagency, and private sector security cooperation and partnership.

PRACTICES AND INCENTIVES

The sharing of cyber best practices can bolster partner capabilities to deal with complex threats. Sharing of techniques for digital forensics or network penetration and resiliency testing could improve technical proficiency. Sharing of procedures for incident management and cyber crime investigation could increase response capacity. Dialogue in areas such as capability development, exercise participation, and workforce training can embrace partner strengths.

As recognized by Larry Clinton in chapter 11, industry is generally wary of partnering with the public sector out of concern that government involvement would lead to overregulation and stifle investment, innovation, and job creation. Still, common interests and shared vulnerabilities provide motivation for cooperation, especially as anarchist cyber-syndicates such as Anonymous and the former LulzSec unite to declare "immediate and unremitting war" on governments, banks, and large corporations. This growing hackivist trend threatens not only governance and commerce but also the privacy and security of individual citizens who utilize the Internet to manage their retirement funds or communicate with family, friends, and colleagues.[27]

Government can utilize market incentives to dispel fears of overregulation and reassure the private sector that investment in cyber security is good business. Cyber security is a costly endeavor, and businesses will inherently make the most cost-effective decisions. By providing tax incentives for cyber security investments, grants for cyber security research, and clear and consistent cyber security standards for award of government contracts, government can make private sector investments in cyber security the financially sound choice.[28]

PARTNERSHIP FORUMS

The rapid pace of change in cyberspace is another reason that military departments, interagency partners, and the private sector should examine new collaborative approaches to cyber security. Public–private sector partnerships can serve to share information about malicious cyber activity and employ protective cyber security measures. These efforts should include means to identify, analyze, and mitigate cyber vulnerabilities in critical infrastructure and key resources.

The National Cyber Security and Communications Integration Center of the US Department of Homeland Security is a promising example of how public and private sector cooperation can effectively counter malicious cyber activities. Since public and private sector users rely on the same cyber networks, systems, and services, they consequently share the same vulnerabilities. The mission of the center is to ensure shared cyber security situational awareness across government agencies, the military, and private sector centers. In addition, the center is responsible for providing defense technical expertise to private sector owners and operators of critical infrastructure and key resources, and coordinating an integrated national response to cyber emergencies.[29]

Shared awareness is one component of an integrated cyber security capability, and response is the other. Under the prescription for aligning the need to cooperate with effective action and resource commitments, which is described by Susan Hocevar, Cyber Emergency Response Teams (CERTs) have emerged from governmental, academic, and commercial organizations to coordinate defense against and response to cyber attacks. For example, CERT agents that focus on industrial control systems (ICS CERT) collaborate with the operational arm of the National Cyber Security Division (US CERT) to develop integrated response procedures for control systems incident response, vulnerability and threat analysis, and intelligence sharing.[30] The utility of integrated CERT response capability was realized in July 2010, as ICS CERT facilities in Idaho orchestrated the coordinated US response to the Stuxnet virus. Following Stuxnet, ICS CERT employed a promising objective review and lessons learned process that incorporated candid recommendations from industry on improving response time and information dissemination into ICS CERT's incident training scenarios and response drills.[31]

DETERRENCE STRATEGIES

The difficulty in monitoring cyberspace, identifying intrusions, and locating the source of attacks in an incident with a high degree of confidence and in a timely manner complicates deterrence and response strategies. The complexities associated with attribution of acts of cyber aggression, according to Kevin Coleman, are compounded by the use of compromised servers, unknowing participants, and noncooperative countries.[32] Botnets, proxy servers, and fake Internet addresses enable attackers and sponsors to operate with anonymity and impunity. Advanced persistent threats conceal or avoid detection of attacker identities and allow plausible deniability by sponsors. If an attack originates from servers linked to nations, is that sufficient evidence to confirm governments endorsed or commissioned the attacks to serve political aims? For example, although the cyber attacks against Google and more than thirty other companies revealed in January 2011 were "tracked back to China, it is impossible to tell whether they were carried out by the Chinese government, by individuals operating with government approval or by rogue hackers."[33]

Problems in detecting attacks or breaches and attributing them correctly delay target identification and speed of execution for prompt or credible retaliatory response. Unlike for kinetic actions that can generally be identified and measured, the failure to detect intentions, moves, and origins in cyberspace stalls preemptive action and could lead to overreactions and miscalculations.[34] Even if the attackers are known with certainty, a challenge exists in determining what incidents justify the use of force in response. For example, do attacks on governmental services, financial enterprises, or media outlets, like on Estonian society in 2007, constitute acts of war?[35] Does a right to counterstrike in self-defense exist if attackers target public sectors or utilities like power grids, communication networks, or critical defense industries? The trigger for in-kind retaliation could be adverse effects such as substantial deaths, secondary kinetic damage, or cascading economic losses.[36]

Even if the origins are traced and fire returned, could collateral damage be avoided if the intrusions were launched through thousands of hijacked computers located in third countries or target nation sites such as the July 4, 2009, attacks on dozens of governments and businesses in the United States and South Korea?[37] A massive counterattack in cyberspace could have cascading effects on civilian computer networks that would escalate to the digital equivalent of mutually assured destruction.[38] Although the Commander, US Cyber Command, contends that "our cyber capabilities represent key components of deterrence," various difficulties complicate preemption, retaliation, and escalation in cyberspace.[39] As Mark Berkowitz eloquently concludes in chapter 9, the optimal approach appears to be denial of benefit through development and deployment of a resilient, layered defense.

SECURITY SYSTEMS

Protecting the computers, networks, and control systems in critical infrastructure and key resource sectors requires a multilayered, defense-in-depth strategy that wields active security defenses that block and hunt intrusions. Implementation of this strategy starts with mapping of the specific geographic location of civilian and military cyberspace physical assets (computers, servers, controllers, cables, transmitters, satellites, and sensors) and their vulnerabilities.[40] Commercially produced capabilities, which include protocol filters, content sensors, behavioral anomaly scanners, leakage detectors, and forensic analysis tools, can then be used to detect and stop or discover and mitigate malicious activity.[41]

The design of active defenses must not only consider present vulnerabilities and threats but also visualize future challenges and the capabilities that will be required to meet them. The armed forces utilize joint operating concepts to contemplate future threat scenarios, using descriptive vignettes to facilitate understanding and identify possible hostile actions and their potential outcomes.[42] The Military Contribution to Cooperative Security Joint Operating Concept reflects the realization that military capabilities must be applied within the context of a broader cooperative security strategy that also incorporates contributions and perspectives from nondefense agencies, private sector experts, and multinational partners.[43]

The Joint Concept for Cyberspace advanced by US Strategic Command endeavors to operationalize integrated security systems through an exhaustive experimentation campaign plan.[44] Concept experiments capitalize on observations drawn from existing military exercises that merge interdomain systems and cyber capabilities and include multinational and interagency partners. Experiments based on plausible future scenarios also help to identify situations where redundant, shortsighted, or poorly coordinated military actions might produce detrimental cascading effects.[45]

Joint concepts and their supporting experiments are constructed to identify capability requirements. Based on joint concept development and experimentation outcomes, the US Army has identified a broad set of capabilities required for ground force cyber network operations. Capabilities that "provide global connectivity to an enterprise communications network" that is "interoperable with joint, Army, interagency, and multinational organizations" enable end-to-end assured support to battle command functions. Capabilities that "monitor for and report cyber threats in real time" and "detect and monitor network intrusions and unauthorized activity in real time" demonstrate awareness of the need for collective systems that provide defense-in-depth from a range of cyber security providers.[46] Although the military may be the lead agent in cyber security campaigns, particularly in austere or hostile environments, the joint force will invariably rely on cyber security partnerships for shared situational awareness and critical network infrastructure provision, protection, and maintenance.

NATO considers cyber attacks in more regional and global terms. The 2010 NATO Strategic Concept asserts that cyber systems "require greater international efforts to ensure their resilience against attack or disruption."[47] The transnational nature of cyber threats is a particular problem for the economically and militarily intertwined NATO nations, who must align member cyber defense capabilities and coordinate cyber security resources for collective defense. In chapter 1, Sandra Leavitt highlights the paucity of organizations like NATO that possess sufficient shared interests and institutional wherewithal to forge and maintain collective action. For this very reason, NATO may be the best entity to organize an international cyber security regime by capitalizing on the relative affluence and shared political and military agendas of its member and partner states.[48] To that end, NATO has nearly tripled its cyber security budget to reinforce cyber security for its unclassified, restricted, and secret communications and information systems.

The new NATO Computer Incident Response Capability will effectively isolate and analyze malware and cyber attacks, deliver network situational awareness and timely threat detection via an advanced sensor array, and provide advanced threat assessment and decision-making tools.[49] Its lead agency, the NATO Consultation, Command, and Control Agency (NC3A), is pursuing an active cyber security defense posture that may set the appropriate tone for other national and collective security arrangements. In the words of the NC3A cyber defense team chief, "NATO is a defense organization. We're defending the territory. We're defending our networks."[50]

NATO members can individually and collectively provide leadership and important contributions across cyberspace and the other domains of the commons. Their ongoing involvement in Multi-National Experiment 7, designed to ensure freedom of action in the commons, is a good start. This experiment brings together multinational and interagency experts and practitioners to explore new planning processes, identify emerging capabilities requirements, share best practices, and develop mechanisms for cooperation within and among the various domains. As Paul Giarra cautions in chapter 8, we must recognize and appreciate the interdomain interactions that underpin international security, commerce, information exchanges, and social interaction in the globalized era. The Multi-National Experiment 7 will explore ways to better understand and shape the interdomain systems that form the basis for comprehensive strategies to protect enterprises that depend on the global commons.

THE commons have become an arena for conflict in the form of intrusion, exploitation, and attack by transnational, regional, and emerging peer competitors. The commons are probed, penetrated, and threatened on a daily basis by provocative actions and unsettling developments. Although the commons serve as operating space for the United States and its partner forces, the vast scope and number of incidents—especially in cyberspace—emphasize that the imperative to prevent, deter, and resolve conflict in the commons is not within the purview of the military alone. Securing the array of indispensable systems operating in the commons mandates the cooperation of national and international instruments of power and elements of influence to identify problems and find solutions. Only through a comprehensive approach that aligns industry with government and defense efforts can unfettered use of the global commons be assured. Recent global initiatives point to an acceptance of this fact and a willingness to cooperate toward common security interests as illustrated by the following measures being taken in the domains:

- At sea, as Gordan Van Hook notes in chapter 10, Maersk Line Limited, the largest US merchant carrier, is working to send organic ship radar system contacts correlated to Automatic Identification System data to a networked data services and analysis system that could be used by a maritime operations center.
- In the air, the International Civil Aviation Organization is bringing civil and military aviation interests together for the first time to share best practices and establish cooperative mechanisms to address airspace congestion and balance the historical need for mission-oriented military airspace control with rapid growth in civil air traffic.[51]
- In space, government customers leverage commercially hosted payload opportunities for attaching responsive military sensor or communication packages to commercial satellites.[52]
- For cyber, Raytheon is partnering with the electrical engineering and computer science departments at West Point to adapt commercially available software to identify insider security threats that could affect forward-deployed military cyber networks.[53]

The global commons serve as the conduit through which communications, commerce, and governance within and among nations flourish. Disruptions in transit and access points indicate the commons remain vulnerable to conflict. In the face of perilous threats, a comprehensive approach is necessary that takes into account the relationships and similarities of the domains operating in concert across the commons. Only by integrating the capabilities of government, industry, and defense can the United States and the international community hope to resolve those problems that are beyond the control and jurisdiction of any one state.

NOTES

The epigraph appeared in new strategic guidance issued by the Secretary of Defense titled *Sustaining US Global Leadership: Priorities for 21st Century Defense* (Washington, DC: Office of the Secretary of Defense, January 5, 2012), 3.

1. Allied Command Transformation, "Global Commons: Asia Pacific Perspective," workshop six report (Norfolk, VA: Allied Transformation Command, November 2010), 3; United States Executive Office of the President, *National Security Strategy* (Washington, DC: The White House, May 2010), 49.
2. Patrick M Cronin, ed., *Cooperation from Strength: The United States, China and the South China Sea* (Washington, DC: Center for a New American Security, 2012), 3–30.
3. Wendel Minnick, "China Becomes Aggressive in South China Sea," *Defense News*, June 13, 2011, 22.
4. Jon Grevatt, "Vietnam Looks to Expand Coastal Defense Assets," *Jane's Defence Weekly*, August 24, 2011, 12.

5. James Hardy, "Hotline to Ease Vietnam-China Tensions," *Jane's Defence Weekly*, September 7, 2011, 15.

6. Trefor Moss, "Interpreting China's Carrier Ambitions," *Jane's Defence Weekly*, September 14, 2011, 47.

7. Wendel Minnick, "China Adds an ICBM Brigade," *Defense News*, September 12, 2011, 38.

8. Robert Hewson, "T-50 Debuts amid Dearth of Orders at MAKS," *Jane's Defence Weekly*, August 24, 2011, 4.

9. National Research Council Committee for the Assessment of NASA Orbital Debris Programs, "Limiting Future Collision Risk to Spacecraft: An Assessment of NASA's Meteoroid and Orbital Debris Programs" (Washington, DC: National Academies Press, 2011), 1, www.nap.edu/catalog.php?record_id=13244.

10. See Clara Moskowitz, "World's First Space Gas Station for Satellites to Launch in 2015," space.com, March 15, 2011, www.space.com/11135-satellite-refueling-mission -space-debris.html.

11. For Russian and Chinese perspectives, see also Pavel Podvig and Hui Zhang, "Russian and Chinese Responses to US Military Plans in Space" (Cambridge, MA: American Academy of Arts and Sciences, March 2008).

12. Jim Finkle and Andrea Shalal-Esa, "Hackers Breached US Defense Contractors," *Reuters*, May 27, 2011, www.reuters.com/article/2011/05/27/us-usa-defense-hackers -idUSTRE74Q6VY20110527; Kelly Jackson Higgins, "China Hacked RSA, U.S. Official Says," *Darkreading*, March 29, 2012, www.darkreading.com/advanced-threats /167901091/security/attacks-breaches/232700515/china-hacked-rsa-u-s-official-says.html.

13. Dmitri Alperovitch, "Revealed: Operation Shady RAT," McAfee white paper, August 2, 2011, 2–14.

14. Associated Press, "China Media Denies Cyber Spying Claim," *Straits Times*, August 6, 2011, C4; Lian Berman, "Iranian Cyberwar: US Must Prepare for Possible Confrontation," *Defense News*, September 12, 2011, 45.

15. William Jackson, "Oak Ridge Lab Shuts Down E-mail, Internet after Cyberattack," *Government Computer News*, April 20, 2011, gcn.com/articles/2011/04/ . . . /oak-ridge-internet-access-still-down.aspx; William Jackson, "Two Weeks after Breach, Energy Lab Back Online," *Government Computer News*, July 14, 2011, gcn.com/articles/2011/07/15 /pnnl-back-online-after-hack.aspx.

16. See Julianne Pepitone and Leigh Remizowski, "Massive Credit Card Data Breach Involves All Major Brands," *CNNMoney*, April 2, 2012, http://money.cnn.com/2012/03 /30/technology/credit-card-data-breach/index.htm.

17. United States Department of Defense, *Strategy for Operating in Cyberspace* (Washington, DC: Office of the Secretary of Defense, July 2011), 4.

18. Alan Joch, "Fighting Back: How the Main Targets of Advanced Persistent Threat Are Responding," *Federal Computing Weekly*, August 8, 2011, 24–25.

19. James G. Stavridis, "The Comprehensive Approach in Afghanistan," PRISM 2 (March 2011): 65–76.

20. North Atlantic Treaty Organization, "A Comprehensive Approach," August 10, 2010, www.nato.int/cps/en/natolive/topics_51633.htm.

21. See Brian Beck, "The Next, Small, Step for Mankind: Fixing the Inadequacies of the International Space Law Treaty Regime to Accommodate the Modern Space Flight Industry," September 2008, http://works/bepress.com/brian_beck/1.

22. Council of Europe, "Convention on Cybercrime," ETS 185, ch. 3, sec. 1, http://conven tions.coe.int/Treaty/EN/Treaties/html/185.

23. UN Convention on the Law of the Sea, 1833 U.N.T.S. 397, December 10, 1982, preamble, articles 38, 42, 44, 125.

24. Council of the European Union, "Code of Conduct for Outer Space Activities," revised draft (Brussels, October 11, 2010), 3–5, 7.

25. Mathew J. Schwartz, "Anonymous Leaves Clues in Failed Vatican Attack," *Information Week*, February 29, 2012, http://informationweek.com/news/security/attacks/232601726; and "Imperva's Hacker Intelligence Summary Report: The Anatomy of an Anonymous Attack," (Redwood Shores, CA: Imperva Headquarters, 2012), 1–17.

26. United States Executive Office of the President, *International Strategy for Cyberspace: Prosperity, Security, and Openness in a Networked World* (Washington, DC: The White House, May 2011), 10.

27. Laurie Segall, "LulzSec and Anonymous Join in Hack Pact," *CNN Money*, June 21, 2011, http://money.cnn.com/2011/06/20/technology/lulzsec_anonymous/index.htm.

28. Business Software Alliance; the Center for Democracy and Technology; the Internet Security Alliance; TechAmerica; and the US Chamber of Commerce, "Improving Our Nation's Cybersecurity through the Public-Private Partnership," March 8, 2011, 2, 10. www.cdt.org/files/pdfs/20110308_cbyersec_paper.pdf.

29. Sean P. McGurk, "The DHS Cybersecurity Mission: Promoting Innovation and Securing Critical Infrastructure," testimony before the Subcommittee on Cybersecurity, Infrastructure Protection, and Security Technologies, US House Committee on Homeland Security, April 15, 2011, 2, www.dhs.gov/ynews/testimony/testimony_1302814781943.shtm.

30. Roberta Stempfly and Sean P. McGurk, testimony before the Subcommittee on Oversight and Investigations, US House of Representatives Committee on Energy and Commerce, July 26, 2011, 6.

31. Robert McMillan, "On the Front Line against the Next Stuxnet," *Computer World*, October 2, 2011, http://news.idg.no/cw/art.cfm?id=9B4D0B77-1A64-67EA-E4998338BAD9277F.

32. Kevin G. Coleman, "US Cyber Defenses Outmatched by Hackers," *Defense Systems*, August 19, 2011, 2.

33. William Matthews, "Chinese Attacks Bring Cyber Spying into the Open," *Defense News*, January 18, 2010, 2.

34. Robert A. Miller, Daniel T. Kuehl, and Irving Lachow, "Cyber War: Issues in Attack and Defense," *Joint Force Quarterly* 61 (2011): 22.

35. Eneken Tikk, Kadri Kaska, and Liis Vihul, "International Cyber Incidents: Legal Considerations" (Tallinn: NATO Cooperative Cyber Defence Centre of Excellence, 2009): 14–32.

36. Siobhan Gorman and Julian E. Barnes, "Cyber Combat: Act of War," *Wall Street Journal*, May 31, 2011.

37. "Cyber attacks enter new phase," *Telegraph* (London), July 10, 2009, http://telegraph.co.uk/news/worldnews/asia/southkorea/5794674/Cyber-attacks-enter-new-phase.html.

38. "Cyberwar: It's Not Just Fiction Anymore," *All Things D*, July 16, 2011, http://allthingsd.com/20110716/cyberwar-its-not-fiction-anymore/.

39. Keith B. Alexander, testimony before the Subcommittee on Emerging Threats and Capabilities, US House of Representatives Committee on Armed Services, March 20, 2012, 7.

40. William Matthews, "Cyber Realities: Push to Map Cyberspace Faces Industry Privacy Hurdles," *C4ISR Journal* (March 2011): 32–34.

41. See the FireEye Malware Protection System (April 2012), http://fireeye.com/products-and-solutions/; and HBGary Products and Services (April 2012), http://hbgary.com/products.

42. United States Department of Defense, "Joint Operations Concepts Development Process," Instruction 3010.02B (Washington, DC: Joint Chiefs of Staff, January 27, 2006), A-2.

43. United States Department of Defense, "Military Contribution to Cooperative Security (CS) Joint Operating Concept," version 1.0 (Washington, DC, December 19, 2008).

44. Amanda Palleschi, "STRATCOM Advances Work on Joint Concept for Cyberspace," *Inside Defense*, August 25, 2011.

45. Michael Collat, "Cyberspace Operations and the Need for an Operational Construct That Enables the Joint Force Commander," *IAnewsletter* 14 (May 2011): 18–21.

46. Headquarters, Department of the Army, "Cyberspace Operations Concept Capability Plan 2016-2028," DA pamphlet 525-7-8 (Fort Monroe, VA: US Army Training and Doctrine Command, February 22, 2010), 46–50.

47. North Atlantic Treaty Organization, "Strategic Concept for the Defence and Security of the Members of the North Atlantic Treaty Organization: Active Engagement, Modern Defence" (Lisbon, November 2010), 4.

48. Kenneth Geers, *Strategic Cyber Security* (Tallinn: NATO Cooperative Cyber Defense Center of Excellence, June 2011), 30–31.

49. NATO Consulation, Command and Control Agency, "NC3A-BE/ASG/11/754, Notification of Intent: NATO Computer Incident Response Capability—FOC (NCIRC-FOC) IFB-CO-13212-NCIRC," Annex A: Summary of Requirements (Brussels, August 31, 2011), and Eleanor Keymer, "NATO Awards Largest Cyber Security Contract to Date," *Jane's Defence Weekly*, March 7, 2012, 10.

50. George I. Seffers, "NATO Set to Strengthen Cybersecurity," *Signal* (August 2011), www.afcea.org/signal/articles/anmviewer.asp?a=2686.

51. Vince Galotti, "ICAO Pursues New Collaborative Frameworks: Why the Time Is Right for Civil/Military Cooperation," *ICAO Journal* 65, no. 1 (2010): 3–9.

52. United States Department of Commerce, "Hosted Payloads," fact sheet (Washington, DC: Office of Space Commercialization, July 19, 2011), www.space.commerce.gov /general/commercialpurchase/hostedpayloads.shtml.

53. Jeanne M. Robinson, "Raytheon and West Point's Information Technology and Operations Center: Partnering to Defend the Cyberdomain," *Raytheon Technology Today* 1 (2010): 30.

Selected Bibliography

Public Documents

North Atlantic Treaty Organization. *Assured Access to the Global Commons.* Norfolk, VA: Allied Command Transformation, April 2011.

———. "Lisbon Summit Declaration." Lisbon: North Atlantic Council, November 2010.

———. *Multiple Futures Project: Navigating Toward 2030.* Norfolk, VA: Allied Command Transformation, April 2009.

———. "Strategic Concept for the Defense and Security of the Members of the North Atlantic Treaty Organization." Brussels: November 20, 2010.

United Kingdom. Ministry of Defence. *Future Character of Conflict.* London: Development Concepts and Doctrine Centre, February 2010.

United Nations. Convention on the Law of the Sea. 1833 UNTS. 397, December 10, 1982.

———. The Treaty on Principles Governing the Activities of States in the Exploration and Use of Outer Space, including the Moon and Other Celestial Bodies. General Assembly Resolution 2222 (XXI). October 1967.

United States Department of Defense. *Joint Operational Access Concept (JOAC).* Washington, DC: Office of the Chairman, Joint Chiefs of Staff, January 17, 2012.

———. *Military and Security Developments Involving the People's Republic of China.* Washington, DC: Office of the Secretary of Defense, 2011.

———. *The National Military Strategy of the United States of America: Redefining America's Military Leadership.* Washington, DC: Office of the Chairman, Joint Chiefs of Staff, February 8, 2011.

———. *Quadrennial Defense Review Report.* Washington, DC: Office of the Secretary of Defense, February 2010.

———. *Sustaining U.S. Global Leadership: Priorities for 21st Century Defense.* Washington, DC: Office of the Secretary of Defense, January 5, 2012.

Unites States Department of Homeland Security. *National Infrastructure Protection Plan.* Washington, DC: Department of Homeland Security, 2009.

Unites States Executive Office of the President. *The Comprehensive National Cybersecurity Initiative.* Washington, DC: The White House, March 5, 2010.

———. *National Security Strategy.* Washington, DC: The White House, May 2010.

————. *National Space Policy of the United States of America*. Washington, DC: The White House, June 28, 2010.

United States Joint Forces Command. *Joint Operating Environment*. Norfolk, VA: February 18, 2010.

Books and Articles

Bedford, Dick, and Paul S. Giarra. "Securing the Global Commons." *RUSI Journal* 155 (October–November 2010): 18–23.

Berdal, Mats R., and Mónica Serrano. *Transnational Organized Crime and International Security: Business as Usual?* Boulder, CO: Lynne Rienner, 2002.

Beyerlein, Michael M., Susan T. Beyerlein, and Douglas A. Kennedy, eds. *Advances in Interdisciplinary Studies of Work Teams: Innovation through Collaboration*. Oxford: Elsevier JAI Press, 2006.

Brown, Michael E., ed. *Grave New World: Security Challenges in the 21st Century*. Washington, DC: Georgetown University Press, 2003.

Buck, Susan J. *The Global Commons: An Introduction*. Washington, DC: Island Press, 1998.

Cawthorne, Nigel. *Pirates of the 21st Century: How Modern-Day Buccaneers Are Terrorising the World's Oceans*. London: John Blake, 2009.

Coleman, Kevin G., and Randy Favero. *Cyber Commander's Handbook: The Weaponry and Strategies of Digital Conflict*. McMurray, PA: Technolytics, December 15, 2009.

Cronin, Patrick M., ed. *Cooperation from Strength: The United States, China and the South China Sea*. Washington, DC: Center for a New American Security, 2012.

Dadush, Uri, and William Shaw. *Juggernaut: How Emerging Markets Are Reshaping Globalization*. Washington, DC: Carnegie Endowment for International Peace, 2011.

Denmark, Abraham M. "Managing the Global Commons." *Washington Quarterly* 33 (July 2010): 165–82.

Edwards, Adam, and Peter Gill. *Transnational Organised Crime: Perspectives on Global Security*. London: Routledge, 2003.

Erickson, Andrew S., and David D. Yang. "Using the Land to Control the Sea?" *Naval War College Review* 62 (Autumn 2009): 53–79.

Flournoy, Michèle A., and Shawn Brimley. "The Contested Commons." *Proceedings* 135 (July 2009): 16–21.

Friedman, Thomas L. *The Lexus and the Olive Tree*. New York: Farrar, Straus and Giroux, 1999.

Hardin, Garrett. "The Tragedy of the Commons." *Science* 162 (December 13, 1968): 1243–48.

Henry, Ryan, and C. Edward Peartree. *The Information Revolution and International Security*. Washington, DC: CSIS Press, 1998.

Hoffman, Frank G. "'Hybrid Threats': Neither Omnipresent nor Unbeatable." *Orbis* 54 (Summer 2010): 441–55.

Jasper, Scott, ed. *Securing Freedom in the Global Commons*. Stanford, CA: Stanford University Press, 2010.

Kaplan, Robert D. "The Geography of Chinese Power." *Foreign Affairs* 89 (May–June 2010): 22–41.

Kaul, Inge, Isabelle Grunberg, and Marc A. Stern, eds. *Global Public Goods: International Cooperation in the 21st Century*. New York: Oxford University Press, 1999.

Kay, Sean. *Global Security in the Twenty-First Century: The Quest for Power and the Search for Peace*. Lanham, MD: Rowman and Littlefield, 2006.

Krepinevich, Andrew F. *Why AirSea Battle?* Washington, DC: Center for Strategic and Budgetary Assessments, 2010.

Lehr, Peter. *Violence at Sea: Piracy in the Age of Global Terrorism*. London: Routledge, 2006.

Lynn, William J., III. "Defending a New Domain: The Pentagon's Cyberstrategy." *Foreign Affairs* 80 (September–October 2010): 97–108.

Mahan, Alfred Thayer. *The Influence of Sea Power upon History: 1660–1783*. Boston: Little, Brown and Company, 1890.

Mulvenon, James C., and David M. Finklestein, eds. *China's Revolution in Doctrinal Affairs: Emerging Trends in the Operational Art of the Chinese People's Liberation Army*. Arlington, VA: CNA Corporation, 2005.

Nordquist, Myron H., and John Norton Moore. *Entry into Force of the Law of the Sea Convention*. Rhodes Papers 1994. The Hague: Martinus Nijhoff, 1995.

Ostrom, Elinor. *Governing the Commons: The Evolution of Institutions for Collective Action*. Cambridge: Cambridge University Press, 1990.

Posen, Barry R. "Command of the Commons: The Military Foundation of US Hegemony." *International Security* 28 (Summer 2003): 5–46.

Redden, Mark E., and Michael P. Hughes. "Global Commons and Domain Interrelationships: Time for a New Conceptual Framework?" *Strategic Forum* 259. Washington, DC: National Defense University Press, October 2010.

Reveron, Derek S. *Exporting Security: International Engagement, Security Cooperation, and the Changing Face of the U.S. Military*. Washington, DC: Georgetown University Press, 2010.

Thachuk, Kimberley L. *Transnational Threats: Smuggling and Trafficking in Arms, Drugs, and Human Life*. Westport, CT: Praeger Security International, 2007.

Tikk, Eneken, Kadri Kaska, Kristel Rünnimeri, Mari Kert, Anna-Maria Talihärm, and Liis Vihul. *Cyber Attacks against Georgia: Legal Lessons Identified*. Tallinn: NATO Cooperative Cyber Defence Center of Excellence, 2008.

Van Toll, Jan, Mark Gunzinger, Andrew F. Krepinevich, and Jim Thomas. *AirSea Battle: A Point-of-Departure Operational Concept*. Washington, DC: Center for Strategic and Budgetary Assessments, 2010.

Williams, Phil, and Dimitri Vlassis. *Combating Transnational Crime: Concepts, Activities and Responses*. London: Routledge, 2001.

Wortzel, Larry M. *The Chinese People's Liberation Army and Space Warfare: Emerging United States–China Military Competition*. Washington, DC: American Enterprise Institute, 2007.

Wu, Shicun, and Keyuan Zou, eds. *Maritime Security in the South China Sea: Regional Implications and International Cooperation*. London: Ashgate, 2009.

Contributors

Ian K. Adam serves in the Royal Navy at the Maritime Warfare Centre, which is responsible for exploiting operational lessons and developing maritime doctrine. Commander Adam was assigned to the Development Concepts and Doctrine Centre within the Ministry of Defence, where he helped inform decisions on strategy, capability development, and military concepts. As a warfare branch officer he has served onboard fourteen ships, including two as commander, and holds a master's degree from King's College, University of London.

Marc J. Berkowitz is a vice president for strategic planning at Lockheed Martin Corporation, where he develops business strategies, strategic plans, and advanced concepts for integrated national security space, intelligence, and information mission solutions. He served previously as the assistant deputy under secretary of defense for space policy and director of space policy in the Office of the Secretary of Defense with responsibility for the analysis, formulation, coordination, and oversight of policy on defense and intelligence activities in outer space.

Larry Clinton is the president and CEO of the Internet Security Alliance, a multisector trade association focused on cyber issues. He has written for and edited professional journals on cyber security, testified before Congress on numerous occasions, and been featured on the *PBS News Hour*, on the *CBS Morning Show*, and on many cable outlets including CNN, C-SPAN, MSNBC, and Fox News. His publications on best practices have been endorsed by organizations ranging from the US Department of Homeland Security to the American Bankers Association.

Kevin G. Coleman is a senior fellow and cyber security strategist and adviser at the Technolytics Institute. He explores cyber warfare doctrine and investigates the current international and domestic military structures as they apply to acts of cyber aggression, including the use of cyber attacks as an instrument of foreign policy. Mr. Coleman is the author of *The Cyber Commander's Handbook* and his work has been cited in the *US Army Cyber Operations and Cyber Terrorism Handbook* and *Critical Infrastructure Threats and Terrorism Handbook*.

Ian Easton is a China analyst at the Center for Naval Analyses. As a former research fellow at the Project 2049 Institute, Mr. Easton conducted Chinese language research and analysis on missile defense and military space competitions in Asia. Prior to that, he worked for the Asia bureau chief of *Defense News* covering Chinese signal intelligence, cyber security activities, and air defense and missile trends in the Taiwan Strait. His latest publication is *China's Electronic Intelligence (ELINT) Satellite Developments: Implications for US Air and Naval Operations.*

Schuyler Foerster is currently Brent Scowcroft Professor of National Security Studies in the Department of Political Science and the Eisenhower Center for Space and Defense Studies at the US Air Force Academy. During a career in the US Air Force, he served as senior adviser on security and arms control. He subsequently became the CEO of an award-winning educational organization. He holds a doctorate in politics from Oxford University and has published two books and several articles on international politics and security studies.

Paul S. Giarra is the president of Global Strategies and Transformation. A strategic planner, wargamer, and security analyst, he is a frequent panelist and commentator on naval strategy and global, regional, and alliance security futures. He is a graduate of the Naval War College and the National Institute for Defense Studies in Tokyo, and also a member of the last Harvard NROTC class. His most recent book chapter is "China's Maritime Salient: Competitive Strategies on the Oceanic Front for the 21st Century," in *Competitive Strategies for China.*

Susan Page Hocevar is an associate professor in the Graduate School of Business and Public Policy at the Naval Postgraduate School, where she teaches in the areas of organizational behavior, negotiation and consensus building, effective teams, and interagency collaboration in stability, security, transition, and reconstruction environments. She received her doctorate in business administration from the University of Southern California. Her current research is focused on diagnosing organizational collaborative capacities.

Scott Jasper is a lecturer in the Center for Civil-Military Relations and the National Security Affairs Department at the Naval Postgraduate School. In the US Navy he commanded a maritime patrol squadron and served on USS *Enterprise* and with US Naval Forces Central Command. As the deputy for Joint Experimentation, Captain Jasper drafted transformation plans at Headquarters, US Pacific Command. He is the editor of *Securing Freedom in the Global Commons* and *Transforming Defense Capabilities: New Approaches for International Security.*

Michael Krepon is the cofounder of the Henry L. Stimson Center, a public policy institute. He also has worked at the Carnegie Endowment for International Peace and the US Arms Control and Disarmament Agency. Mr. Krepon has written or edited thirteen books, including *Space Assurance or Space Dominance: The Case against Weaponizing Space; Open Skies, Arms Control and Cooperative Security; Commercial Observation Satellites and International Security;* and *Better Safe than Sorry: The Ironies of Living with the Bomb.*

Sandra R. Leavitt is the executive director of the Center on Contemporary Conflict and a research assistant professor of national security affairs at the Naval Postgraduate School. She specializes in the social mobilization of nonstate actors and internal conflicts in Southeast Asia, policymaking in developing states, nationalism, and security cooperation. She received her doctorate from the Department of Government at Georgetown University and is coauthor of "A Framework for Addressing the Risks of Counterterrorism Technology Transfer: Implications for Russia and Eurasia."

Thomas G. Mahnken is the Jerome Levy Chair of Economic Geography and National Security at the Naval War College and a visiting scholar at the Philip Merrill Center for Strategic Studies at the Johns Hopkins University's Paul H. Nitze School of Advanced International Studies. From 2006 to 2009, he served as the deputy assistant secretary of defense for policy planning. His books include *Technology and the American Way of War since 1945*. Dr. Mahnken is the editor of the *Journal of Strategic Studies*.

Scott Moreland is a lecturer, trainer, and research associate in the Center for Civil-Military Relations at the Naval Postgraduate School, where he directs interagency and multinational peacekeeping and crisis response exercises. Mr. Moreland serves as a facilitator and lecturer with the International Defense Transformation and Civil-Military Relations Mobile Education and Training programs for foreign defense officials and military officers in South America, Europe, and the United States. His latest publication is a chapter on integrated training in *Securing Freedom in the Global Commons*.

Mark A. Stokes is the executive director of the Project 2049 Institute. Previously he served as vice president and Taiwan country manager for Raytheon International, executive vice president of Laifu Trading Company, a senior associate at the Center for Strategic and International Studies, and member of the board of governors of the American Chamber of Commerce in Taiwan. Lieutenant Colonel Stokes served as an attaché in Beijing and a director for China and Taiwan with the Office of the Assistant Secretary of Defense (International Security Affairs).

Sam J. Tangredi is the director of San Diego Operations for Strategic Insight, Limited. One of the nation's top defense strategists, he has written over 100 publications and received eleven literary awards. Prior to retiring from the US Navy as a captain, he served as a surface warfare officer. In his last assignment he established the Strategic Planning and Business Development Directorate in the International Programs Office. Dr. Tangredi is the author of *All Possible Wars?* and *Futures of War* and the editor of *Globalization and Maritime Power*.

Eneken Tikk serves as legal adviser, scientist, and legal and policy branch chief at the NATO Cooperative Cyber Defence Centre of Excellence in Tallinn, Estonia. Earlier she practiced Internet technology law as an attorney for a number of Estonian agencies. She also lectured in the field of international law and law of armed conflict at the Estonian Military College. In addition, she was lead author of the NATO report titled "Cyber Attacks against Georgia: Legal Lessons Identified."

Gordan E. Van Hook is the senior director for innovation and concept development for Maersk Line, Limited, where he works on ways to leverage best practices for energy efficiency, sustainment, and commercial ship conversions. In addition, he headed the Maersk crisis response team during the *Maersk Alabama* hostage incident in 2009. A retired naval officer, Captain Van Hook commanded USS *O'Bannon* and served as the Fifth Fleet operations officer during Operation Enduring Freedom. He has published numerous articles dealing with maritime domain awareness, energy, and maritime security.

Index

Regional Cooperation Agreement on Combating Piracy and Armed Robbery against Ships in Asia, 124, 130–32

Republic of China (Taiwan), 52, 76–79, 82, 90, 92, 96–99

rogues, 53n37; actors, 3, 237; cyber rogues, 9; hackers, 241; states, 42, 45, 55, 115, 188

Royal Air Force. *See* United Kingdom

Royal Australian Navy. *See* Australia

Royal Navy. *See* United Kingdom

Russia, 76, 95–99, 106, 115, 155, 187, 203, 206–11, 222, 234; Arctic claims, 79, 81; cyber attacks, 106, 116, 159t, 215, 221, 223; nuclear deterrence, 57–58; proliferation threat, 98, 150; and space arms control, 162, 235. *See also* Soviet Union

seabasing, 75–76, 83, 136

Second Artillery. *See* People's Liberation Army

Second Nuclear Age, 58, 61–63

Secret Service, 186, 191

Secret Service (MI5). *See* United Kingdom

Security and Accountability for Every Port Act, 135

short-range ballistic missiles. *See* ballistic missiles

Singapore Strait, 128

South China Sea, 11, 80; and China, 82, 96, 234; Spratley and Paracel Islands, 79; and Vietnam, 79, 234, 245

South Korea, 3–4, 53n37, 175, 214

Southern Command, 179

Soviet Union, 43, 57–58, 61–64, 83, 208–9, 226; antiship ballistic missiles, 63, 77; arms control, 99, 162, 203; naval forces, 76; nuclear capabilities, 62; space policies, 59, 148, 205, 207; and strategic deterrence, 57, 163

Space Code of Conduct, 14, 53n39, 163, 213; for cyberspace, 64, 108, 165; for space, 10, 49, 165, 201–2, 205, 207–12, 235, 238

Space Surveillance Network, 29

Spratly and Paracel Islands. *See* South China Sea

Strategic Arms Limitation Treaty, 204

Strategic Arms Reduction Treaty, 204, 209

Strategic Command, 158, 242

Stuxnet, 5, 107–8, 113–14, 159t, 187, 240

surface-to-air missiles, 45, 97, 100n1

Taiwan. *See* Republic of China

Taiwan Strait, 76–77

Telstar, 159t

Tongasat, 159t

Transportation Command, 150

Treaty on the Prevention of the Placement of Weapons in Outer Space, the Threat or Use of Force against Outer Space Objects (draft), 162

Twitter, 110

unified communications, 189

United Kingdom: Royal Air Force, 144; Royal Navy, 73–74, 143–44; Secret Service (MI5), 221

United Nations: Agreement Governing the Activities of States on the Moon and Other Celestial Bodies, 201, 204; Conference on Disarmament, 211, 228–29; Convention on International Liability for Damage Caused by Space Objects, 204; Convention on the Law of the Sea, 10, 23, 78–79, 82, 123, 237–38, 234; Convention on Registration of Objects Launched into Outer Space, 206; International Court of Justice, 78, 81, 222; International Maritime Organization, 130, 177–80

Verizon, 188, 191

Vietnam. *See* South China Sea

Voiceover Internet protocol. *See* Internet

Volpe Center, 178

weapons of mass destruction, 31, 38n52, 58, 99, 109, 114, 117, 145, 158, 162; in outer space, 202–3; proliferation of, 2, 6, 25, 76, 98

World Wide Web. *See* Internet

Yellow Sea, 79, 86n42